The Kubrick Facade

Faces and Voices in the Films of Stanley Kubrick

Jason Sperb

The Scarecrow Press, Inc.
Lanham, Maryland • Toronto • Oxford
2006

SCARECROW PRESS, INC.

Published in the United States of America
by Scarecrow Press, Inc.
A wholly owned subsidiary of
The Rowman & Littlefield Publishing Group, Inc.
4501 Forbes Boulevard, Suite 200, Lanham, Maryland 20706
www.scarecrowpress.com

PO Box 317
Oxford
OX2 9RU, UK

Portions of chapters 1, 2, 3, 4, and 7 originally appeared in "The Country of the Mind in
Kubrick's *Fear and Desire*," *Film Criticism* 29, no. 1 (Fall 2004): 24–37.
Chapter 4 appeared in a slightly different version in "The Magic of Words: Voice-Overs
and Storytelling in Kubrick's *Dr. Strangelove* (1964)," *Storytelling: A Critical Journal of
Narrative* (Summer 2006).
Chapter 5 appeared in an earlier, condensed form in "I Can Feel It: Sounds, Intensities
and Subjectivities in *2001* (1968)," *Interactions* 14, no. 2 (Fall 2005): 147–59.

British Library Cataloguing in Publication Information Available

Library of Congress Cataloging-in-Publication Data

Sperb, Jason, 1978–
    The Kubrick facade : faces and voices in the films of Stanley Kubrick / Jason Sperb.
    p.   cm. Filmography: p. Includes bibliographical references and index.
    ISBN-13: 978-0-8108-5855-8 (pbk. : alk. paper)
    ISBN-10: 0-8108-5855-X (pbk. : alk. paper)
    1. Kubrick, Stanley—Criticism and interpretation.   I. Title.
PN1998.3.K83S64   2006
791.4302′33092—dc22   2006007581

⊚ ™ The paper used in this publication meets the minimum
requirements of American National Standard for Information
Sciences—Permanence of Paper for Printed Library Materials,
ANSI/NISO Z39.48-1992. Manufactured in the United States of
America.

For H. D.

*Sometimes the truth of the thing
is not so much in the think of it,
but in the feel of it.*

—Stanley Kubrick

Contents

Preface

𝒯he first and only Kubrick first-run film I ever experienced with an audience in a movie theater was *Eyes Wide Shut* in July of 1999 at Sony College Park on the north side of Indianapolis. Around that same time, I had managed to catch a rerelease of *A Clockwork Orange*, once and only once, at the Castleton Arts theater nearby. How fleeting, how ephemeral, those cinematic experiences have truly become—I recently found out that this old "arts theater" (Indy's only, once) has closed its doors for the last time, just last month. When I saw *Capote* and *Shopgirl* there in November, I had no idea just how soon I was to lose the visceral *entirety* of that event, forever. I can still remember, of course; I can even drive up there and see the abandoned building again; but to go back there would be to never look outside the past (at something present). What an appropriately sad way to think one last time about my project on the films of Stanley Kubrick. I can never return to those moments; I can never even return to that theater—the site of so much cinephiliac joy at one point some time ago, including that one-time midnight showing (what a crowd!) of *A Clockwork Orange* as part of the passing Warner Bros. Festival in that intense, brilliant summer. Almost exactly two years after seeing *Eyes Wide Shut* and *A Clockwork Orange*, I saw *AI* at a multiplex in Crawfordsville, Indiana, about ninety minutes west of Indianapolis.

In many ways, there is only one experience (one first one, that is), and I have always already been trying to work my way back to the initial experience of the films of Stanley Kubrick. This book is no exception. I have not spent most of my life in this state, yet my cinematic experiences of Kubrick's films (along with *AI*) all have been in Indiana. And so it seems oddly appropriate, then, that I conclude this project on the films of Stanley Kubrick four and a half years later just down the road from Indianapolis in Bloomington. It is all the more remarkable that I have ended up back here considering that I have just finished living in four very different states over the course of three very different years, writing and rewriting about Kubrick the whole way. It is past time to bring those journeys to an end.

Indeed, this book has been a journey through many states, many academic programs, and many film courses—it wouldn't be a stretch to say that the present project has spanned the length of my graduate career. There are some passages here that still remain intact from my writings as a first-year master's student at Oklahoma State University. For example, professors Walker and Walkiewicz both allowed me to write papers on Kubrick in their respective seminars way back in 2002—my first formal workings about the director, both of which in different ways tried to come to terms with the sounds of his films. Though very little here actually resembles those first two awkward efforts, the research overall did reflect an indescribable intensity I sensed in the films, and it did introduce me to *Fear and Desire*, thus planting the seed for this project.

Detours through Castleton, Indianapolis, Crawfordsville, and so forth have not been entirely arbitrary, any more than this brief detour through my past has been. For, as I hope to reveal in the following pages, this is ultimately a very intimate (scholarly) intervention into the films of Stanley Kubrick. They are about the *experiences* of his films. My experiences. And my experiences with the experiences of others. But let me just close by saying I am not trying to memorialize past cinematic experiences. Those summers are gone, and the sadness comes in accepting I cannot retrieve them. Instead, I am trying to open up the possibilities for new cinematic experiences. There are encounters with Kubrick's body of work still to come, not yet passing, and the joy comes in anticipating what will be next. In whatever forms it took along the way, *The Kubrick Facade* began and concluded in Indiana. But beyond this journey, *the experience of Kubrick continues. . . .*

Acknowledgments

Window
gazing . . .
a / thing
Kubrick can
cure? Keep or
give away.

—L

$\mathcal{T}$here is great sadness in writing an acknowledgment page. I find myself not celebrating a particular accomplishment so much as I am looking back softly and thoughtfully at so many experiences and journeys irretrievably gone. Sure, people may remain (somewhere); but the moments do not. And what good are memories, really, after the experiences have passed? Reading over this manuscript one last time, I am overwhelmed with memories of places I've visited, and of the people I've known, and of the people I've been. Each paragraph here takes me back to a different experience—to theaters in Indianapolis, to apartments in Charleston (Illinois), to seminar rooms in Stillwater, to hotels in Oklahoma City, to coffee shops in Gurnee, to airports in Tulsa, to basements in Royal Oak, to parks in Detroit, to offices and spare rooms in Bloomington. But even that list somehow misses it. And going back through those memories again, it's only now dawning on me just how *long* this book has taken me, in a way quantified beyond time. For there is something there lost forever in a kaleidoscope of time—after the ship explodes (as it always does), we each hurl irreversibly in our own directions, never to return to those bittersweet moments again. It *is* so hard to make the good things last.

But, perhaps, giving thanks is not a way to prolong the good, but simply to acknowledge it. There are many people along the way to whom I owe a debt of gratitude. At Oklahoma State University—Robert Mayer, for workx *Acknowledgments*

ing with me the most closely and the most patiently, especially in those grueling times when it seemed as though neither of us any longer retained any faith in my project; Edward P. Walkiewicz, Jeffrey Walker, Leonard J. Leff, Edward Jones, Carol Moder, Arthur Redding, and Scott Balcerzak, who were all—in their own way—present and helpful in the project's early formation. Additionally, I am grateful to Thomas Nelson of San Diego State University for his outside advice and guidance during my time in Oklahoma. As the project moved beyond Stillwater, several other people proved quite valuable—in particular, Tony Williams; Rod Munday; Steven Shaviro and the English Department at Wayne State University; and finally, Joan Hawkins and James Naremore at Indiana University.

Parts of this work have appeared before in various journals, and appropriately I'd like to thank many in that field as well—Lloyd Michaels and the anonymous readers at *Film Criticism* for offering constructive criticism on improving my work and for first recognizing and appreciating the research that eventually led me here; likewise, Bonnie Plummer, Elizabeth Foxwell, and the reviewers at *Storytelling* for perseverance and patience; and Sebnem Toplu and the editors at *Interactions* for their support and feedback. As well, a very sincere debt of gratitude is owed to Stephen Ryan, Jessica McCleary, and Patricia MacDonald at Scarecrow Press.

Finally, I offer the simplest but deepest thanks to the best advisors I have yet had—my late grandfather and my parents. This project is dedicated to them.

Introduction: Experiencing Faces and Voices

> The feel of the experience is the important thing, not the ability to
> verbalize or analyze it.
>
> —Stanley Kubrick[1]

There is one visually striking shot among many in *The Shining* (1980)—a long slow zoom on Jack Nicholson's face as he stares at a scaled-down model of the Overlook Hotel's overgrown labyrinth maze. The increasingly cool light bounces off the right side of his face, echoing many such images of blank expressions in the film. This shot then cuts to an overhead shot of the outdoor maze itself, as his wife and child try to navigate their way through the incomprehensible web. On the surface, the operative effect (for lack of a better term) is fairly clear—the mind as a maze, something to be entered with caution and navigated with great trepidation. Thomas Allen Nelson, in the most comprehensive book yet on the films of Stanley Kubrick, reiterates this imagery in *Kubrick: Inside a Film Artist's Maze* (2000). In the first edition, the book cover features a dense purple maze over an image of a middle-aged Stanley Kubrick while shooting *Barry Lyndon* (1975). The cover of the second edition is even more pronounced—a thick black outline of a maze over a close-up shot of an older Kubrick. In both that moment from *The Shining* and on the cover of both editions of *Inside the Film Artist's Maze*, there is a sense that Kubrick's films were obsessed with the mind as a dense object of mystery, something impenetrable but that beckons those who experience it to investigate further than that cold facade.

But what are Kubrick's films ultimately saying about the mind? Or, put another way, what does the mind itself ultimately have to say, in all its marks, in Kubrick's films? In one way, Kubrick's early films (prior to *Dr. Strangelove* [1964]) suggest a very strong reliance on the mind and its ability to understand experience. Going back far enough into the trajectory of his films, we can sense that the mind initially had quite a bit to say. This is particularly evident in its deployment of the voice-over narration.[2] These early films reveal for me a continuous attempt to organize the content and meaning of diegetic experiences through the power of nondiegetic language. As I discuss in the next chapter, the narrative power attempted in Kubrick's first feature-length film, *Fear and Desire* (1953), allows me to articulate how the opening voice-over narration of each early Kubrick film—often the form of an omniscient third-person voice—revealed a strong desire for projecting narrative assumptions and asserting narrative control, however stable, over the events that thereafter unfold. *Fear and Desire*, in its simplest form, is the tale of four soldiers trapped behind enemy lines during an unnamed war. By explicit design, they are purely abstract characters who are fighting a purely allegorical war, fighting in "no other country but the mind." We see here the maze of the mind imposed upon the foggy forest of the story. Deriving from this opening voice-over declaration, I take the idea of "the country of the mind" as my central front for issues of narrative control. In a much different sense than we see in a later film such as *The Shining*, the country of the mind is the first of many Kubrickian preoccupations with the maze of the mind. "*Fear and Desire* is not meant to be a war film in the conventional sense of the term," writes Paolo Cherchi Usai, "but rather insists on the fact that the only reality with which characters contend is psychological, not physical. . . . [The film] instead proclaims a much more ambitious intent, the exploration of the unconscious."[3] To posit a country of the mind—as all the earlier Kubrickian voice-over narrators do (from *Fear and Desire* through *Killer's Kiss* [1955], *The Killing* [1956], *Paths of Glory* [1957], and *Spartacus* [1960])—means to claim that all events within the story world can be thematically and narratively mediated through a marker of perception—not just sensed or intuited, but cognitively captured and explained. As I develop and define more fully in the next chapter, the country of the mind is not the narrator or the narration by itself but rather is an effect of the narration, the thematic and discursive *vision* of the narrator himself (and the narrators in Kubrick's films are always in some way male). Interestingly, however, later Kubrick films, such as *The Shining*, seem to critique this same claim to narrative authority. There is an increasing apprehension—such as with Jack Torrance's writer's block—over the ability of the mind and language to come to terms with experience. Thus, Kubrick's films increasingly reveal the country of the mind as an arbitrary and often illusory means of representing the experience. It is progressively more a facade that masks the ambiguity of the story world beyond. Yet the early films seem content with the thematic and narrative power of the voice-over.

In chapter 4, I attempt to further illuminate this turn I see in emphasis from narration to ambiguity in *Dr. Strangelove*. I focus on this film predominantly as a site of possible transition in part because the film features both a third-person narrator who opens the film and three characters who work as implicit first-person narrators for each of their respective settings (Major Kong [Slim Pickens] in the B-52 cockpit, General Ripper [Sterling Hayden] at the Burpelson Air Force Base, and General Turgidson [George C. Scott] in the War Room). Yet, importantly, none of them ultimately seems to have any clue as to what goes on in other parts of the story world, and thus all prove to be inadequate "narrators." We see for the first time in a Stanley Kubrick film how much the mind is not only a maze but also invariably un-*plot*-able. The cognitive effects of the mind (such as a voice-over) cannot navigate the experiences of the story, as was the case with the country of the mind in *Fear and Desire* or Davy's first-person narration in *Killer's Kiss*. One of the more striking examples of this is Turgidson's obsession with the War Room's "Big Board"; he is more concerned with *how the world is being plotted* up there, on the surface of a map, than with what is going on with actual encounters in the course of the narrative (of which even we ourselves as the audience see only bits and fragments). Put another way, the map on the Big Board offers a visual instance for the country of Turgidson's mind, another facade, rather than presents a sufficient accounting of the experience itself. And this, in turn, becomes his primary narrative understanding of what is actually occurring within the diegesis of *Dr. Strangelove*.

Focusing exclusively on the mind may be indeed the dominant way of *thinking* about the films of Stanley Kubrick. According to Gilles Deleuze, "If we look at Kubrick's work, we see the degree to which it is the brain which is *mis en scene*. . . . For, in Kubrick, the world itself is a brain, there is an identity of brain and world."[4] At the end of *The Shining*, Jack becomes trapped and then frozen (literally and figuratively) within his own mind when he fails to find his way out of the maze and thus collapses and freezes to death in the harsh winter. It is a completion, in one sense, of the unification between the brain and the surrounding world. "In *The Shining*," Deleuze adds, "how can we decide what comes from the inside and what comes from the outside, the extra-sensory perceptions or hallucinatory projections?"[5] To a certain degree, we cannot. *The Shining*'s emphasis on subjectivity negates any attempt to distinguish between the two—inside and outside. Yet, this dilemma of destructive "hallucinatory projections" (which results from the mind and produces only violence in the film) may compel us to think outside perceptions and projections entirely—outside the inside, outside the mind. We are compelled outside the mind, even as we self-reflexively question how we can come to sense this endeavor.

Deleuze himself does not equate the entire world in Kubrick's films with the brain—he argues only that the brain attempts to contain and compact the totality of the world. "The identity of world and brain, the automaton," he writes, "does not form a whole, but rather a limit, a membrane which puts an outside and an inside in contact, makes them present to each other, confronts them or makes them clash."[6] There is something that escapes the brain, even as it attempts to see the world in its own image. For example, rather than think about where Jack goes (or what happens in his mind) after he freezes to death, this final plot turn in *The Shining* instead may push us in a radically different direction—away from the mind and the narrative authority of *Fear and Desire*. We may find ourselves considering another possibility besides just the mind as a maze—rather, the mind as a *quagmire*, within which one can be easily (irreversibly) caught up in the trappings of conscious and subconscious thoughts. Jack becomes resigned to the maze in a way not unlike how Turgidson is wedded to his map. The objects are both symbolic products of the mind, but they are both worthless in experiencing and sensing a world outside the direct cognition of the characters. One of the great joys of *The Shining* (and perhaps maddening to horror buffs who expect more overt bloodletting and graphic terror in the film) is that for all the film's emphasis on subjectivity ("shining")—and it is considerable—the film isn't really privileging the mind or its violent projections at all. At least, *The Shining* isn't privileging the mind in any exhaustive or affirming fashion. *The Shining* more precisely centers on the gaps between those subjectivities that "shine."

In *The Shining*, it is not so much the mind we see as it is the face. We see very little of the world beyond the surface of projections and perceptions. There are of course many violent moments of mental images in the film, but they produce nothing constructive in the world of the story and constitute mere slivers of time within long periods of narrative uncertainty and ambiguity. The distinction between the mind and the face here is akin to the difference between being caught up inside one's thoughts and being entirely shut out of those same introverted reflections—forced out into the external experiences the mind cannot grasp. Though framed from his point of view, the tracking shots of Danny (Danny Lloyd) on the tricycle attempt to pull us out of the mind and into the chaotic, yet fluid and unbroken, experience of the Overlook Hotel—the endless shots of the corridors; the continuous, repetitive sounds of his tricycle riding on the carpet and the floors. When Danny finally stops, confronted by the twin girls at the end of the hallway, it only heightens the sense that Danny cannot outrun the violence of the mind in the expressionistic experiences of the hotel. Yet the ephemeral intensity of the diegetic experiences prior to and after this sequence are moments curiously outside the overt mindscreens we see projected by Danny, Hallorann (Scatman Crothers), and Jack. In *The Shining*, the mind is violence—both in what it produces and in what it sees. The mind is regression—"all work and no play makes Jack a dull boy." Survival is outside the maze; survival is *outside the mind*, outrunning the mind, outthinking (unthinking) the mind. According to Geoffrey Cocks, "Kubrick, while admiring reason and technology, also *feared* the consequences of thought."[7] Kubrick's films likewise force us to fear the consequences of thought and, I would argue, thus think outside the mind. And so this dilemma of unthinking the mind may compel us to look elsewhere. The experiences of the films may push us beyond the facade that the mind and those faces project to an unthought realm where mutual experience and interaction exists. But how can we think in a way that tentatively attempts to *unthink* these films?

This is my project—to begin articulating the ways in which one might return to the experiences of Stanley Kubrick's films, not in a formalist way, but in an affective one. When looking at the cinematic body of Stanley Kubrick, it's irrefutable to me that there was something about the human mind that these films were always trying to come to terms with (and perhaps they do). And yet, when I think of the mind and ask what it does, I cannot separate it from the body. Indeed, as though beckoned by the words of Kubrick himself, when we approach the "feel of the experience," it is through our bodies and not just our minds. It is something we sense and then react to—not just construct in our own heads. There is something outside the mind and outside our thoughts, and it can only begin to approach us through the senses. But can we think of a Kubrick body of work without this—an intrinsic connection between thought and the senses?

As for the films of Stanley Kubrick, there is something outside of our understanding and of our discussions of his films, and—likewise—I think we can only begin to approximate it by considering what exists there in those experiences on a preconscious, sensory level. It may have been the mind that preoccupied his films, but only in so much as it reacted to the experiences of the body. Kubrick famously noted that "sometimes the truth of the thing is not so much in the think of it, but in the feel of it,"[8] and yet I wonder if this much-celebrated quotation has been fully considered when critically approaching his films, especially when approaching those films *not* titled *"2001"* (1968). Of course, what Kubrick had to say in his time about his movies, or about film more generally, only matters so much. But I sense his films—whether intended or not—force us into a similar dilemma about thinking and feeling. Kubrick may have been on to something when attempting to articulate that moment when we are confronted with the "experience," and I wonder why so many of us—myself included—keep feeling compelled again and again to try to "verbalize and analyze" his films.[9]

If there is one unifying assumption to my journey here—through the separate, but interconnected, surfaces that make up the films of Stanley Kubrick, the criticism of Stanley Kubrick, the idea of Stanley Kubrick, the history of Stanley Kubrick, and the auteurism of Stanley Kubrick—it is that there is something not merely in my head, or that I impose upon his films; rather, that particular something is in the *experience* itself of "Stanley Kubrick," however one has or will wish to label him (or not)—a director, a historical figure, a critical metaphor, a perfectionist, a filmmaker, a myth, a recluse, a literary adaptor, a body of work, and yes, an auteur. There is something to experience beyond these facades. As I look to each of his works, it is the "feel of the experience" that draws me back again and again to write and rewrite about the films of Kubrick, and I cannot help but feel that the senses of the body are at least as important, if not more so, than the thoughts of the mind—only the latter of which seem presently to preoccupy Kubrick criticism. "What cannot be experienced," writes Brian Massumi, "cannot but be felt—albeit reduced and contained. For out of the pressing crowd an individual action or expression will emerge and be registered consciously."[10] While scholars and critics must write and speak to articulate the experience of his films, registering consciously what we thought we saw and heard, we must write and speak of something that has already been expressed, thus slipping off our critical surfaces and into the virtual spaces of film studies—what "cannot but be felt."

Kubrick once said that "there are certain areas of feeling and reality which are inaccessible to words."[11] Again, I'm not saying that Kubrick had it all figured out, either (he couldn't have); I am instead wondering aloud why we continue to *think* about Kubrick's films, at some supposed conscious and subconscious levels, when the effect of his films and his words may push us elsewhere. For example, Cocks attempts to unlock the subconscious desires and interests driving Kubrick's films in his recent book *The Wolf at the Door: Stanley Kubrick, History, and the Holocaust* (2004). In particular, he attempts to go inside Kubrick's mind to find the reason explaining so much of the filmmaker's obsession with self-destructive societies. "For Kubrick, at varying levels of consciousness," he writes, "the Holocaust was at the center of the harsh realities of the modern world entire that made up the subject matter of his films. His thirteen feature films all in one way or another address human struggles with and over power and violence."[12] As with the opening of this present study, Cocks's book also focuses in particular on *The Shining*. For him, the filmmaker's one horror film opens up rich possibilities for psychoanalytic Freudian and post-Freudian readings of Kubrick's intentions, which—whether "conscious, intuitive, or unconscious—must be given primary consideration in any evaluation of his films."[13] *The Shining* contains "a deeply laid subtext that positions the Holocaust as the modern benchmark of evil. An analysis of otherwise inexplicable visual and aural aspects of *The Shining* demonstrates that this film was an artistic and a philosophical response to the horrors of the Second World War."[14] Cocks's work presents us with some interesting and provocative possibilities about Kubrick's intentions and about his subconscious thoughts. My argument about *The Shining*, however, would consider that if there are indeed "otherwise inexplicable visual and aural aspects" to the film, then perhaps we need to look right at the surface. Conceivably, these aspects are totally and literally inexplicable; they do not *mean* anything. That is to say, we are not compelled to go further into the mind to find explication, but instead we could embrace their essentially enigmatic nature as they compel us to run from the mind. I wonder how much further into the maze Kubrick critics and scholars can go before we too collapse in exhaustion and freeze to death, thus trapped for eternity in our own fixed, suspended understandings—safe, habitualized assumptions that do not adequately account for the shifting, ephemeral experiences of Kubrick's films.

Moving away from a strict emphasis on reading intention (and the more implicit logic of origin), I propose an auteur study that focuses as much on the *consistent effects* Kubrick's films achieve on those who attempt to understand the experience as on reading what comes on or before the text itself. The far more urgent intervention into the critical receptions of Stanley Kubrick's films seems to be not how we think about his films, or about how other forms of thinking may have influenced that thinking—all that nonsense is simply the quagmire logic of the maze. The only point inside of the maze is to get back outside it, to the outside of the mind. Rather than stay trapped inside thoughts, we instead may have cause to consider how we *feel* with his films—not so much in an emotional way (as James Naremore recently did[15]), even though much ground remains there to be made. Instead, I argue that Kubrick's films progressively advocate that we start—as much as one can— outside the mind entirely, at the *pre*conscious sensory level of sight and sound.

And even these two senses are themselves inadequate, for they only begin to approximate what I would try to qualify as the affect of his films.[16] Kubrick's thoughts are not a definitive answer to the films' "meaning." Rather, they are a more usefully articulated way to think of the following question: What can we think of the "feel" of his films? Feelings not only resist words but also precede them. If we wish to better understand the ambiguity of Kubrick's films, we may need to first touch base with a sense of affect before going on to contemplate the effects of the mind. While it is not particularly original to regurgitate how ambiguous and nonverbal Kubrick's films are, I nonetheless feel that these indisputable qualities only begin to approach the impact of his films. In the rush to suspend and explain away the ambiguity of these movies, I wonder if existing criticism has thus far missed a crucial aspect—the *affect* of the films of Stanley Kubrick; not only on our minds but specifically on our bodies as well—that is to say, I do not think about Kubrick's films any more than I sense them. In this book, meanwhile, I do not hope to document how I read Kubrick's films; rather, it is much more how I feel the films themselves compel us to construct an always tentative remapping of the movies we experience, through the way Stanley Kubrick's body of work always already *sounds* and *looks*. "There is as much thought in the body," writes Deleuze, "as there is shock and violence in the brain."[17] In criticism, of course, we think of the mind and we use the mind, but only as a translator of what first our bodies experience. In other words, I argue that there is a *sense* to his films—both in their affective powers and in the discursive logic these powers compel us to.

Yet, as I will show, it is also a sense paradoxically expressed through the chaos of the films. Kubrick's later films propose to us minimalist narratives and overt narrators, but only in their relation to failed narrations. In other words, we sense narrative resisting chaos in his films, and chaos resisting narrative. In a remarkably provocative and useful side note in a chapter looking at the films of Stanley Kubrick, Fredric Jameson points out in *Signatures of the Visible* that

> *The Shining* may be read as Kubrick's meditation on the issues raised by his previous film and on that very impossibility of historical representation with which the achieved perfection of *Barry Lyndon* so dramatically and paradoxically confronts us. For one thing, the conventional motifs of the occult or supernatural thriller tend to distract us from the obvious fact that *The Shining*, whatever else it is, is also the story of a failed writer.[18]

Jameson's observation here is so pointedly simple, so efficiently quick, and yet so potentially far-reaching that his overtly Marxist concerns (as well as the novelty of Kubrick's working within the genre conventions of the "supernatural thriller") may also equally distract us from the less obvious point that Kubrick's films were *quite often* the story of a failed writer. More precisely, Kubrick's films were often the story of a doomed narrator, someone who can no longer make cohesive sense of the surrounding story world. Jack Torrance doesn't just fail to write his novel; he fails to understand the story of his life, his job, his family, and his importance to them and thus resorts to violence instead. The world he thought he inhabited proves to be a false one, as one might rightly assume would happen. But Jack cannot adjust to this rupture and realign the glimpses of reality he experiences with his narrative expectations (of which we see bits and pieces in his conversations with Grady and the hotel manager). In other words, his world just doesn't make any sense to him. But this is not just to emphasize here (as I and others previously have[19]) the ambiguity of Kubrick's films—something unshakably there in *The Shining*, *2001*, *Eyes Wide Shut* (1999), and so forth. Rather, drawing out the ambiguity of his films is instead to reveal first a specific *act* of failed narration in the film, which thus forces us to confront the possibilities of an emerging chaos outside the grasp of that narrative. And to articulate such doubt and uncertainty is to argue—as I will here—that Kubrick's later films specifically highlight how characters, such as Jack Torrance, attempt to find meaning in the world around them, how they fail, and (most crucially here) how we might be able to *sense* what's beyond that failure.

The de-emphasis on verbal and aural authority points to a scholarly moment for remapping the themes of Kubrick's films as emerging from a virtual, affective space. That is to say, even while emotions, themes, motives, and so forth may still remain, they shift outside the direct scope of narrators and narrations—outside the mind. And with this newfound awareness—the knowledge of the inability to grasp the totality of events and motives within the story world—comes the emergence of self-consciously failed, or incomplete, narrators, those who can sense the inadequacy of arbitrary cognitive order. This transition from attempts at authority by voice-over narration to individual characters as failed storytellers, such as Jack Torrance and Bill Harford (Tom Cruise), is emphasized by what I designate as a distinctly Kubrickian look, a key concept that most explicitly signifies the post-*Lolita* (1962) failure of narrative authorities. In Kubrick's later films, such as *The Shining*, *Full Metal Jacket* (1987), and *Eyes Wide Shut*, this blank face of a main character signals "the look," a now silent narrator—the voiceless voice-over—failing to understand the story world, possessing markedly less narrative authority. The look marks a heightened sense of the limits of these characters' ability to understand the experience—they can look, but they cannot see the world with any cohesive order or logic. As I elaborate in chapter 6, these faces look at nothing, but *to look* is itself the key. That blank face offers me nothing but a feeling, but this nothingness is itself a sense of what the film offers narratively. Through our senses, this face narrates narrative ambiguity—something we sense but do not receive at the level of cognition. Thus, I propose here the possibility of Kubrickian protagonists narrating not only in a voice-over (as in the earlier films) but also in a *voiceless voice-over*—this *look* that invites us to an ambiguity we can otherwise never understand, this look that marks and intensifies for us some narrative possibilities for sustaining narrative ambiguity. When his characters can no longer narrate (and this is the crucial event for the "failed writer" in the many films of Stanley Kubrick), it is the silence, and their blank faces, that compels us to a narrative void.

These faces represent those who try—like *Killer's Kiss's* Davy and the voice-overs in earlier films—to understand their surroundings, to impose a narrative on the events. But they instead find only that their attempts at understanding are frustrated, marked by moments where they retreat behind the look—perhaps able only to live in the country of their own minds. These withdrawals are a strikingly consistent stylistic occurrence beginning with *Dr. Strangelove*, where one character stares blankly into space, resigned to having his own understanding of events in the film defied by either competing characters' narratives, or a complete lack of narrative clarity. Jack Torrance's increasing withdrawal from his family in *The Shining*, marked by long takes on his blank expression, offer one of many examples of the Kubrickian look. It is a facade overwhelmed by the experience. And indeed I sense that it was this, Nicholson's empty face, the feeling of that appearance, that first compelled me to write about the films of Stanley Kubrick. With this look, the filmic image focusing on the face, the character becomes detached and isolated—acknowledging the failure to relate to, or engage with, the other characters in the experience of the story, or to think about the events in any constructive way. The climax of *Eyes Wide Shut*, for another example, centers not on a moment of disclosure but on one of acquiescence. Bill Harford must accept that he does not know how or why the prostitute died, and he never will. Little can be learned definitively of the film's true events by either the main protagonist or the film's audience, thus destabilizing the country of Bill's mind as a practically worthless narrative tool, forcing him to retreat behind his own look. From there, he can emerge only after he has begun to experience and engage the world again, without the fog of his own faulty assumptions and beliefs.

Seeking to better draw out the markers of narrative authority and failure throughout the films of Stanley Kubrick, this project next explores the role of voice-over narration in both *Fear and Desire* and, to a lesser extent, the other pre-*Dr. Strangelove* movies in Kubrick's filmography. Specifically, I hope to show how the use of voice-over creates a sense of narrative clarity—the discursive vision of the country of the mind—that attempts to clearly establish the tone and structure of the remainder of the respective films. Such a strategy suggests an unmistakable belief in what Kubrick himself once called the "magic of words,"[20] the way in which filmic reality can be filtered and framed through the effect of the country of the mind. However, *Dr. Strangelove* offers a subtly different experience with the power of voice-over narration. The fourth chapter of this book examines how both the third-person narrator and the implicit first-person narrators—General Turgidson, General Ripper, and Major Kong—suggest a breakdown in the ability of narrators to tell a story with the same clarity that *Fear and Desire* offered. The stories constructed within *Dr. Strangelove* by various narrators openly contradict each other. Moreover, the film first points toward an awareness of the look, of the voiceless narrator. As Ripper realizes his failures, he begins to withdraw to silence and blank expressions, clearly retreating to a world, perhaps toward a country of the mind that exists beyond the one he brought to the eve of destruction in the film. The next part then reconsiders *2001* as the post-apocalyptic wasteland leveled by the end of *Dr. Strangelove*, where the spectacularly failed attempt at narration in the earlier film leads directly to the latter film's emphasis on diegetic sound and its ease with constant silence and the often empty use of language—in other words, *2001*'s willingness to resist narrative authority, to resist the often destructive inhabitation of the country of the mind, in the wake of *Strangelove*'s verbal and narrative onslaught. We can feel *2001*, and it's a particular feeling that marks a departure from Kubrick's earlier films.

The sixth and seventh chapters interrogate the inadequate, voiceless narrators in later films such as *A Clockwork Orange* (1971), *The Shining, Full Metal Jacket*, and *Eyes Wide Shut*, describing how their attempts at narrative control bring us to the edge of cognition, to a point where both they and we can sense the emergent chaos. In some ways, this newly frustrated narrator is best exemplified by Alex in *A Clockwork Orange*—a character at once both allowed a free range of verbal expressions and, at the same time, forced to confront the failure of oral communication and narrative construction—his own and others. Alex and Jack illustrate how violent these individuals can become when they surrender any understanding of the world as they thought they knew it—or more precisely, their reactions to the unwillingness of others to bend to the narrative desires that suggest how they think things should be. Danny and Hallorann, meanwhile, tap into seemingly supernatural visual representations, rather than voice-over narrations, as a way to make sense of the chaotic world before them in *The Shining*. In *Full Metal Jacket*, Joker and Pyle offer contrasting examples of the older Kubrickian narrator (voice-over) versus the later one (the look), respectively. Finally, Bill Harford's journey throughout *Eyes Wide Shut* reveals a consistent pattern whereby his understanding of events fails to align with others'. And, in each instance, these Kubrickian characters and their expressions constitute a look of blank faces, characters who are often denied their voices, left without the power over filmic reality once possessed by the opening voice-overs of *Killer's Kiss, The Killing, Paths of Glory*, and so forth.

I conclude, finally, with a few thoughts on the process of narrating and narration in Steven Spielberg's *AI* (2001) and what the construction of narrative may or may not reveal, both about the affect of Kubrick in the younger director's sci-fi film (which Kubrick originally developed) and about the larger tendency to receive and dismiss the elder director's later films. In this respect, I hope to show how the tendency to map out narrative and thematic clarity carries equal significance for both narrators in the films and for their audiences. Kubrick remains as an affect beyond the facades of his films. But I also hope to use those same facades—the country of the mind, the Kubrickian look—to remap our own narrative assumptions about (and the experiences of) the films of Stanley Kubrick.

This project argues for a renewed emphasis on the experience of Stanley Kubrick's films—that both the faces (in later films such as *The Shining*) and the voices (in early films such as *Fear and Desire*) open up equally new avenues for examining narrators and narrative authority, for examining the affect of the cinematic experience, and for examining the unembodied mediation (i.e., the country of the mind) within the rupture between the mind and the body. Moreover, this project also posits that a striking stylistic reoccurrence running throughout his later films—this Kubrickian look—serves as a direct rebuttal to the earlier voice-overs by showing how the human mind and its language, as demonstrated in texts such as *Dr. Strangelove*, fail to fully comprehend any notion of filmic reality. Later Kubrickian narrators are thus left with nothing more than a blank, even dumbfounded, stare. Starting with *Fear and Desire*, the purpose here is to show the cognitive and affective tensions associated with narrative authority—while also pointing us back to the emergence of the body's importance to the preconscious experience—and to provide a new point for mapping and remapping a body of work, always shifting, always evolving, but also always already there.

This project began with an unexplainable disturbance for me, an ephemeral reaction, somewhere after the first emergence of Jack Nicholson's blank face—that facade within the larger facade of *The Shining*. So, what is a Kubrick facade? It is the mind. Or, put another way, it is a projection of the mind. The faces and voices in his films. And the films themselves. It is surface. It is what we gaze at or listen to—what we are intrigued by or guided by. But it means nothing. The faces and voices mean nothing; instead of pointing back to some central conscious or subconscious truth, these faces and voices alter something within us. Their importance is in their effect. There is nothing beneath the facade, or in the mind, that *by itself* means anything. What matters instead is how the facade affects the viewer, how the facade is a point of orientation away from some supposed deeper meaning and toward the transient, fleeting cinematic experience. The power of the Kubrick facade is not in what it means but in what it creates outside itself. How the film affects something in us. The facade is nothingness. But it is a *nothingness that narrates.* That is why the blankness and the silences are so powerful. And, perhaps, this is why Kubrick's films seem so cold and alienating to some, even when they (we) cannot look away.

Though I cannot get outside the thoughts of my own mind, I do wish to begin moving back to that affective moment where I first saw Nicholson's frozen gaze and sensed the power of nothingness—not to reclaim or preserve that instant but to acknowledge it and to allow for the possibility of other such experiences. Here in this book, I want to quantify the ways in which the films of Stanley Kubrick compelled me to write about them (and, implicitly, why so many of us are compelled to write about his films again and again). From there—the initial experience of watching his films—older facades guided me here, to *The Kubrick Facade*, and I hope this project may start to lead the reader (viewer) back. While Stanley Kubrick is always already there and gone, "Kubrick" is always already here. From here, I hope to offer an alternative guide to what we may hope to find when the time comes to journey back into "the Cinema of Stanley Kubrick" I thought I experienced.

NOTES

1. As quoted in Gene Phillips, *Stanley Kubrick: A Film Odyssey* (New York: Popular Library, 1975), 173.

2. In this context, "voice-over narration" refers to the definition previously established by Sarah Kozloff, who explains how "the term [*voice-over narration*] has often been used quite loosely." To clarify, Kozloff defines the term as follows: "basically, in 'voice-over narration' all three words are fully operative. . . . *Voice* determines the medium: we must hear someone speaking. . . . *Over* pertains to the relationship between the source of the sound and the images on the screen: the viewer does not see the person who is speaking at the time of hearing his or her voice. . . . *Narration* relates to the content of the speech: someone is in the act of communicating a narrative—that is, recounting a series of events to an audience." *Invisible Storytellers: Voice-Over Narration in American Fiction Film* (Berkeley: University of California Press, 1988), 2–3.

3. Paolo Cherchi Usai, "Checkmating the General: Stanley Kubrick's *Fear and Desire*," *Image* 38, no. 1/2, (Spring/Summer 1995): 13. I am deeply indebted to James Naremore for calling my attention to this article. Eerily similar to the reception of *Fear and Desire* itself, most Kubrick scholars have overlooked this well-written and well-researched piece of scholarship on his first film, failing even to note it in bibliographies on the director. Until recently, I was guilty of a similar omission.

4. Gilles Deleuze, *Cinema 2: The Time-Image*, trans. Hugh Tomlinson and Robert Galeta (Minneapolis: University of Minnesota Press, 1989), 205.

5. Deleuze, *The Time-Image*, 206.

6. Deleuze, *The Time-Image*, 206.

7. Geoffrey Cocks, *The Wolf at the Door: Stanley Kubrick, History, and the Holocaust* (New York: Peter Lang, 2004), 122.

8. As quoted in Piers Bizony, *2001: Filming the Future* (London: Aurum Press, 1994), 137.

9. Something about Kubrick's films compels a strong critical and intellectual reaction. There is *something* there. Although there are few truly outstanding and comprehensive scholarly studies of Kubrick's films (particularly in comparison with the literature on other such classical auteurs as Hitchcock, Welles, and Ford), there continues to be a considerable number of books relating to the director being released, despite the fact that Kubrick's last film and his death occurred more than seven years ago. The last four years alone have given us Michel Chion's *Eyes Wide Shut* (London: British Film Institute, 2002); Christiane Kubrick's *Stanley Kubrick: A Life in Pictures* (Boston: Little, Brown, 2002); Stuart Y. McDougal's edited collection *Stanley Kubrick's* A Clockwork Orange (New York: Cambridge University Press, 2003); Paul Duncan's *Stanley Kubrick: The Complete Films* (Los Angeles: Taschen, 2003); Cocks's *The Wolf at the Door*; Alison Castle's *The Stanley Kubrick Archives* (Los Angeles: Taschen, 2005); Rainer Crone's *Stanley Kubrick, Drama and Shadows: Photographs, 1945–1950* (New York: Phaidon, 2005); and *Depth of Field: Stanley Kubrick, Film, and the Uses of History*, ed. Geoffrey Cocks, James Diedrick, and Glenn Perusek (Madison: University of Wisconsin Press, 2006). What's more, there are two more projects forthcoming in the near future. There is a collection featuring more new essays on Kubrick's entire body of work, edited by John Springer and Gary Rhodes, due soon from McFarland. Additionally, noted film scholar James Naremore is finishing his own critical study on Kubrick, surely destined to be one of the definitive books in the field.

10. Brian Massumi, *Parables for the Virtual: Movement, Affect, Sensation* (Durham, N.C.: Duke University Press, 2002), 30–31.

11. As quoted in Phillips, *A Film Odyssey*, 181.

12. Cocks, *The Wolf at the Door*, 2.

13. Cocks, *The Wolf at the Door*, 3.

14. Cocks, *The Wolf at the Door*, 2.

15. In a provocative essay on *AI*, Kubrick, and Spielberg, Naremore begins with a discussion of the sci-fi epic's highly emotional conclusion and thus attempts to uncover partly why "I've watched it five times, and on each occasion I've been moved to copious tears." "Love and Death in *AI: Artificial Intelligence*," *Michigan Quarterly Review* 94, no. 2 (Spring 2005): 258. In some respects, it is a remarkably personal look at the effect of *AI* on Naremore, as he notes that "in the concluding shot/reverse shot, when [David] hears his mother's declaration of love and embraces her, I weep—and I feel in tune with the film, because tears are one of its most important motifs" (258). I, of course, do not intend foolishly to refute Naremore's own reading of his personal experience with *AI*; I just want to start thinking of an affect in Kubrick's body of work that is decidedly less cognitive, more subjectless (i.e., something preceding even a qualified feeling of sadness, as Naremore articulates here).

For example, Steven Shaviro, in a provocative essay on the film *Strange Days* (1995), offers a brief but highly useful introduction to theories of affect, ones that move away from the cognitive emphasis Naremore attempts to untangle. "I would like to talk about affect without a subject," he writes, "affect that comes, instead, before or after the subject." "Regimes of Vision: Kathryn Bigelow, *Strange Days*," *Polygraph* 13 (2001): 59. In his article, Shaviro differentiates a more subjectless feeling than emotion, "which continues to designate the more familiar sense of a personal, subjective feeling. An affect [a type of feeling that I am attempting to articulate in Kubrick's films] is something that comes before the subject has arrived, or that subsists after the subject has departed, or that happens alongside the subject, affecting it but not being integrated within it" (60). Thus, we cannot quite grasp the affect of Kubrick's films—it is not something in us, even though it is there, in the experience of the movies, and in turn engages us as spectators.

Additionally, it is not what we think but what we feel. To think is to attempt to capture a feeling that has passed. "I want to avoid making a binary opposition," Shaviro writes, "between thought and feeling; but I would still insist that affect is resistant to cognition, or that it happens at a point where thought reaches its limit. To put the point differently: an affect that is re-cognized by thought, or expressed in language, is thereby turned into emotion. Affect per se is the irreducible ground of emotion, that evades being captured by cognition or by language; or else it is the residue of emotion, the *part maudite* that is not reducible to cognition or to language" (60).

16. Here, I define affect according to the recent work of Massumi (which influenced Shaviro's writing), where affect is the sensation of the body, situated on a particular event, that compels us to thought. "The body doesn't just absorb pulses or discrete stimulations," Massumi writes, "it unfolds *contexts*, it unfolds volitions and cognitions that are nothing if not situated." *Parables for the Virtual*, 30. Working off Massumi's theories, meanwhile, Shaviro emphasizes how

> there is another, perhaps counterintuitive, sense, in which I would like to say that affect or feeling is not, strictly speaking, personal. A feeling can take me outside myself. It can make me lose control of myself, turn me into a different person. A certain feeling may be too much to bear. Or it may just be that a feeling doesn't seem to fit. It's a tonality, a quality, something that colors the way I perceive the world. But I'd swear that it isn't just my projection, because it has come to me from somewhere else. It isn't mine, but something alien to me: something from far away, that has managed to insinuate itself within me. (*"Strange Days,"* 59–60)

My experiences of Stanley Kubrick come to me from "somewhere else." In the process of unthinking Stanley Kubrick's body of work, I also hope to show how it attempts to unthink itself. And, importantly, how the films themselves compel me—through a feeling—to unthink them. It is not "just my projection" but something in the experience of his films that colors how I receive and perceive them.

17. Deleuze, *The Time-Image*, 205.

18. Fredric Jameson, *Signatures of the Visible* (New York: Routledge, 1992), 92–93.

19. Criticism on Kubrick has long noted such ambiguity. In one of my earlier publications on Kubrick, I wrote that "the absence of narrative meaning—making sense of *Eyes Wide Shut*'s story world—is not just a theme, but actually emerges as a subject of Kubrick's last film." "The Country of the Mind in Kubrick's *Fear and Desire* (1953)," *Film Criticism* 29, no. 1 (Fall 2004): 26. Meanwhile, Mario Falsetto writes that this last Kubrick film was "full of ambiguity and profundity." *Stanley Kubrick: A Narrative and Stylistic Analysis*, 2nd

ed. (Westport, Conn.: Praeger, 2001), xiii. As for earlier films, Bizony writes that *"2001 was unapologetically ambiguous." Filming the Future*, 16. This is a conclusion noted by many, including famous Kubrick scholar Alexander Walker, in Walker, Sybil Taylor, and Ulrich Ruchti, *Stanley Kubrick, Director: A Visual Analysis* (New York: Norton, 1999), 192. Most recently, Cocks reiterates how "his films, particularly since *2001*, employ an 'open narrative' that requires the audience to derive meaning actively rather than passively instructed, entertained and manipulated." *The Wolf at the Door*, 6.

The list of such observations is exhausting. Most intriguing to me (and perhaps a nice summary of ambiguity and affect here) is Thomas Allen Nelson's observation that "Kubrick felt strongly that the visual powers of film made ambiguity an inevitability as well as a virtue." *Kubrick: Inside a Film Artist's Maze*, 2nd ed. (Bloomington: Indiana University Press, 2000), 14.

20. This was Kubrick's take on think tanks and their discussions of policies. By the mid-1960s, Kubrick was skeptical of such excessive dependence on language and the illusion of fixing problems through elaborate statements in governmental reports and policy, which he of course exploited and mocked to great comic effect in *Dr. Strangelove* (as quoted in Walker, Taylor, and Ruchti, *A Visual Analysis*, 184). I return to this interview and to the magic of words at greater length in the beginning of chapter 4.

· 2 ·

We're All Islands: Seeing and Hearing the Country of the Mind in *Fear and Desire*

One suspects that [Kubrick] did not find it disagreeable to know that the only traceable print of [*Fear and Desire*] was in private hands and not easily available for public screening.

—Alexander Walker[1]

*T*here are ways through which we too can begin to think about how others may have similarly sensed the failures at play in *Fear and Desire*—a projection of authority, but the affect of uncertainty. For me, yes, but for others, too. Indeed, if there is one thing most commonly ascribed to his work, Kubrick's films are not models of narrative clarity. Many of his most famous films, such as *2001: A Space Odyssey* and *The Shining*, seem as concerned with what remains hidden as what is shown. His last film, *Eyes Wide Shut*, for example, takes narrative ambiguity—antithetical storytelling—almost as its main subject. "Suppos[e] there is nothing more" to *Eyes Wide Shut*, writes Michel Chion, in his perceptive book-length study of the film, "suppos[e] there are only signifiers with nothing signified."[2] *Eyes Wide Shut* "tells us," he goes on to write, "that motives do not matter and that we cannot know them."[3] The climax of *Eyes Wide Shut* centers not on a moment of revelation but on a moment of resignation—the acknowledgment that little can be learned definitively of the film's events by either the protagonist, Bill Harford, or the film's audience. As Chion implies, the ambiguity is not only something we sense but is also in the experience of the film itself. There is nothing in *Eyes Wide Shut*. Or, put another way, nothingness is *in* the film. The aforementioned *2001, A Clockwork Orange, Barry Lyndon,* and *The Shining*, all point toward the possible ambiguity of narrative events—taking us to the limits of narrative understanding and forcing us to confront the affect of a chaos beyond. But *Eyes Wide Shut* takes this problem one step further by highlighting the emerging possibility that no definitive, authoritative meaning can ever

17

be established in the story—the motives and intentions behind events, and thus the moments themselves, are ultimately unmediated and unrepresentable. They are filled with meaninglessness. *Eyes Wide Shut*, moreover, posits a Kubrickian protagonist who may finally, if only vaguely, feel this ambiguity. Thus the absence of narrative meaning—making sense of *Eyes Wide Shut*'s story world—is not just a theme; it actually becomes the subject of Kubrick's last film. At the end of Stanley Kubrick's career, authority seemed to be a failed pursuit in the face of so much ambiguity, the kind that pervades *Eyes Wide Shut*.

Yet Kubrick's films were not always so ambiguous in their content— "meaning," however defined or substantiated, seemed of paramount importance. This point, meanwhile, is not focused on nearly as much by insightful scholars such as Chion. On the contrary, Kubrick's early films, such as *Killer's Kiss*, *The Killing*, and *Spartacus*, foreground the mind's seeming potential for mapping out narrative assumptions and points of orientation through the story world—for, in a sense, mapping out meaning. The overlapping points of view; the complicated, often nonlinear narrative structures; the voice-overs; the dramatic, nondiegetic "signifying" music[4]—all these elements of the early films suggest narratives preoccupied with (to borrow Chion's term) people's "motives" (i.e., why heists fail and military institutions rest on the verge of self-destruction). In a nice, concise summary of Kubrick's narrative evolution (or devolution), Luis M. Garcia Mainar argues that Kubrick's early films reveal diametrically opposed views for the possible forms (and absences) of storytelling:

> Voice-over narration in Kubrick's films evolves from an element that shows the mastery of the text by itself, an element of coherence that assures the perfect fitting of each element in the first films, to a more detached, ironic relationship of narrator to text that hints at the growing feeling in the later films that reality cannot be controlled and that the text is unable to present it to us in a clear, reassuring way. This passage seems marked by the absence of voice-over narration in *2001*, a reference to the organizing, clarifying function it had fulfilled in Kubrick's films up to then, which would not have been coherent with the spirit of this revolutionary film.[5]

Mainar astutely points out the break in Kubrick's career in respect to attitudes toward narration, from that of a "mastery" to that of a "more detached, ironic relationship." Something clearly shifts near the middle of his body of work. The mind—typified by the abandoned voice-over in *2001*— can no longer understand the experiences of the body. The "feel" becomes the important thing. And this project will later argue that this break more subtly occurs with *Dr. Strangelove* and its use of the strangely irrelevant third-person narrator. This shift comes one film sooner than the curious and no-doubt telling decision to eliminate the third-person, omniscient, and scientific voice-over in *2001* that is highlighted by Mainar, to which I return in chapter 5.

Mario Falsetto, in his narratological study of Kubrick's body of work, also points out, in relation to *The Killing*, that "the use of an omniscient voice-over commentary is associated with a certain kind of filmic authority."[6] Both Mainar and Falsetto thus focus on voice-over narration as the key to how Kubrick's films either do or do not construct "an element of coherence"—or do or do not map stories that will guide audiences to some assumed narrative and thematic resolution. Indeed, voice-over narration best offers us initially the first opportunity to begin reexploring an ever-changing dynamic within the films directed by Stanley Kubrick. Before moving to trace a sense of affect in his later films, the voice-over first allows us to rechart a path that builds from an early belief that storytelling could be best and most explicitly rendered visible by the verbalizing and explaining of the mind. This then evolves, as I see it, to a later sensation that such clarity and certainty were, at best, elusive, ephemeral, fleeting—just like the mystery of the dead woman that Bill Harford will never solve in *Eyes Wide Shut.* Paolo Cherchi Usai correctly notes how "Kubrick's 'invisible' narrator, whose presence is so common in the director's [post-*Fear and Desire*] films—defining the twisted temporal framework of *The Killing* and presiding over the ample dramatic trajectory of *Barry Lyndon*—is here already omniscient" in the director's first film.[7] There are ways, however, in which the omniscient narrator of *Barry Lyndon* will not affirm "its control over the storytelling process"[8] in a way Kubrick's first film does. In later Kubrick films, the experience of the story itself confounds the failed symbolic (and occasionally literal) writer trying to react to it. The shift in attitude toward voice-over narration, certainly, points us to an act of failed writing, just as the failure of Jack Torrance as a writer pushes us to the ambiguity of *The Shining.* This is not, however, the issue with the voice-over narrator in *Fear and Desire.*

The present project begins with voice-over narration, something both theorists have approached before.[9] Yet Mainar and Falsetto leave unexplored the one Kubrick film that best illustrates how well voice-over narration can attempt a "certain kind of filmic authority" and show "a mastery of the text by itself." This is the one Kubrick film that I sense was perhaps the most dependent upon what the filmmaker later in his career referred to as "*the magic of words.*"[10] It is no small part of my project here to show how the first appearance of a slowly evolving shift from narrative clarity and authority to "a growing feeling that reality cannot be controlled"—as well as the clues to thinking about Kubrick's production more peripherally—lies in the experience of his little-seen 1953 film *Fear and Desire*, a project hitherto largely passed over, unnoted, by Kubrick scholars. As I will show in this chapter, *Fear and Desire* offers a stronger starting point for remapping the boundaries of narrative authority and diegetic chaos within the films of Stanley Kubrick. In a celebrated career that spanned more than forty years but astonishingly produced only thirteen feature-length films, *Fear and Desire* stands as the last exhumed text through which to better grasp the artistic evolution of one of cinema's most preeminent contributors.

Sensing and recharting the virtual—themes, meanings, motives—in this cinematic body requires mapping new points of orientation while also unearthing maps that journeyed before. This project is not merely my own imagined territory, somewhere between these pages and the films discussed. It is also a negotiation with the prior narrative imaginations—namely, the impressions drawn from the work of other critics, as well as the acts of narrators and narrations throughout Kubrick's films. To draw a map through the experience of these films, I first look back to the maps within the films themselves. And like many of Kubrick's later films, *Fear and Desire* opens with a voice-over narration (David Allen). Unlike the later films, however (save, perhaps, the third-person narrators who open *Spartacus* and, to a lesser extent, *The Killing*), the voice-over narrator begins *Fear and Desire* by plotting out for the audience some ambitious, if vague, philosophical ground. He intones seriously:

> There is a war in this forest. Not a war that has been fought, nor one that will be, but any war. And the enemies that struggle here do not exist unless we call them into being. For all of them, and all that happens now is outside history. Only the unchanging shapes of fear and doubt and death are from our world. These soldiers that you see keep our language and our time, but have no other country but the mind.

In this low-budget, once forgotten effort, the third-person narrator opens the film by declaring that the narrative structure and its characters exist in "no other country but the mind." The narrator in the film thus attempts to envision a map, charting out for us a narrative orientation to the story world. The narrator, writes Usai, "immediately imposes direct control over the course of the story."[11] The implication is that everything that happens in *Fear and Desire* thus exists through the mediation of this country of the mind—an illusory, narratively engaged realm that presumes authority over the characters and events within the film. In the early films of Stanley Kubrick, the country of the mind is but another facade—a way through which the mind imagines the country. But it is inadequate to the experience. The country of the mind is not the story world per se, and it is not in itself a map—the country of the mind is the *understanding* of a figurative or literal map, that which is marked as the orientation of a narrating consciousness to the story world beyond. The country of the mind is the narrative assumption about the story world therein charted. It is what the map orients us to within the story world. The country of the mind is an unembodied mediation between the narrator and the story world—a nonrepresented country expressed by, but also externalized from, the mind. It can be denoted figuratively by a voice-over, an expressionistic image, a sound—it can even be that which is denoted by the nuclear montage at the end of *Dr. Strangelove*, or charted by the Big Board. Kubrick's films point to the country of the mind whenever a cinematic moment marks ephemeral narrative assumptions about the story world.

All Kubrick's films situate instances of this facade (i.e., the country of the mind). What shifts and fluctuates is the rupture between the reliability and durability of these maps, the narrators, and the territories they seek to chart. The voice-over at the beginning of *Fear and Desire* supports the first instance of this kind of mapping and gives us little reason to doubt that the country of the mind varies much from the existential forest in which the battles play out. Yet in *Eyes Wide Shut*, events as they are mediated through the country of Bill's mind—where women are murdered in order to be silenced, and he is stalked because of his past behavior—may not be what he experiences in the story world at all. In *Fear and Desire* and *Eyes Wide Shut* (and in every Kubrick film in between), I envision the country of the mind as that which the explicit or implicit narrator sees as the story world unfolding, though it is rarely if ever synonymous with the story world itself. Nor is the country of the mind the narration itself, either, but rather a consequence of the narration, the thematic and discursive *vision* of the narration.

Of course, the country of the mind is also a deeply presumptuous, even pretentious, concept, and it well symbolizes the overconfidence of the film's formal and narrative ambitions. Norman Kagan regards *Fear and Desire* as a "fascinating effort"[12] (if also the work of "high school intellectuals at play"[13]). Perhaps on this point, I do not deviate much from Kagan, though I do hope to offer much more than plot summary. But—like Kagan—I too regard the film not as a polished cinematic masterpiece but as a fascinating effort that, in any case, points to new ways of perceiving the films of Stanley Kubrick.

This present study, despite all the previous criticisms—both valid and over-stated—of *Fear and Desire*, starts from the premise that we can learn a good deal about Kubrick's body of work by looking carefully at his first film. I do want to establish the backlash Kubrick's film faced. This hopefully calls atten-tion to how the young filmmaker may have been especially conscious of *Fear and Desire*'s weaknesses—as illustrated in the Warner Bros. press release described later in the chapter—and may have gradually, over the course of his career, rethought his style and production according to them. In the first part of this chapter, I wish to explore the stylistic decisions of *Fear and Desire* that Kubrick later refined, such as the use of voice-over narration, music, and multiple story threads[14]—all important elements in constructing an authori-tative narrative presence. We find in *Fear and Desire*'s opening voice-over, for instance, a crucial clue to understanding the filmmaker's early desire to elevate storytelling into and through the country of the mind. Specifically, I argue here that *Fear and Desire* allows us to rechart the journey of an artist from one who believed in the power of film as a transcendent medium, showing an ambitious understanding of the world and its own story space, to one who believed that film was most effective when letting go of its own obsession with meaning.

Because the characters and events exist seemingly as a projection of the mind of the narrator, *Fear and Desire* explicitly foregrounds an authoritative mediator between story and audience, asking viewers to trust the voice-over while the film attempts to play out this meditation on humanity and war. As one of the few to write on the film at length, Usai defends the film vigorously, in particular crediting the film's visual style; however, even he concedes that "the verbal flamboyance of the prologue, and of the film as a whole, overloads the narration with explicit philosophical metaphors."[15] Through the use of multiple story lines, manipulative music, and voice-over narration, *Fear and Desire* posits an authoritative representation of the film's story world—a com-plete reversal of Kubrick's later films, which broke free from and even criticize the seeming obsession with narrative authority and claims to thematic clarity. In contrast to previous critical discussions of the filmmaker's body of work, this study will show that Stanley Kubrick's career can and should be reconsid-ered in substantive ways through the lens of his very first feature directorial effort. To this end, I argue that *Fear and Desire* was not just the director's first feature-length film but also the first important one—not because his first effort was or was not a particularly good film (does it even matter?) but because *Fear and Desire* provides some crucial cues to understanding the ways in which narrative meaning can (and cannot) be constructed within and by a film. I believe we can better appreciate the later films by viewing them in light of Kubrick's first feature.

Like the later *Paths of Glory* and *Full Metal Jacket* (as well as less overt antiwar films such as *Dr. Strangelove* and *Barry Lyndon*), Kubrick's first film takes a moral stand against war; however, unlike his subsequent antiwar movies, which focus mostly on military establishments—the definitions of *cowardice* and *desertion*, boot camp, and the ominous War Room—*Fear and Desire* attacks war both more transparently and more vaguely, as a crime against humanity, and pays almost no attention to the institutional forces at work within the military unit (conversely, Kubrick's other antiwar films often become so preoccupied with the inner workings of the military that their respective wars, such as WWI and Vietnam, seem secondary). Within *Fear and Desire*'s relatively brief running time, these four main soldiers kill other enemy soldiers and kidnap an otherwise innocent country girl (later killed by one of the men, who lusts after her and subsequently lives in guilt for his actions) before eventually confronting more enemy soldiers, who are the doubles of the original soldiers (played by the same actors). After killing the enemies, their symbolic "twins," they finally escape on a raft to their home territory. Even without much use for a guide, the themes of *Fear and Desire*—war as humanity battling against itself, with soldiers struggling to fight the demons within—would seem apparent enough to most. In contrast to his other antiwar films, however, the use of allegory in *Fear and Desire* illustrates how much the filmmaker explicitly points out his views on war to audiences rather than allow such ambitious themes to develop through the organic and dramatic experience of the film itself. As one example, *Paths of Glory*'s court-martial proves more subtle and effective as symbolic of war as self-defeating than *Fear and Desire*'s method of twin casting.

Within *Fear and Desire*, additional uses of voice-over, mood music, and multiple story threads attempt to impose narrative meaning through this film's country of the mind. The dramatic, booming score of Gerald Fried plays over the film's credits, indicating early on the tendency to allow explicit narrative elements to establish *Fear and Desire*'s tone. Fried, meanwhile, would continue this type of mood music in *Killer's Kiss*, *The Killing*, and *Paths of Glory* (while Alex North—whose overt, potentially intrusive score for *2001* was also deleted, like the planned voice-over, from the sci-fi epic—would assume such duties for *Spartacus*). Later in *Fear and Desire*, as the four fleeing soldiers march through the forest, the film overlays their respective voice-overs, as each man discusses his anxiety about being trapped behind enemy lines. Such lines as "Nobody's safe here," "Are they watching me?" "They're all scared," "We're gonna hang from the trees tonight," and "I'm so scared" emanate from the men's minds and echo in rapid succession over a montage of the men working their way through the forest floor. Stating how "they're all scared" recalls the explicit opening discussion of "the unchanging shapes of fear and doubt." This particular kind of intense, multiple first-person subjectivity—the overlapping countries of the mind—would never again be deployed in Kubrick's films. Even the highly subjective narrative structure of something like *A Clockwork Orange* only serves to critique Alex's violent asociality, hatred, and self-absorption rather than win him sympathy and allegiance. There is no real *affirming* or *constructive* subjectivity in Kubrick's later films—by which I mean positive and constructive in the way the early voice-overs guide the audience or construct some semblance of meaning. The "interviews" in *Full Metal Jacket*, where characters answer questions to the camera (perhaps a moment of overt subjectivity or mindscreen), do not attempt to explain the emotions of the latter film's soldiers in the way that *Fear and Desire*'s voice-over had earlier; they may even detach the emotions and further undermine narrative authority in *Full Metal Jacket* by portraying the soldiers as generic and uninteresting in their discussions. In contrast to that style, however, *Fear and Desire* relies on the ability of each man to verbalize his mental and emotional state rather than to display such anxieties dramatically or between the lines of a standard military interview, as in *Full Metal Jacket*.

When the tense music returns in the next scene, as the soldiers approach the river, *Fear and Desire* yet again reminds audiences of the emotional tension being signified within the story. This kind of mood music returns shortly thereafter when the four men unexpectedly spot an enemy cabin; the music suggests that this location soon will be the sight of a dramatic confrontation, an emotional setup much like the drums that always play in the background, counting off the moments leading up to the executions at the climax of *Paths of Glory*. As the men approach the shack, the music becomes even louder and more forceful, building up the anxiety while awaiting their violent attack on the enemy soldiers inside (a similar musical buildup occurs when Sidney [Paul Mazursky] is left with the girl and the sequence leads slowly, but deliberately, to an attempted rape). The soldiers kill the men in the cabin, after which the third-person voice-over narrator returns, again attempting to put the themes within *Fear and Desire* into words, as Lt. Corby (Kenneth Harp) looks out silently over the murdered enemy soldiers:

> We spend our lives running our fingers down the lists in directories, looking for our real names, our permanent addresses. No man is an island? Perhaps that was true a long time ago, before the ice age. The glaciers have melted away and now we're all islands—parts of a world made of islands only.

It is difficult to pinpoint just what exactly the narrator is talking about while "running [his] fingers down the lists in directories." The metaphor Kubrick and screenwriter Howard O. Sackler employ here does not seem to fit the context of the massacre, other than as a (under)statement on each human's inability to connect with other people—"we're all islands." This idea, though, establishes what would go on to be perhaps *the* dominant theme of Kubrick's films and serves as an important way in which we can both remap Kubrick's films and think about the country of the mind's essential isolation from the same world it seeks to mediate.

Characters—all the way up to Bill Harford in *Eyes Wide Shut*—cannot relate to the people around them and must therefore fall back on their own mostly faulty assumptions about the world and its meaning. Thus, to avoid complete chaos, they resort to mapping out an arbitrary discursive order to make sense of their surroundings rather than beginning to move outside themselves and their own minds (off the isolation of the island), engaging actively with others, even at the risk of uncertainty and narrative chaos. This line also highlights *Fear and Desire*'s penchant for vague abstractions—common in the dialogue in the film—where the distance for the men to the front lines is "only a short distance, the distance between life and death." *Fear and Desire* also returns to this idea of people as islands at several other points, such as when Sidney begins to lose his mind and mumble incoherently. Positioning humans as being "islands" not only lays out a major theme of alienation within *Fear and Desire* (and many Kubrick films) but also again foregrounds the film's focus on the issue of narrative authority. Such a moment in the film is not unlike when, for example, Mac (Frank Silvera) floats down the river in a raft—literally his own "island" as a consequence of the country of the mind. This sequence, which I return to later, is also accompanied appropriately by Mac's voice-over. More generally speaking, rivers signified, ironically, social stagnation and estrangement in Kubrick's films, if we pair the events along the river in *Fear and Desire* with those moments later on in *A Clockwork Orange* and *Barry Lyndon*, where each film's protagonist retreats to gazing contemplatively by a river, both having been shut out from their respective societies and—as the latter film's third-person narrator suggests—met with "coldness . . . and resentment."[16]

After Sidney is left by the other three soldiers with the kidnapped girl, multiple story threads begin to emerge in *Fear and Desire*, and the elusive authority that first called these characters "into being" now begins using montage to draw explicit connections and meaning, about such themes as sanity, compassion, an animal instinct for survival, and basic human desires such as jealousy and lust, from the parallel sequences. The film cuts back and forth between Sidney (and the girl by the tree) and the other soldiers down by the river. This use of multiple story threads (echoed by both Davy's flashback and Iris's flashback within a flashback in *Killer's Kiss*) reached its highest form in *The Killing's* extremely complicated juggling of events and chronology leading up to the heist (well documented and dissected by Falsetto). Intriguingly, this elaborate intertwining of conflicting story lines was in fact prominently displayed in Kubrick's first few films and, just as importantly, rejected in later films. After *Dr. Strangelove*, his later works focused linearly on single protagonists—Alex, Jack, Bill—or confined groups, such as *Full Metal Jacket's* two military units and *The Shining's* family unit. After experiencing the three isolated settings in *Strangelove*, we never see more than one dominant point of view within the same story world of a Kubrick film. The point here is that the process of orienting audiences to events within the diegesis—in essence, the act of mapping a country of the mind—becomes less foregrounded as overt events within the film become more spatially limited and confined. For example, though we can presume that much happens outside the scope of Bill's perceptions within the story world of *Eyes Wide Shut*, there is no dominant, omniscient narrator who reveals it to us. Unmistakably, Bill is that film's narrator—and he is wholly incompetent at the task.

Once Sidney kills the girl (then runs off in hysterics as Mac watches, understandably befuddled), the three remaining soldiers regroup and decide to try to kill the enemy general. Mac goes down the river in a makeshift raft, while the other two prepare to assassinate the leader. At this point, the film adopts its most complicated narrative structure, as the story moves between Mac on the river, Corby and Fletcher (Steve Coit) outside the enemy headquarters, and the general himself inside his office. Meanwhile, as Mac rides down the river, his own first-person voice-over emerges:

> It's better . . . it's better to roll up your life into one night and one man and one gun. It hurts too much to keep hurting everyone else in every direction and to be hurt with all the separate hates exploding day after day. You can't help it. The curse buzzes out of your mouth with every word you say. And no one alive can tell which is which, or what you mean. Yeah. You try door after door when you hear voices you like behind them. But the knobs come off in your hand.

Like the third-person narrator in *Fear and Desire*, Mac's first-person voice-over attempts to stress his emotional state as well as the general ideas behind the film—humanity confronting itself, the desire for soldiers to stop fighting and killing, and how these desires subsequently eat away slowly at a soldier's sanity—emotions never explicitly stated in *Paths of Glory* or *Full Metal Jacket*, where the desires of the soldiers are no more clear than the con-

stant blank facade on the face of Leonard Lawrence, "Pyle" (Vincent D'Onofrio). The general's speech, meanwhile, reiterates this parallel descent into
madness, as he lectures about waiting to kill and to die and about preparing
for death. In one of the narrative's most visually explicit moments, *Fear and
Desire* cuts between Mac and the enemy general's respective speeches about
self-loathing and awaiting death, clearly attempting to strike a thematic connection between the two men as equally disgusted with, and exhausted by,
the act of war (echoing a similar parallel between the speeches of Spartacus
[Kirk Douglas] and Crassus [Laurence Olivier] years later). During these
moments, *Fear and Desire* intersplices the story thread of the other two soldiers, Corby and Fletcher, as they approach and eventually attack the enemy
compound, with these men's "doubles," the general, and his aide subsequently
gunned down. In the film's final moments, these claims to narrative authority—through dramatic mood music, the various speeches on war, and the
complicated parallel editing—work the audience deliberately toward *Fear and
Desire*'s violent conclusion. Thus, *Fear and Desire* repeatedly portrays a
human mind as attempting to provide authoritative order to, and impose
meaning on, the world this mind thinks it experiences. This notion offers a
fascinating avenue through which to better understand not only differing
forms of narrative order—those forms offered separately by such elements as
the voice-over and music in early films, then attempted with less success by
characters, such as Torrance and Harford, in later ones—but also the importance of the previously overlooked *Fear and Desire*. The formal and thematic
properties in Kubrick's films can be understood not apart from but instead
through the lens of his first film, *Fear and Desire*.

It is not terribly surprising that *Fear and Desire*—though not all that bad and,
in any aesthetic case, extremely important when examining Kubrick's entire
body of work—quickly fell out of circulation. "After 1956," writes Usai, *Fear
and Desire* "virtually disappears from critical discussions of the director. Two
years passed before Kubrick could bring himself to speak of the film, which
he remembered with almost excessive embarrassment."[17] As a result of such
apparent shame, it is equally predictable in retrospect that it took nearly forty
years after its original debut for Kubrick's first film to reemerge for audiences.[18] "Despite the opposite intentions of its creator," adds Usai, "*Fear and
Desire* soon began to acquire the status of a myth—a myth of failure, a work
with flaws of such number and magnitude as to require this total suppression
both of critical discussion and of all attempts to bring the film back to light."[19]
    When the film finally resurfaced in 1991 at the Telluride Film Festival,
Fear and Desire was understandably highly anticipated; the film, however, dis-

appointed many devoted Kubrick followers and most cineastes. Anticipating such a negative response, the filmmaker asked Warner Bros. to prepare a press release, stating that Kubrick "considers [the film] nothing more than a 'bumbling, amateur film exercise,' written by a failed poet, crewed by a few friends, and 'a completely inept oddity, boring and pretentious.'"[20] Despite the harshness of the words, Kubrick's self-criticism was not without justification. Although Kubrick's own personal opinion of the first film he directed is not essential for understanding either *Fear and Desire* or his larger body of films (it may even, the evidence so far suggests, inhibit it), such self-awareness does serve as the first of many points that may help indicate why the film was overlooked for so long. Kubrick's self-consciousness over *Fear and Desire* in particular is especially striking. For example, Usai finds it rightly perplexing that the filmmaker was so anxious to distance this film above all, asking, "Why was Kubrick so adamant about suppressing *Fear and Desire*, but not his early shorts, or *Killer's Kiss*"?[21] There is something there that caused Kubrick so much artistic anxiety for so long, and it would seem only fair to speculate that this artistic self-consciousness influenced the production of his later films. While some have kindly (and not inaccurately) written the movie off as "an initial practice piece,"[22] Thomas Allen Nelson nails *Fear and Desire*'s faults more specifically:

> While the themes of *Fear and Desire* crudely reflect a number of later Kubrick-
> ian preoccupations, their expression resembles that youthful grab-bag of 1950s
> bohemian negativism and existential self-congratulation that a fledgling direc-
> tor no doubt found attractive during the period when he and his first wife lived
> in Greenwich Village.[23]

As a blatantly allegorical war film, *Fear and Desire* suffers from a transparent obsession with trying to make profound yet ultimately thin and abstract statements on life—the work of an ambitious filmmaker who had a vague sense of what he wanted to say about such issues as war and mortality but had yet to find an effectively cinematic way of saying it. Or at least, Kubrick revealed in *Fear and Desire* a film that was reaching through a "grab-bag" of provocative potential, without actually accomplishing much in terms of meaning. As the opening suggests, *Fear and Desire* believes in the mediating narrative power of the country of the mind—where meanings and intentions within the story world could be brought apparently to the level of direct perception. Supposedly, Kubrick himself attempted to market the film in the early 1950s as an "allegorical" and "poetic" drama of "'man' lost in a hostile world—deprived of material and spiritual foundations—seeking his way to an understanding of himself, and of life around him."[24] Interestingly, the emphasis on the relationship with "the hostile world" directly foreshadows an identical phrase from the discarded opening narration of *2001*, made fifteen years later. The conscious effort to omit such didactic words was no doubt intended in some way to avoid the pretension of Kubrick's first film. Also echoing reactions to *2001*, Kubrick boldly predicted that *Fear and Desire* "will, probably, mean many things to different people, and it ought to."[25] This last note certainly is also an ironic prediction—not only because this will be an appropriate response to many later Kubrick films but also because *Fear and Desire*'s use of the voice-over makes such a response to the film problematic, at best. There is little room for ambiguity in the film's message, save perhaps in relation to its heavily muddled abstractions—abstractions that even the concepts in the title itself allude to (likewise echoed in the film's original working title, the equally vague and distracted *The Shape of Fear*). Yet—lest I risk trampling too far here—it should be noted that I do not consider *Fear and Desire* to be a horrible film overall, just a flimsy dramatic exercise that collapses quickly under the considerable weight of its own narrative and thematic aspirations.

And indeed when the film first opened in 1953, the response was not overly negative. *New York Times* movie critic Bosley Crowther noted that despite the fact that *Fear and Desire* "is uneven and sometimes reveals an experimental rather than a polished exterior," the filmmakers still "succeed in turning out a moody, often visually powerful study of subdued excitements."[26] Reportedly, legendary film critic and screenwriter James Agee even took Kubrick out and bought the young filmmaker a drink, declaring, "There are too many good things in [*Fear and Desire*] to call it arty."[27] Nonetheless, the film, for all its stylistic and thematic ambitions, still lacked a strong narrative and relied more on telling *Fear and Desire*'s themes than on showing such themes; from what can be uncovered in the film, Kubrick and Sackler apparently believed too much in the expository power of the abstract word. Even Crowther criticized the script as "more intellectual than explosive."[28] Indeed, among other characteristics, *Fear and Desire* repeatedly portrays the human mind as verbalizing abstract thoughts and providing authoritative thematic meaning and narrative order to events within the film. Fifteen years later (while working on *2001*), Kubrick himself would dismiss *Fear and Desire* as "a very inept and pretentious effort."[29] Kubrick should not have been so afraid of the film and its circulation, yet the fact remains that his own artistic self-consciousness had a deep effect on criticism.

Subsequently, most scholars have seemed anxious to follow Kubrick's lead, moving past the film and deemphasizing its place, along with *Spartacus* (another underconsidered effort), in the Kubrick canon. The limited availability of the film only further encouraged this dismissal, no doubt, but I suspect that *Fear and Desire*, however easy to access, was not initially an important stopping point for those—in the 1970s and 1980s—mostly interested in explicating the supposed awe-inspiring genius of *Dr. Strangelove*, *2001*, and *A Clockwork Orange*. But now, it is more relevant for a new wave of scholarship to go back to places previously marginalized, well aware that so much terrain has already been otherwise scoured. Still, Kubrick's first film is not without its scholarly detours—some critics have attempted to acknowledge and investigate *Fear and Desire* over the years, though those same few scholars generally dismiss *Fear and Desire* shortly thereafter, perhaps because of its thematic weaknesses or amateur production values.[30] Typically, the film is mentioned in passing, such as when Michel Ciment observes (almost as an aside) that with *Full Metal Jacket*, Kubrick "was doing a remake of his first film, *Fear and Desire*,"[31] an interesting possibility otherwise unsupported and unelaborated upon. No doubt, some scholars avoided the film because, as with its director, they simply felt it wasn't any good (or good enough). My own intention here is not to add to the critical negligence by arguing that Kubrick should have known better than to tell a story allegorically, or to criticize him for making a film that on the surface seems highly pretentious. Instead, I only wish to establish the strong backlash Kubrick's film faced and call attention to how we can specifically sense the ways in which the young, noted perfectionist may have been particularly sensitive to *Fear and Desire*'s weaknesses and subsequently worked to refine them.

Almost definitely, the most comprehensive look at *Fear and Desire* thus far has been Usai's "Checkmating the General: Stanley Kubrick's *Fear and Desire*," which was appropriately published in the George Eastman House's own artistic and scholarly journal, *Image*.[32] In this article, Usai attempts to unpack the history of the film and its crucial thematic and formal qualities. In fact, Usai goes so far as to argue that *Fear and Desire* "seemed instead to conceal—under the appearance of an eager but failed attempt—the essential nucleus of Kubrick's world, the institutions that would lie dormant for almost twenty years, emerging finally in his two latest films [at the time of his writing], *The Shining* and *Full Metal Jacket*."[33] In particular, Usai compares the opening voice-over narration of *Fear and Desire* ("outside history") to "*Full Metal Jacket*'s depiction of military training and action as a timeless expression of human behavior."[34] In other words, *Full Metal Jacket* shows what *Fear and Desire* only tells, according to Usai. Such a connection between these two particular antiwar Kubrick films is not entirely a coincidence, as Usai implicitly develops the argument that Ciment only hints at—that *Full Metal Jacket* is in some ways a reworking or rewriting of *Fear and Desire*. Such an argument would have particular historical urgency for Usai, as *Full Metal Jacket* was the most recent Kubrick film at the time of his article (originally appearing in the late 1980s and then republished in English in the mid-1990s). Usai builds the argument that the film's abstractions make *Fear and Desire* "a rather ambiguous war story"[35]:

> Some of its elements are classic [to the war genre]: a lost platoon, a mission to accomplish, an impossible escape, men of differing temperaments, feminine presence reduced to a minimum, and, underlying the narrative, an apparent pacifism. But, if the film lacks heroes, where are its antiheroes? What in fact is the mission? And why do the same actors play two different roles?[36]

Usai is less reserved in his praise for the film than other Kubrick scholars overall—not rejecting the film entirely or (as I argue here) showing how the film serves as a specific point for rethinking the evolution of Kubrick's narrative sensibilities. Usai in fact goes so far as to suggest that—in some respects—*Fear and Desire* was not a practice piece, but rather the *quintessential* Kubrick film, right out of the gate, and that this transparency in a way is what may have troubled the filmmaker so much ultimately. It was, in a sense, too explicitly "Kubrick" for even Kubrick's own liking. Looking over Kubrick's entire body of work, Usai argues:

> A comprehensive, in-depth study of Kubrick's iconography, and of the themes that recur throughout his work, would be likely to show that an impressive number of these concerns are most fully and explicitly realized in *Fear and Desire*. . . . Thus it is no surprise that Kubrick wanted to rid himself of such an explicit film, one that revealed far too much of his personal agenda. Kubrick tried to suppress and perhaps destroy it, as if to deny its existence, not just because *Fear and Desire* seemed to him nothing but a pretentious and amateurish effort, but because the film proclaims with uncalculated immediacy the major creative strategies of the director's oeuvre that would follow in the coming years.[37]

In a way then, Usai argues that (for Kubrick, at least) *Fear and Desire's* serious flaws were not that the film failed to realize Kubrick's later themes but that it realized them all too well. I am tempted to argue that Usai gives Kubrick a bit too much credit here—suggesting that Kubrick wanted to be a little more elusive and shifty in his deployment of the themes he apparently had already mastered as a storyteller, even though he had yet to make a feature-length film.

There is the oft-repeated chess metaphor here—"Kubrick, the consummate chess player, had committed in his youth the most unforgivable mistake of the game: announcing his strategy for capturing the adversary's king (or general) with his opening move."[38] Surely the other problem here is that it may be a bit too presumptive to suggest that Kubrick already knew exactly what he wanted to say. Certainly I agree that what have already been identified as several Kubrickian themes appear to be already in play in *Fear and Desire*. However, if we take one of the strongest effects from this first film to be the need to resist putting meanings into words, to resist meanings entirely, then perhaps it would be a mistake to assume automatically that there is a definite "agenda" or "strategy" beneath the surface of Kubrick's later films. Perhaps Kubrick was not so much rethinking his cinematic chess game as he was unthinking it. For me, Nelson's metaphor of the "youthful grab-bag of 1950s bohemian negativism and existential self-congratulation" works better than that of "the chess player" for attempting to articulate Kubrick's ambitions or to conceptualize the production of *Fear and Desire*'s thematics. Chess implies that Kubrick had it all figured out—the fully formed, fully mature, old-school auteur, toying with his audience's assumptions and expectations. The grab-bag, on the other hand, suggests that Kubrick was a young, talented, and ambitious artist still in training, who was overreaching to say anything and everything he thought might have an effect on its audience. The grab-bag metaphor implies a soon-to-be great filmmaker who—despite great energy and effort—had not yet figured out what to say, or how to say it. As his career evolved past *Fear and Desire*, Kubrick conceivably did not attempt to go further into the country of the mind but rather attempted to move outside it entirely. Usai argues that the main revision Kubrick made after *Fear and Desire* was in better hiding his plan, crafting a more subtle cinematic story. Certainly, Kubrick and the rest of the film's crew could not have been expected to master the filmmaking and storytelling process so quickly—an important point all these film critics openly acknowledge. I, meanwhile, do not disagree with these previous sentiments—I only wonder if perhaps Kubrick's response to his first film is better thought of not in terms of telling a story better but as trying not to tell so much of a story at all. The story becomes—literally in *The Shining*—that *there is no story.*

NOTES

1. Alexander Walker, *Stanley Kubrick Directs* (New York: Harcourt Brace Jovanovich, 1972), 14.

2. Michel Chion, *Eyes Wide Shut*, trans. Trista Selous (London: British Film Institute, 2002), 41.

3. Chion, *Eyes Wide Shut*, 84.

4. In her book on an otherwise undertheorized topic, Claudia Gorbman asks rhetorically, "What and how does music signify in conjunction with the images and events of a

story film?" *Unheard Melodies: Narrative Film Music* (Bloomington: Indiana University Press, 1987), 2. In this study, I focus on what Gorbman's discussion delineates as the signifying qualities of film music. In particular, this study employs the assumption that this type of music is a "signifier of emotion" ("soundtrack music may set specific moods and emphasize particular emotions . . . a signifier of emotion itself") and a vehicle for "narrative cueing" ("music gives referential and narrative cues, e.g., indicating point-of-view, supplying formal demarcations, and establishing setting and characters") (73).

5. Luis M. Garcia Mainar, *Narrative and Stylistic Patterns in the Films of Stanley Kubrick* (Rochester, N.Y.: Camden House, 1999), 58.

6. Mario Falsetto, *Stanley Kubrick: A Narrative and Stylistic Analysis*, 2nd ed. (Westport, Conn.: Praeger, 2001), 5.

7. Paolo Cherchi Usai, "Checkmating the General: Stanley Kubrick's *Fear and Desire*," *Image* 38, no. 1/2 (Spring/Summer 1995): 13.

8. Usai, "Checkmating the General," 13. While Usai makes connections between the different third-person narrators in Kubrick's films, he does not highlight the later voices' sense of narrative detachment and thematic irony, which mark them in sharp contrast to the early films—especially, but not only, *Fear and Desire*.

9. Most rigorously, Falsetto attempts to explicate a few of Kubrick's voice-over narrations yet abstains from identifying any trends or ruptures among them, other than to differentiate first-person from third-person narrators in the different films. Falsetto clearly believes that the unreliable voice-over narrator goes back at least to *The Killing*, where he uses two instances of "temporal errors" to argue that there is an attempt by Kubrick to "undercut the conventional faith in the authority of the voice-over." *Narrative and Stylistic Analysis*, 5. In his book, Falsetto attempts a very strict formal reading of the filmmaker's most famous films (with the conscious intent of avoiding the one popular film Kubrick's exact control over has been the most debated: *Spartacus*). Falsetto's main focus is on the visual properties of Kubrick's films, such as editing, the manipulation of camera shots, and point of view. Though Falsetto does break down the pattern of plotting in films such as *The Killing* and *Dr. Strangelove*, he shows a greater interest in shot composition than in the dynamics of story and discourse. Overall, Falsetto tries to prove that Kubrick employed very careful and precise manipulation of temporal and narrative ordering, without focusing on a particular overall thematic argument.

Written five years later, Mainar's work extends Falsetto's discussion. Yet Mainar also attempts to bridge such an analysis of Kubrick's films with less formalist approaches—primarily, the thematic and explicatory approach, usually influenced by the auteur theory that most prominent existing Kubrick scholars employ. Mainar singles out the following studies for this group: Alexander Walker's *Stanley Kubrick Directs* (1972; expanded, with the help of Sybil Taylor and Ulrich Ruchti, into *Stanley Kubrick, Director: A Visual Analysis* in 1999), Norman Kagan's *The Cinema of Stanley Kubrick* (1972), Gene D. Phillips's *Stanley Kubrick: A Film Odyssey* (1975), Thomas Allen Nelson's *Kubrick: Inside a Film Artist's Maze* (1982; revised and expanded in 2000), Michel Ciment's *Kubrick: The Definitive Edition* (1983; revised in 2001), and Robert Philip Kolker's *A Cinema of Loneliness* (1988; most recently revised in 2000). Mainar also identifies two distinct trends in Kubrick scholarship since the early 1970s, when such critical efforts first began emerging—"a formalist [approach] based on the analysis of style and narrative patterning, and a completely symptomatic [using David Bordwell's definition of the word] study that draws on different interpretative cues present in the films and that generally leads the critic to postmodernist issues." Mainar finds both areas lacking, with the former being "mere evaluation that stems from stylistic analysis" and the latter being a "consideration of postmodernist issues that at times seems completely disconnected from the films." Subsequently, Mainar seeks to join the two divergent schools of thought, with the intention of bridging "the gap between structure and ideology." *Narrative and Stylistic Patterns*, 2.

10. As quoted in Alexander Walker, Sybil Taylor, and Ulrich Ruchti, *Stanley Kubrick, Director: A Visual Analysis* (New York: Norton, 1999), 184.

11. Usai, "Checkmating the General," 13.

12. Norman Kagan, *The Cinema of Stanley Kubrick* (New York: Holt, Rinehart, and Winston, 1972), 18.

13. Kagan, *The Cinema of Stanley Kubrick*, 11.

14. I define "multiple story threads" as a narrative structure that has several distinct story lines moving simultaneously. I see these structures as instances of a narrative authority because they directly call the audience's attention to a narrative presence that—by juxtaposing certain diegetic moments—is attempting to impose meaning on the story world.

15. Usai, "Checkmating the General," 13.

16. Usai argues that the river in *Fear and Desire* is that "which the film's explicit allegory identifies as the endless flow of time." "Checkmating the General," 27. Such a reading would not be incompatible with *A Clockwork Orange* and *Barry Lyndon*, too, if we see their respective moments of contemplation as also a time for their acknowledging growing up and, even, growing old.

17. Usai, "Checkmating the General," 9.

18. It may not have been only artistic embarrassment that caused Kubrick to marginalize and disown the film for so long. In a parenthetical aside, Usai suggests that

> [Kubrick's] divorce from Toba took place the same year in which the film was shot; and, according to James B. Harris, the producer of some of Kubrick's subsequent films, the director approached him in his desperate search for the money needed to complete the project, and even asked him to try and sell *Fear and Desire* to television networks, among other ploys. "Checkmating the General," 9.

19. Usai, "Checkmating the General," 10.

20. Quoted in Vincent LoBrutto, *Stanley Kubrick: A Biography* (New York: Donald I. Fine, 1997), 91.

21. Usai, "Checkmating the General," 9.

22. Walker, *Stanley Kubrick Directs*, 44.

23. Thomas Allen Nelson, *Kubrick: Inside a Film Artist's Maze*, 2nd ed. (Bloomington: Indiana University Press, 2000), 22.

24. These quotes come from a letter written by Kubrick to *Fear and Desire*'s eventual distributor, Joseph Burstyn. As quoted in Usai, "Checkmating the General," 3.

25. Usai, "Checkmating the General," 3.

26. Bosley Crowther, "*Fear and Desire*," *New York Times*, 1 April 1953, 35.2.

27. As quoted in Gene Phillips, *Stanley Kubrick: A Film Odyssey* (New York: Popular Library, 1975), 18.

28. Crowther, *"Fear and Desire,"* 35.2.

29. As quoted in Kagan, *The Cinema of Stanley Kubrick*, 16.

30. Aside from biographers such as Vincent LoBrutto and John Baxter, scholars Norman Kagan, Thomas Allen Nelson, and Gene Phillips give *Fear and Desire* the most scrutiny in relation to Kubrick's larger body of work, though only Kagan devotes more than a page or two of criticism, much of which is plot summary.

31. Michel Ciment, *Kubrick: The Definitive Edition*, trans. Gilbert Adair (New York: Faber and Faber, 2000), 234.

32. At the time of the article, Usai was a senior curator at the George Eastman House, one archive where pristine prints of film are still available, despite Kubrick's attempts to remove the film from circulation. Thus, Usai's decision and ability to write such a detailed article on the film is not so surprising.

33. Usai, "Checkmating the General," 11.

34. Usai, "Checkmating the General," 11.

35. Usai, "Checkmating the General," 8.

36. Usai, "Checkmating the General," 8.

37. Usai, "Checkmating the General," 27.

38. Usai, "Checkmating the General," 27.

· *3* ·

Taking Life Too Seriously: Imposing Narrative Authority from *Killer's Kiss* to *Lolita*

> It's crazy how you can get yourself in a mess sometimes and not even be able to think about it with any sense and yet not be able to think about anything else. You get so you're no good for anything or anybody. Maybe it begins by taking life too serious. Anyway, I think that's the way it began for me.
>
> —Davy Gordon, *Killer's Kiss*

Killer's Kiss also begins with voice-over narration, though this time the dialogue is in the first person. Instead of a gravely serious, impersonal voice, we hear the film's protagonist, a boxer named Davy Gordon (Jamie Smith), who tells us he gets himself in a "mess" by "taking life too serious." On one level, Davy's words read as little more than standard *noir* fare from the 1940s and 1950s (typical and probably derivative of such contemporary films as *Double Indemnity* [1944], *The Killers* [1946], and *Sunset Boulevard* [1950])—a recounting of regret and loss that then opens the door for the rest of the film to be told primarily in flashback. However, the opening voice-over narration also crucially creates the effect of a kind of personal confession from Kubrick himself, and perhaps from writer Howard Sackler as well, as though the young collaborators were implicitly aware of how *Fear and Desire* took the cinematic representation of life "too serious"—that is to say, imposing too much meaning on the story world. This particular way of remapping the opening voice-over of *Killer's Kiss* (i.e., as a response to the prior film) takes on even greater resilience when one considers that "taking life too serious" is not even a particularly strong theme in the narrative that follows. If *Killer's Kiss* is not interested in taking life too seriously, it does so by virtue of the fact that the latter film has a much less ambitious narrative and thematic plan than *Fear and Desire*; instead of a meditation on war and humanity, this later film seeks only to tell a relatively simple tale about a boxer; his crush on a beautiful neighbor, Gloria (Irene Kane); and his run-ins with the New York underworld. If *Killer's Kiss* lacks the thematic ambition of *Fear and Desire*, however, the later film does show a greater interest in breaking away from allegory and in telling a story more realistically. Almost undoubtedly influenced by Kubrick's earlier documentary work,[1] much of *Killer's Kiss* seeks a realistic representation of the city surrounding the primary characters, even if one heavily filtered, as I discuss later, through the country of Davy's mind.

Starting with a subsequent film such as *Killer's Kiss*, the roots of the voice-over in Kubrick's early films—the continuing need to chart out a way of receiving story events—can be traced all the way back to *Fear and Desire*'s declaration that the film exists in the country of the mind. There, we first see the cognitive ambitions for the country of the mind, ambitions that continue through *Lolita*. Meanwhile, it is manifestations of the country of the mind subsequent to *Fear and Desire* that I attempt to document in earnest in this chapter. Similar narrative authorities continue the trend. *The Killing* begins with a third-person narrator discussing how one of the film's characters "had as much effect on the final outcome of the operation as a single piece of a jumbo jigsaw puzzle has to its predetermined final design. Only the addition of the missing fragments of the puzzle would reveal whether the picture was as he guessed it would be." Here, *The Killing* returns the audience to the same narrative and thematic clarity used to delineate *Fear and Desire*, which explicitly reminded the audience that everything that happened in the film occurred "outside history." Later, *The Killing* reinforces the idea of narrative as a jigsaw puzzle when introducing Johnny Clay, the heist's mastermind, as "perhaps the most important thread in the unfinished fabric [and the person who] furthered its design."

Paths of Glory (1957), moreover, opens with a similarly omniscient narrator declaring that "successful attacks [during the trench warfare of WWI] were measured in hundreds of yards and paid for in lives by hundreds of thousands." Though not an allegory, *Paths of Glory*'s opening voice-over—like that of *Fear and Desire*—does as much as the narrator in Kubrick's first film to tell audiences what they should think about these historical events and how they should feel about them as anything else. As though the general horror of war (as well as the image of war that *Paths of Glory* depicts shortly thereafter) was not sufficient by itself, the narrator explicitly repeats to audiences the terrible toll suffered in armed conflict. *Spartacus*'s opening voice-over also preaches about how "the [Roman] Republic lay fatally stricken with a disease called human slavery. The age of the dictator was at hand, waiting in the shadows for the event to bring it forth." As with *Fear and Desire*, *Spartacus* shows no interest in allowing the film's themes to develop dramatically during the experience of the film. The voice-over narrator plots out exactly what he hopes events in *Spartacus* are intended to be about thematically. Whereas *Fear and Desire* tells the audience about humanity being at war with itself, *Spartacus* talks about the "disease" of slavery, as though such a human tragedy could not speak, had not already spoken, for itself.

Then, decades later, in *Eyes Wide Shut*, Bill Harford suggests Kubrick's final (failed) narrator—one far removed from the third-person narrators (who were omniscient and all-knowing) in *Fear and Desire*, *The Killing*, and *Spartacus*—whose attempts at narrative authority and meaning are constantly undermined by other characters in the film. When Bill goes to see the woman's corpse in the morgue, to verify her death, we hear a voice-over of the woman saying, in an aural flashback from the earlier scene, that their behavior could cost the lady her life and possibly his, as well. A product of Bill's mind, this voice-over explicitly foregrounds how Bill is taking two fundamentally separate events (her words from one scene and his image of her body in another) and constructing in the country of the mind a narrative of murder and sacrifice to connect the two. Thus, the film highlights an increasingly rare use of voice-over narration—an overt instance of Bill as narrator—as an arbitrary reconstruction of the human mind and not as a moment of narrative clarity (the black and white expressionistic images of his wife [Nicole Kidman] engaged in a sexual act with an anonymous naval officer being another instance). Importantly, this is one of the only instances of something approximating a voice-over narration in *Eyes Wide Shut*, with Bill recalling her words as though they were a voice-over (the other instance is very similar—as Bill recalls his wife's verbal description of the said hypothetical sex act in an aural flashback while he is staring at her, sitting at the kitchen table and talking to their daughter). Dominant from *Fear and Desire* through *Killer's Kiss*, *The Killing*, and so forth, up until *Dr. Strangelove*, voice-over narration becomes an increasingly irrelevant, even nonexistent device in Kubrick's films. This stylistic change perhaps begins at the end of the first half of *Barry Lyndon*, when the film literally tunes out the third-person narrator halfway through his dictation to the audience. By the time Kubrick came to make his last work, the director had stripped away such rhetorical devices (or kept them, but only to critique their foolish assumptions), moving further away from any explicit notion of narrative clarity or verbalizing—"the mastery of the text by itself"—in both the structures and, importantly, the characters of his films.

KILLER'S KISS

In *Killer's Kiss*, we can first see Kubrick's films beginning to refine the issues of narrative authority presented in *Fear and Desire* by way of this subtle shift away from some of the verbal abstractions previously displayed. *Killer's Kiss*, if nothing else, shows a vague awareness of how words can kill sounds and images with too much meaning. Structurally, however, *Killer's Kiss* is not a complete rebuttal of his earlier film, even with the thematic awareness that it may be easy to take life too seriously. Kubrick's second film still relies on a frame narrative, and almost all of the film is told through Davy's memory. Much of the story in *Killer's Kiss* still exists through the mediation of an overt country of the mind—only the "mind" in question is now Davy's. Here, Davy is an authoritative narrator, with whom the audience is clearly meant to align itself. He is the hero of the film—a small-time boxer who struggles through the ugly world of promoters, dance hall owners, and gangsters to find peace and happiness with his lover at the film's end. In other words, *Killer's Kiss* adopts Davy's point of view without reservation; we follow him and have no reason to doubt his character or dependability as a storyteller.[2] Almost the whole film is told as Davy's flashback. This device allows the film to align with Davy's point of view without disruption—save for one curious sequence.

Halfway through the film, Gloria tells the story of her dead sister, Iris. In these few minutes, Gloria assumes complete control of the narrative structure, with her dialogue with Davy bleeding into a first-person voice-over. Gloria's narration, meanwhile, plays over the image of her sister, a ballerina, dancing alone on a nameless stage, surrounded by darkness and illuminated only by a single, harsh light. Gloria proceeds to tell the story of how, little by little, she began to be jealous of her sister's success and how her jealousy led to her lashing out at Iris after their father's death and, subsequently, led additionally to Iris's suicide shortly thereafter. This shift to Gloria's point of view adds little to the film, other than to continue the film's thematic discussion of loss and regret. Arguably, a break also exists between Davy's narration and Gloria's filmic image,[3] as though Davy, the film's narrator, could not possibly see the memories inside Gloria's mind and thus reconstruct them as a memory for the audience; however, I would argue that the filmic image derives not from Gloria's mind but instead, as with much of the rest of the film, from Davy's. The sparseness of the image itself—the bare, darkened stage, with the ballerina at a distance and thus denied many distinct features—suggests that Gloria's narration is not in fact accompanied by images from Gloria's specific memory but rather is Davy's own reconstruction of Gloria's story.

Killer's Kiss, as previously noted, suggests a less pretentious route of overtly narrating by switching from a third-person omniscient authority to a more realistic first-person narrator who does not pretend to know as much about such grandiose issues as "the unchanging shapes of fear and doubt" as the *Fear and Desire* narrator claims to. However, even the opening narration of *Killer's Kiss* suggests a desire to put something abstract into words and not to let the story events go uncharted. By stating that one could "not even be able to think about *it*" and that "*it* begins by taking life too serious," Davy hovers around a concept and tries to approximate "it" linguistically without directly stating whatever "it" is he means to discuss. He speaks of a "mess," yet such a description does little to clarify the situation that causes the problem. In other words, Davy repeats many of the same errors that *Fear and Desire*'s narrators had previously committed—he speaks in broad generalities, hoping that some kind of intangible and universal meaning, rather than specific dramatic point, will arise between the linguistic cracks. His voice-over must *mean* something. Moreover, his difficulties with locating "it" suggest an emerging awareness of narrative and thematic chaos and foreshadows the later difficulty of subsequent Kubrickian protagonists to locate the meaning of events before them.

As with the other openings of Kubrick films, *Killer's Kiss* relies on Davy's voice-over narration to compress the thematic and story content of *Killer's Kiss*, providing a very clear chart through the story world. During one breakfast scene, Davy's voice-over (where he talks about [ironically] talking about himself) about being a "wash-up" as a boxer and about one day returning to Seattle supplants the actual diegetic conversation running concurrently with Davy's nondiegetic words. This discussion then leads into Gloria's voice-over about her family. At the conclusion of the flashback (within the flashback), *Killer's Kiss* then cuts to Davy at the train station, where he was at the opening of the film. This move certainly reminds the audience that the whole story is told in flashback—yet the scene of a reminiscing Davy, who tells the audience about how Gloria "got dressed and we went out for a walk and I bought her an ice cream and saw her laugh for the first time," actually compresses a lot of expository information in *Killer's Kiss* and shows the extent to which Davy has a narrative command of story events. In addition to Gloria's emotional shifts, the two young people also fall in love and decide to spend the rest of their lives together in a matter of a few minutes of exposition here. Moreover, the audience not only hears Davy's description of events, but the film also denies the viewer an image of what actually happened (or at least, how Davy remembered and perceived things as happening), showing instead an image of the young boxer pacing slowly in the train station. In this moment, Davy becomes the only source of information, having denied the audience both diegetic sound and image from the flashback. We see his blank face, but his voice continues to guide us through the story. There is no overt narrative chaos and tension, as we feel in later films. Such moments occur several times in *Killer's Kiss*; Davy describes what he thinks and feels and even, sometimes, what he physically does in the course of the narrative, in place of our own visual or aural experiences with these described internal reactions and external behaviors.

Early in *Killer's Kiss*, Davy sits on the subway and reads a letter from his aunt and uncle, the contents of which are realized cinematically by the uncle's voice-over. The music—clearly aligned with Davy himself—that accompanies this scene evokes a sentimental feeling for home. This kind of slow jazz, composed by Gerald Fried (who also scored *Fear and Desire*), returns again and again throughout the film, which comes close to suggesting a vague sense of nostalgia—perhaps as an inherent part of Davy's flashback into the past, though also possibly as a kind of general evocation of the mood and atmosphere of crime films of the time. Through words and music, the film repeatedly emphasizes Davy's narrative authority.

THE KILLING

Even more so than *Killer's Kiss*, *The Killing* relies heavily on voice-over narration; however, this later film uses the same device to much the same end—simple story exposition. While *Killer's Kiss* uses first-person voice-over to compress story information, decrease dubbing problems, and include the audience in Davy's thought processes, *The Killing* uses its one third-person omniscient narrator to give coherence to the many story threads running through the extremely complicated film. The specific, matter-of-fact narration contrasts sharply with the more general voice-overs that opened other films:

> At exactly 3:45 on that Saturday afternoon in the last week of September, Marvin Unger was perhaps the only one among the 100,000 people at the track who felt no thrill at the running of the sixth race. He was totally disinterested in horse racing and held a lifelong contempt for gambling. Nevertheless, he had a five-dollar win bet on every horse in the fifth race. He knew, of course, that this rather unique system of betting would more than likely result in a loss, but he didn't care. For after all, he thought, what would the loss of $20 or $30 mean in comparison to the vast sum of money at stake?

In these few sentences, *The Killing* at once both focuses the voice-over narration on a single person with specific preoccupations (gambling, horse races), rather than on abstract ideas—such as "fear," "doubt," or a "mess"—and establishes the film's main subject of "the vast sum of money at stake." However, Kubrick then follows up this opening moment of *The Killing*, after a couple of sequences of dialogue, with yet another general third-person voice-over discussion—one that, as with previous films, maps out the structural and thematic ambitions of the film rather transparently:

> Waiting for the race to become official, he [Marvin] began to feel as if he had as much effect on the final outcome of the operation as a single piece of a jumbo jigsaw puzzle has to its predetermined final design. Only the addition of the missing fragments of the puzzle would reveal whether the picture was as he guessed it would be.

Dana Polan claims that many Kubrick voice-overs, especially *The Killing*, suggest a sort of "self-parodic blandness," using specific examples from *Killer's Kiss*.[4] Perhaps, within the world of film noir, such a voice-over narrator by 1956 would seem to parody genre conventions of the time. Indeed, there are some humorous moments in the voice-over as well, though not to the extent that one could safely argue that such humor obviously and consciously derived from a smug and clever self-awareness. If there is parody in the film, it is just as easily unintentional as intentional. While Polan's argument about *Killer's Kiss* and *The Killing* might work if it locates its place along an alternate historical trajectory of film noir, it neglects to take into account how such heavy-handed, overly explanatory exposition was very common in Kubrick's early films. Looking across this body of work, the opening narrations—from *Fear and Desire* to *Spartacus*—do not support the argument of a self-aware parody in *The Killing*, even if they are sometimes absurd and often bland (find me a pre-*A Clockwork Orange* voice-over that isn't bland). Alexander Walker, on the other hand, offers a detailed and convincing explanation of Kubrick's insistence on voice-over as an authoritative narrative presence, at least early on, specifically in relation to *The Killing* (and it is worth quoting at length):

> It may be pertinent to note that Kubrick's first short, *Day of the Fight*, was deliberately aimed at the same market as *The March of Time*. Of course, his fondness for narrative exposition cannot be explained away this simply. Kubrick, it is worth remembering, belongs to a pretelevision generation whose sense of drama was still shaped to some degree by the aural impact of radio. Narration is a strong identity mark of his films. It is one way, as he once remarked, of cutting directly through stage convention and conveying essential information without tedious use of dialogue or other expository scenes. One grants him this. Yet the narration, usually brief and resonant with foreboding even when it has a ticker-tape succinctness, as in *The Killing*, is like an aural note he strikes to which he tunes the rest of the film.[5]

Walker's defense, I think, is crucial here. The influence of radio on his generation would encourage Kubrick to use words early on as a form of authoritative narration, at least until he had begun to develop a more cinematic voice. And the third-person narrator in *The Killing*, as Walker suggests, establishes the rhythm, like a news report, for the entire structure while also attempting to impose meaning on the events within the film. For all his wordiness, pretension, redundancy, and absurdity, *The Killing*'s narrator emerges as an authoritative narrator—a necessary discursive tool—the country of whose mind is crucial to the tightness and efficiency of the story's movement. As with Kubrick's other early films, *The Killing*'s narrator extends from the "aural impact of radio." Here was a time when voice-overs were not only an authoritative source of exposition but also, essentially, the only source (save, perhaps, music and dialogue) of background exposition (this idea is reinforced in *The Killing* later, when—after the heist occurs—a radio broadcaster describes the events of the crime, not unlike the narrator would). Through the remainder of the film, the voice-over narrator returns not only as an interpretive guide but also as *The Killing*'s authoritative narrator, mediating the importance of each separate character's story line with the others.

Throughout the film, the country of the mind—the vision of Kubrick's authoritative narrator—continually returns with the voice-over narrator to connect the story lines explicitly for audiences. After the first scene featuring Marvin, another scene introducing Officer Kennan is established: "About an hour earlier that same Saturday afternoon in September in another part of the city, Patrolman First Class Randy Kennan had some personal business to attend to." After Clay is brought into the narrative, Mike, who "a half an hour earlier at approximately 6:30 . . . came home," follows him. Likewise, George is introduced in a similar manner: "At 7:15 that same night, George Peatty, the track cashier, arrived at his apartment." The narrator's highly specific chronological ordering of events continues still: "Three days later at 10:15 on a Tuesday morning, Johnny Clay began the final preparations [for the racetrack heist]." In these scenes, the narrator attempts to situate every character in the diegesis in relation to each other, as well as every moment in connection to every other moment, giving narrative order to the story world. The third-person narrator becomes so descriptive of the events occurring within *The Killing* that at one point he even tells the audience that "four days later [after Clay rents a motel room], at 7:30 a.m., Sherry Peatty was wide awake," leaving less room for audience interpretation of the scene and illustrating the extent to which the narrator within the film's discourse attempts to verbally control the perception of *every* story event in the film. Although the narrator does not attempt to tell audiences why she was wide awake, that this fact is specifically pointed out reiterates how the narrator attempts to construct a narrative context for the scene immediately as it begins, pointing the audience's attention directly to Sherry. Indeed, the narrator always returns at the beginning of a sequence, as though *The Killing* must always narratively establish a set way of receiving the story events—in this case, focusing our attention on Sherry (or Clay, Mike, Kennan, and so forth) as the centering point for the scene.

When the day of the heist begins unfolding, the voice-over narrator continues to overtly guide audiences through the story: "Earlier that morning, at 5:00, Red Lightning [one of the horses] was fed only a half portion of feed in preparation for the seventh race that afternoon, the $100,000 Landsdowne Stakes." Shortly thereafter, "at 7:00 that morning, Johnny Clay began what might be the last day of his life." Here, the narrator not only moves forth the action but also adds an extraneous commentary in an attempt to heighten the audience's awareness of what is at stake. Moreover, the narrator describes every action Clay takes—his visit to the airport at exactly 7:00, his trip to the florist at 8:15, his stop at the bus station at 8:45, and his arrival at Mike's apartment at 9:20—before moving on to the specific events of each one of the heist members, including Mike O'Reilly (who goes through a series of similarly described events at home, at the bus station, and at work at the race-track's bar) and Officer Kennan, who also "set into motion his phase of the operation." After the policeman refuses to help a woman in need who comes running to him, the third-person narrator explains to the audience:

> He had timed the trip to the track on half a dozen different occasions and he knew at just what point he should be at precisely what time. He knew that the entire success of the plan depended on his accuracy in arriving at the track at exactly the correct moment. A minute or two early was allowable, but ten seconds late would be fatal.

Yet such an explanation—as with most of what *The Killing*'s narrator offers—while not overt parody, is superfluous and excessive, pointing toward the self-awareness of the third-person narrator who opens *Dr. Strangelove* (and is quickly pushed aside), as audiences could clearly glean from the meticulous planning of the heist why the policeman would be unable to take the extra time to help the middle-aged women in distress. Far from ironic or limited (though still, perhaps, excessive), Kubrick uses the third-person narrator in *The Killing* as a necessary narrative tool—the enabler of an authoritative country of the mind—helping the audience better understand the events of the story. It is in this film that Paolo Cherchi Usai's chess metaphor—the auteur meticulously planning every detail—works much better than in later films.

The use of nondiegetic jazz within the narrative returns even more prominently in *The Killing*, where Fried's score, a much more frenetic, up-tempo version of the kind of music he wrote for *Killer's Kiss*, appears almost as often as the third-person narrator. This hectic, rushed score consistently reminds audiences of the hectic, rushed nature of the film's narrative structure. *The Killing* opens with a booming, thunderous score playing over shots of the horses preparing for the race. The music of this sequence, like the voice-over narrator, establishes the serious tone of the film for audiences and returns throughout the film—after Mike checks on his wife; when Clay first arrives at the motel (and later, when Clay inspects the room, in the same scene); when Mike arrives at the track and then watches the money moved into the counting room; during the riot scene by the racetrack bar as the security guards run to help; when Clay walks up to the same bar and then moves into position to sneak inside the racetrack's back rooms; just as Clay prepares to enter the money room and begin the robbery; and when Clay frantically puts the money away in a suitcase after avoiding the bloody shoot-out at the scheduled rendezvous point. Moreover, the score builds progressively louder over the course of the film, building the tension as *The Killing* moves toward its centerpiece—the extended heist sequence inside the race-track, which is complemented by Fried's music at nearly every moment, like when Clay prepares the money for the drop-off out the window, changes clothes, and finally works his way out of the post-riot and post-horse-shooting mayhem at the racetrack, along with the rest of the general crowd. The nondiegetic music in this scene highlights for audiences both Clay's urgency as he attempts to escape unnoticed and his brief triumph, having, at least temporarily, successfully pulled off the robbery without incident. When, however, the heist ultimately fails at the airport, the score again heightens the audience's expected anxiety over Clay's impending arrest in the film's final moments.

In the sense that Kubrick depends so heavily here on the country of the mind—the trace of an unquestioned narrative authority—to tell the story and explain exactly why certain events happen as they do, *The Killing* could be regarded as a rather flawed film. This is another example, like *Fear and Desire* and *Killer's Kiss*, of authorial choices that Kubrick would later change. I mention this only because Kubrick scholars have mostly praised this film as the first genuine beginning of Kubrick's career,[6] but for all the praise lumped on the film, I would argue that *The Killing* was not a polished, flawless master-piece that suddenly and miraculously emerged, marking the beginning of a "career," but instead was still very much just another practice piece (albeit, more entertaining and accomplished) along the trail for the young Kubrick, who continued experimenting with the boundaries of film discourse. The fact that Kubrick would never again work with such a complex narrative structure (in regard to blatant temporal and spatial manipulation) illustrates how Kubrick's films later rejected the same kind of innovative cinematic storytelling for which *The Killing* is celebrated. Only later would Kubrick's films reveal an understanding of film as a truly cinematic medium, one that did not require the magic of words, or the "aural impact of radio."

PATHS OF GLORY

In *Paths of Glory*, however, there is only one moment of voice-over narration, yet its presence is still telling. At the very beginning of the film, a third-person narrator summarizes the events of World War I in France leading up to the point in the war where *Paths of Glory*'s narrative begins:

> War began between France and Germany on August 3, 1914. Five weeks later, the German army smashed its way to within 18 miles of Paris. There, the battered French miraculously rallied their forces at the Marne River and in a series of unexpected counterattacks, drove the Germans back. The front was stabilized and shortly afterwards developed into a continuous line of heavily fortified trenches zigzagging their way 500 miles from the English Channel to the Swiss frontier. By 1916, after two grisly years of trench warfare, the battle lines had changed very little. Successful attacks were measured in hundreds of yards and paid for in lives by hundreds of thousands.

Although not as heavy-handed as other Kubrick voice-overs, the opening of *Paths of Glory* still works with his other early films as articulating very specific points of orientation for the experience of the film's audience. As with most of the voice-over narration in *Killer's Kiss*, this use in *Paths of Glory* does little more than summarize events. While Walker refers to this opening as "brief and brilliant,"[7] I instead find the narrator's purpose to be simply a reminder for audiences of the general historical context in which *Paths of Glory* takes place, with didacticism thrown in near the end. The narration here is mostly a narrative shortcut, transmitting information neither particularly dramatic nor necessary for understanding the small-scale human tragedy about to unfold. The rest of the film, meanwhile, establishes the not-particularly original theme, seen in Kubrick's first film, that war is nothing more than humanity fighting with itself. To *Paths of Glory*'s credit, this theme is played out much more dramatically—the French military seem more concerned with court-martials and executing their own soldiers than in defeating the Germans—than in its first Kubrickian antiwar predecessor (a trait that the absence of a continuing voice-over narrator in the film also perhaps points to). Unlike *Killer's Kiss* and *The Killing*, *Paths of Glory* depends as much on nonverbal elements—the sounds of trench warfare, the look of tired soldiers, and the unspoken agendas of military commanders—as on words to tell a story. Yet for all of *Paths of Glory*'s overall effectiveness as an antiwar film (and it is a brilliant, beautiful work of art—even with Kirk Douglas's typical overacting), the continued reliance on the voice-over, the need to situate concretely the historical and thematic stakes of the story in the early moments, illustrates Kubrick's films' continuing struggle to break free from narrative authority and the country of the mind.

Paths of Glory also continues the trend of signifying music, most strikingly realized when one soldier stumbles upon the dead body of another soldier, killed by friendly fire. The loud, intrusive rush of music parallels the sudden shock of the image of the dead soldier. Also, the consistent use of drums playing in the background of the film plays up the building tension as the different leaders prepare for battle and then conspire to try their own soldiers for cowardice after a failed attack. As all effective signifying music must, the beating of the drums increases the audience's anxiety. These sounds become literal by the end of the film, when the presumably diegetic drums anticipate the execution of the three doomed soldiers.

While *Paths of Glory* does not disrupt chronological order in the way *The Killing* did, the latter film does, however, weave several story threads together simultaneously. In *Paths of Glory*, the discourse moves between the individual stories of Colonel Dax (Kirk Douglas), General George Broulard (Adolphe Menjou), General Paul Mireau (George Macready), and several of the soldiers (such as the three doomed men—Joe Turkel's Private Pierre Arnaud, Ralph Meeker's Corporal Philippe Paris, and Timothy Carey's Private Maurice Ferol). Each of these men moves along with his own story line and agenda, only occasionally intersecting, such as the central courtroom scene and the subsequent executions near the end. Unlike the squad in *Full Metal Jacket*, these French soldiers live their own separate lives, even if within the same war. Despite the absence of a disordered discursive chronology, *Paths of Glory* nonetheless continues *The Killing*'s complex manipulation of story lines. *Paths of Glory* opens with Broulard and Mireau discussing a new military offensive to take the "Ant Hill"—the same mission that will set into motion the eventual court-martials. The film then cuts to the front line, when Mireau meets up with his men in the trenches. In particular, he speaks with the three soldiers who will be executed eventually for "cowardice." During the extended tracking shots through the trenches, Mireau's story line leads to crucial additional story lines, culminating in his meeting with Colonel Dax.

As each important character is introduced to the narrative, *Paths of Glory* begins an explicit, complex juggling of story lines, with audiences becoming more and more aware of the discourse as it manipulates the multiple threads. The film moves from the friendly-fire death of one of the soldiers, to the preparation of the Ant Hill invasion, to two soldiers talking about how they would prefer to die—carefully juggling each story line in much the same way as *Fear and Desire* had previously. During the failed attack, meanwhile, *Paths of Glory* cuts back and forth between the soldiers on the field and Mireau's observation of the events unfolding, which leads eventually to his ordering an assault on his own men. After the attack, subsequently, the multiple story lines continue, as Mireau instigates the court-martial for cowardice, Broulard half-heartedly inquires about another "friendly-fire incident" (where Mireau ordered the mortar firing on his own men), Dax carries out the orders, and the three doomed men prepare to defend their lives in front of the military court. The setting of the court-martial itself calls attention to the multiple story lines working within *Paths of Glory*; Mireau and Broulard watch as Dax futilely attempts to defend the men one by one against the charges of coward-ice presented by Major Saint-Auban (Richard Anderson). As the film moves toward its inevitable execution, the discourse moves back and forth between the executioners' preparations, the doomed men as they prepare for death and pray with a priest, and Dax's different scenes—he interviews Lieutenant Roget (Wayne Morris) about his reasons for picking Corporal Paris for the court-martial and to inform him that he will be leading the firing squad; he uncovers the truth about Mireau's actions the day of the attack; and he confronts Broulard over the general's inaction as everything unfolds. Five years after *Fear and Desire*, Kubrick was still telling an antiwar parable through multiple intertwining story lines, the kind of parable he would streamline considerably, plotwise, by the time he made the minimalist *Full Metal Jacket*, which focused on one contained and isolated military unit in Vietnam. By that time, the country of the mind's durability—bridging the gap between narration and events, between order and chaos—would be markedly weakened.

SPARTACUS

Like *Paths of Glory*, *Spartacus* features only one sustained instance of voice-over narration, and as with the prior film, this device occurs only at the begin-ning. Yet the voice-over that opens *Spartacus* differs from its predecessor in at least one crucial way—an overt didacticness and pretentiousness highly reminiscent of the opening of *Fear and Desire*. Sliding back to that earlier facade, the latter film echoes the earlier's explicit statement of the film's intended themes:

In the last century before the birth of the new faith called Christianity, which
was destined to overthrow the pagan tyranny of Rome and bring about a new
society, the Roman Republic stood at the very center of the civilized world.
"Of all things fairest," sang the poet, "first among cities and home of the gods
is golden Rome." Yet, even at the zenith of her pride and power, the Republic
lay fatally stricken with a disease called human slavery. The age of the dictator
was at hand, waiting in the shadows for the event to bring it forth.

As with *Fear and Desire*, *Spartacus* shows no interest in allowing the
film's own themes to develop dramatically over the course of the film. The
voice-over narrator states exactly what *Spartacus* (at least) hopes it is
about—in part—thematically. One senses here that the ambitious epic palate
Kubrick was working with in this particular film may have to some extent
reawakened the overreaching ambition displayed earlier on in the narrative
structure of *Fear and Desire*, as though, for a moment, Kubrick felt like a new
filmmaker again, with new technical possibilities. Whereas *Fear and Desire*
tells the audience about humanity being at war with itself, *Spartacus* boldly
orients us to the "disease" of slavery. Also, the last line, where the narrator
talks about how "the age of the dictator was at hand, waiting in the shadows
for the event to bring it forth," similarly recalls the overgeneralizations of the
openings of previous Kubrick films. This is a realistic possibility, if for no
other reason than the very real fact that—as with *Fear and Desire*'s discussion
of "running our fingers down the lists in directories"—it is difficult to tell just
what exactly the narrator is talking about. Like Davy's "mess," the "event" in
Spartacus demands more clarification (or less explicit meaning, as I would be
inclined to argue). This passage could be a reference to Spartacus's eventual
uprising, yet such an interpretative conclusion is by no means a given. Could
this passage also be a foreshadowing of the American Civil War, or any other
slave rebellion or war in human history? Certainly, the ambiguity (perhaps
born from the need to universalize these themes beyond *Spartacus*) exists to
such an egregious point that, as with *Fear and Desire*, the statement ends up
essentially meaningless for all practical purposes of thematic and narrative
development.[8] That said, however, the opening voice-over narration does
eventually particularize on the character of Spartacus:

In that same century, in the conquered Greek province of Thrace, an illiterate
slave woman added to her master's wealth by giving birth to a son whom she
named Spartacus—a proud, rebellious son who was sold to living death in the
mines of Libya before his thirteenth birthday. There, under whip and chain
and sun, he lived out his youth and his young manhood dreaming the death
of slavery 2,000 years before it would finally end.

The story of the character Spartacus, the hero of the film, is thus introduced. However, the voice-over narrator once again extends the discussion
beyond Spartacus's particular tale itself, turning the slave's plight into a representative (not to mention, preachy) statement on the entire history of slavery
as "a living death." Certainly, Spartacus—the man himself living during the
Roman Empire—does not look 2,000 years ahead to "the death of slavery"
but is concerned instead with the problems he faces in his immediate surroundings as a Roman slave in the hot desert sun. Moreover, referring to
slavery as a "living death" adds little to the thematic development and dramatic movement of the film, instead speaking only to the didactic nature of
the entire opening. In many ways, then, *Spartacus*'s voice-over narration ends
up often being as vague as *Killer's Kiss* and as directive and pretentious as *Fear
and Desire*. The voice-over narration shows a first glimpse of the extent to
which *Spartacus* will depend on an overt narrative authority to tell its story,
something also illustrated by the use of multiple story threads and mood
music.

Likewise, *Spartacus* continues a similarly ordered narrative as *The Killing*
and *Paths of Glory*, albeit stretched over a much greater length (the first
Kubrick film to exceed three hours, *Spartacus* is twice as long as *Paths of
Glory*[9]). Although *Spartacus* does not disrupt chronological order, either, this
1960 film does maneuver between the story lines of Spartacus (Kirk Douglas),
Crassus (Laurence Olivier), Gracchus (Charles Laughton), Batiatus (Peter
Ustinov), Caesar (John Gavin), Glabrus (John Dall), and several other smaller
characters. The story world in *Spartacus* bears the mark of an authoritative
narrator, demanded by such a complicated narrative structure, not unlike *The
Killing* and *Paths of Glory*. Aside from the use of voice-over narration to open
the film, the country of the mind is also suggested in *Spartacus* through the
form of multiple story threads, which run throughout the film. After the
film's overture, *Spartacus* begins with the film's hero at a slave camp. Soon
after, Batiatus is introduced, and the film continues to bring in many more
characters over the course of its three-hour time frame. Batiatus, a slave
owner and gladiator trainer, purchases Spartacus and takes him away to his
camp. During this long series of scenes, the threads of Crassus and Glabrus,
both of whom visit the camp, are also introduced. Even early on, Kubrick
starts weaving story thread within story thread, and subsequently, the audience begins depending upon the reliability of the country of the mind to
maintain continuity with the different story lines. Shortly after he receives his
training and survives a duel to the death with a fellow gladiator, Spartacus
leads a revolt among the slaves and wins his freedom. Scenes inside the
Roman senate then follow the revolution, where Gracchus and Caesar are
introduced in the narrative.

At this point, almost a third of the way through the film, the full scope of *Spartacus*'s epic story begins to be revealed. As the Roman politicians and warriors—Crassus, Gracchus, Caesar, and Glabrus—begin scheming their way to power and finding a way to defeat the rebellious slave, they become just as important to the narrative as Spartacus himself. The narrative follows these men as much as it follows Spartacus's group throughout the film. Later on, Batiatus, having been exiled from his own home by the slaves, returns to the narrative and begins plotting with Gracchus and, later still, with Crassus. The latter character, meanwhile, continues on his own story thread, scheming with Glabrus and Caesar and lusting after a young slave played by Tony Curtis, who himself will return to the narrative when he joins up with Spartacus's group—illustrating the complicated and extended intricacies of the story threads by showing the many points at which different characters in the film intersect (a point repeated in the scene when Glabrus is captured by Spartacus). During this time, Spartacus also falls in love with another slave, Varinia (Jean Simmons), adding yet another story line to an already complicated narrative.

After the intermission, *Spartacus* continues its complex manipulation of threads as the stories of the senate and those of the slaves work through the narrative and toward their inevitable clash. The discourse carefully balances the smaller story lines within the two larger ones, evenly cutting back and forth between the stories of Spartacus and the slaves and those of Crassus, Gracchus, Caesar, and Glabrus. This parallelism is best illustrated more than two hours into the film, when Spartacus's speech to the thousands of freed slaves, as they prepare to march to Rome, is intercut with Crassus's introduction to the Roman masses as the new commander in chief of the Roman armies (a parallel montage that echoes an earlier one in *Fear and Desire*). Cutting back and forth between the two grandiose speeches not only calls attention to the two men as symbolic and literal leaders of their respective people but also highlights their respective roles at the front of two distinctly different story lines—divided not only by ideology and geographical location but also (as the consistent editing points out) by the film's discourse, even while momentarily united in the country of the mind (here defined as the surface of the montage). This authoritative narrative manipulation of various events' meaning and importance suggests the mark of a country of the mind, reminding the audience of the narrative authority keeping the multiple story threads clearly defined within the narrative structure. In this context, the film's celebrated battle climax, featuring thousands of men in bloody hand-to-hand combat, meanwhile plays—like the executions in *Paths of Glory*—as much as a clashing of these multiple story threads as it does anything else.

Spartacus, featuring Alex North's haunting score, also relies heavily on signifying music as an authoritative narrator within the film's story. Most prominently, *Spartacus*'s score is displayed in the overture, the credits, and the entr'acte—three instances where the importance of the film's authoritative narrative presence is crucial to situating the film in an emotional context. *Spartacus* is intended to be a sweeping, grand story of romance, triumph, resilience, tragedy, and redemption, and the grandeur of the score in these sequences tries to orient us to this goal, even before the story itself has begun to unfold. The romantic score returns when Spartacus is first introduced to Varinia, his eventual love interest. Later, during that same scene, the score's tone shifts to a more dramatic one when Spartacus is taunted by Batiatus for not sexually assaulting Varinia while she is in his cell. When Spartacus is left alone with her, meanwhile, the romantic score returns, as though highlighting the supposedly strong connection being built between them (this same musical motif returns every time Spartacus and Varinia are together—that which engages the country of the mind, through this particular piece of music, tries very hard to emphasize the romantic link between the two). Also early in the film, a loud, more dramatic score emphasizes the seriousness and intensity of the images seen during the gladiator-training montages. In fact, much of the first part of *Spartacus* is an extreme juxtaposing of nondiegetic music—between the softness of the love theme in certain scenes and the harshness of the gladiator music in the other sequences. Such melodramatic and dramatic music also highlights other moments in the film—Crassus's introduction, when he first visits Batiatus's gladiator-training camp, along with friends and with Glabrus; the anticipation, execution, and ugly aftermath of the first gladiator duel; the gladiator revolt; the introduction of Rome to the story; Spartacus's return to the slave camp; the several scenes where the former slaves march together across the plains; Spartacus and Varinia's reunion by the lake and their subsequent walks through the forest; the ex-slaves' assaults on Roman outposts and march into Metapontum; at the end of the parallel speeches given by Crassus and Spartacus (discussed in the section on multiple story threads) and the marches to war that follow; and during the quiet anticipation and tragic aftermath of the climactic battle between the Roman army and the freed slaves. Certainly, however, the most dramatic instance of North's score comes at the very end of the film, when Varinia and her son meet briefly with a crucified Spartacus for the final time. When Varinia sees her husband, and the dying Spartacus looks down and sees his newborn son for the first time, she tells him that she will carry on the legacy of Spartacus and the freedom he fought for; when Varinia tells Spartacus she loves him and rides away with Batiatus, the music swells to its dramatic climax. For Kubrick, *Spartacus*'s score is absolutely essential to the narrative structure of the film—a source of narrative authority—because (more so than even *Fear and Desire*, *Killer's Kiss*, and *The Killing*) the nondiegetic music, whether romantic, dramatic, rousing, or tragic, in almost every single scene highlights how the audience is supposed to feel at that given moment in the narrative and again illustrates the narrative authority's attempt to impose order on the story world.

LOLITA

Arriving after *The Killing*, *Paths of Glory*, and *Spartacus*, *Lolita* also depends on voice-over narration; however, unlike every film up to this point, *Lolita* does not *open* with a voice-over narration. In this respect, the beginning of this latter film indicates how the audience sits in much less comforting territory as the film frame follows a lonely car through dense fog—as though, for the first time, there may initially be no narrative authority to frame the story. The fog that seems to follow Humbert (James Mason) down that lonely road in *Lolita* may likewise serve as a possible avenue for envisioning the country of the mind, symbolically situating itself between the narrator and the story world. Thus, the fog becomes an embodiment of the narrative vision of the narrator of the story world. It similarly recalls the fog on display in the opening of *Fear and Desire*. Importantly, this fog obscures our vision of the experience far more than it clarifies it. It may not be a bit of a stretch to argue that the fog that covers the opening terrain of *Fear and Desire* and *Lolita* signifies the country of the mind or some other cognitive barrier, clearly obstructing our view of the story world as much as something can (much like the way a voice-over narration actually impedes our own sense of the story world).

   If *Lolita*'s world will reveal anything—will allow abstract thoughts to be verbalized—such revelations will be leaked out in pieces, or in the experience itself, not blatantly stated in the opening seconds. Of course, ironically, *Lolita* does give away the film, in a sense, when the story's conclusion (the death of Quilty [Peter Sellers]) is moved to the beginning of the film. Also significant here is that having this knowledge of Humbert Humbert's future, knowing he will eventually kill someone for sexually abusing a minor (and for jealousy), orients the audience to the story *prior* to his eventual voice-over narration (the first first-person narrator in a Kubrick film since *Killer's Kiss*), which will offer Humbert's own perspective on events. Unlike previous films, we experience *Lolita* before Humbert gets his chance to guide us. Humbert's first-person voice-over narration certainly suggests another narrative authority within the film, but the shift in temporal order—moving Quilty's murder to the beginning and thus establishing events within the film's world as separate from this particular narrative presence, the introduction of which *follows* that opening scene—points to forms of overt narrative authority as increasingly weakened in later films and proportionally unable to understand the story world in the manner such an authority previously had. Humbert's first voice-over words come later in the film, just after the murderous prologue in the discourse and four years earlier in the story:

> Having recently arrived in America, where so many Europeans have found a haven before, I decided to spend a peaceful summer in the attractive resort town of Ramsdale, New Hampshire. Some English translations I had made of French poetry had enjoyed some success and I had been appointed to a lecture-ship at Beardsley College, Ohio, in the fall. Friends had given me several addresses in Ramsdale where lodgings were available in the summer.

Such an emotionally indifferent voice-over (in some respects, as detached as earlier third-person narrators)—where Humbert talks about his early days in Ramsdale yet makes no connection between this beginning of the flashback and the story's violent conclusion—suggests an obliviousness that in part prevents the audience from aligning with the narrator. Yet it would be premature to disregard Humbert's words as completely limited because of this narrative rupture, as the narration still attempts to pass along important information about why he is in Ramsdale—not essential information, but still plain and straightforward enough not to call credibility into account. Moreover, the voice-over allows the audience to glimpse what is going on in the man's head (an especially important point, from a censorship point of view, considering the subject matter—pedophilia—in which Humbert will eventually be involved[10]). Indeed, the next use of voice-over occurs after the audience catches on to Humbert's infatuations—a topic the protagonist himself addresses:

> What drives me insane is the twofold nature of this nymphet . . . of every nymphet, perhaps. This mixture in my Lolita of tender, dreamy childishness and a kind of eerie vulgarity. I know it is madness to keep this journal, but it gives me a strange thrill to do so and only a loving wife could decipher my microscopic script.

Certainly, Humbert's "strange thrill" also indicts the audience for actively seeking out the contents of his journal entries. However, it may also be important to note that, considering what Humbert does (lusts after a minor and murders another human being) throughout the film, the film's discourse perhaps could not, in 1960, be allowed to align too closely with the main character.[11] *Lolita* exposes Humbert as a criminal before turning over the narration to him, as though denying too tight a relationship between narrator and spectator. Indeed, Humbert's declaration of "my" Lolita suggests a departure between the two; the audience's Lolita is not, presumably, the Lolita that Humbert constructs—or, in other words, Lolita is not the audience's Lolita, nor, importantly, the Lolita in the country of Humbert's mind.

All of this, however, is not to state that Humbert is a source of dishonest or deceptive narration, even if he seems distant, both in tone and in behavior.[12] There is also an honesty in Humbert's voice. He does not try to trick himself or the audience into believing contradictory perceptions of events in the filmic image. If anything—and this is why I think a rupture between explorer and territory has not quite fully occurred in *Lolita*, even if the country of the mind seems increasingly illusory—Humbert may be too honest as a narrator, whatever his beliefs or behavior. He does not project a vision of the world completely out of touch with actual events, or explicitly incompatible with other visions, as will be the case with General Turgidson, Major Kong, and General Ripper in the next Kubrick film, *Dr. Strangelove*. After marrying Lolita's mother, Charlotte, only to be closer to the daughter, Humbert remarks:

> The wedding was a quiet affair and when called upon to enjoy my promotion from lodger to lover, did I experience only bitterness and distaste? No, Mr. Humbert confesses to a certain titillation of his vanity, to some faint tenderness, even to a pattern of remorse daintily running along the steel of his conspiratorial dagger.

Important here is that, even while Humbert clearly plays with language to manipulate this mapping of himself, he is not lying per se. For all his flippancy and irony, Humbert sincerely appears to be both titillated and remorseful about his new relationship with the Haze family. A few scenes later, Humbert continues his narrative confession, when plotting the possible demise of his new wife and allowing the audience to clearly see his intentions:

> No man can bring about the perfect murder. Chance, however, can do it. Just minutes ago she said it wasn't loaded. What if I had playfully pulled the trigger then? "She said it wasn't loaded. It belonged to the late Mr. Haze. She was having her morning tub. We had just finished talking about our plans for the future. I decided to play a practical joke and pretend I was a burglar. We were newlyweds and still did things like that to each other. As soon at it happened, I called an ambulance, but it was too late." Simple, isn't it? The perfect murder!

The voice-over leaves no room for motivational uncertainty on the part of Humbert as he holds the gun, even while also encouraging audiences to remove themselves emotionally from *Lolita*'s protagonist and narrator, who seems on the verge of committing homicide. Even while Humbert plays out his potential deception of the police ("She said it wasn't loaded"), there is no overt attempt to trick the audience, however ill-conceived the plan might seem. Humbert's speculation suggests the potential power of a limited narrator in this scene by showing the deceptive possibilities of narrative construction (a planned murder becomes verbally narrated as an accident) yet does not ask the audience to accept this deception as well. In other words, what is important here is that, despite the fact that Humbert is deliberately putting on a performance, the audience is clearly aware of who is being tricked by the acting (the authorities) and who is not (them), thus suggesting a limited split between the country of Humbert's mind and the possible meanings of the events in *Lolita* as they occur (or as we perceive them as occurring). Humbert's understanding that the audience would find his plan "simple" indicates how he does not attempt to explicitly manipulate the film's audience in the same way he imagines manipulating the surrounding story characters. When Humbert, meanwhile, cannot bring himself to actually shoot Charlotte, his voice-over again tells the audience exactly that—he could not make himself "put her to death." The filmic image, which shows a remorseful, even disgusted Humbert, subsequently reinforces this additional confession visually.

In *Lolita*, the melodramatic music also returns repeatedly, such as when Lolita runs up the stairs to say good-bye to Humbert early in the film and right after Humbert is told that Charlotte is dead from the car wreck.[13] However, the main point I wish to make here is that the use of nondiegetic music emerges in *Lolita*—like the voice-over narration—only after the opening murder of Quilty, as though such music exists only concurrently with the narrative authority (like Davy) established by Humbert's flashback. This quality of isolating signifying music from the opening sequence's objectivity[14] may, in and of itself, point the way toward the narrative structures displayed in later films, where any claims to narrative authority will be more overtly isolated from events. The mind and its powers begin to be questioned. In this respect, *Lolita* points us toward the ambiguity of experience in later films. And, too, there are ways in which we can sense that *Lolita*, while not quite a break from earlier forms of narrative authority, might at least be aware of the pretension and fallibility of those earlier forms. Halfway through the film, Humbert leaves Beardsley with Lolita, claiming to attend a "Hollywood engagement." Humbert tells them and us that he "was to be . . . chief consultant in the production of a film dealing with existentialism, still a hot thing at the time." The exact film title within *Lolita* remains a mystery (the actual film presumably does not even exist but rather is presented as a ruse to deceive others). Yet the film Humbert works on could just as easily have been something like *Fear and Desire*, where Kubrick, as a young filmmaker, previously fell for the "hot thing" of existentialism as a transparent filmic subject.[15] In this sense of *Lolita*, Kubrick implicitly shows a clear understanding of the thematic and dramatic shortcomings of his first film, along with a determination to detach himself from the trap of taking cinematic life "too serious." And perhaps, we can see here an attempt to work out that artistic self-consciousness to some degree within the narratives of his later films. A shift in stylistic tendencies was already under way in *Lolita*, where Humbert loses a grip on his authority over the film's story. Additionally, the hot topic of existentialism—no less than that of the country of the mind—which quietly pervades the narrative structures of such films as *Fear and Desire* and *Killer's Kiss*, is brought to our attention, but only as it is highlighted and mocked.

Lolita reveals for us a heightened awareness of the trappings of the maze. Words possess a little more elusiveness here. In an article for *Sight & Sound*, written around the time *Lolita* was being released, Kubrick himself wrote about the difficulties of attempting to adapt a novel to the screen. It is a particularly intriguing article—appropriately titled "Words and Movies"—because the filmmaker reveals a much different attitude toward words and their meaning than his earlier films had evinced. Focusing on the inner life of characters, writes Kubrick, will liberate actors from "deliver[ing] literal statements of meaning."[16] In some ways, we see this unfolding in *Lolita*. The didactic voice-overs of *Fear and Desire* and *The Killing* give way to someone slightly shiftier in his use of language. "I think that for a movie or a play to say anything really truthful about life," he adds, "it has to do so very obliquely, so as to avoid all pat conclusions and neatly tied up ideas."[17] It is hard not to see here—as in *Lolita's* "existentialism"—Kubrick's own response to *Fear and Desire*. It is hard not to see Kubrick beginning to imagine the possibilities of experience that remain outside literal statements—surface voice-overs that do not verbally contain these moments but feebly and weakly attempt to freeze them in language. By the time Kubrick made *Lolita*, he was no doubt as much an informed observer of films as he was a filmmaker. And he points in this article to a new type of storytelling—one that I sense will approximate more closely (outside words) his later films:

> At best, realistic drama consists of a progression of moods and feelings that play upon the audience's feelings and transform the author's meaning into an emotional experience. This means that the author must not think of paper and ink and words as being his writing tools, but rather that he works in flesh and feeling.[18]

Although Kubrick is commenting on literary style here, there is the sense that film can follow the same pattern. The audience's feelings and emotional experience become more relevant in such a way as to transcend words—writing instead through "flesh and feeling"; writing through the body as much as through the mind. If *Fear and Desire* privileges the contents of the mind, if *Killer's Kiss* privileges the explicit, reliable voice-over narrator, if *The Killing* privileges the cognitive ability to manipulate space and time, then Kubrick's subsequent films will embrace the body—the "flesh"—as a means of moving outside the confining arrogance of the mind and into the liberating chaos of indescribable experience. Kubrick's next two films will more fully reveal the failure of words, the ways in which "ideas have to be discovered by the audience"[19] in an increasingly preconscious way.

NOTES

1. I refer here to *Day of the Fight* (1951), *The Flying Padre* (1951), and *The Seafarers* (1953). The first film details twenty-four hours in the life of a boxer, Walter Cartier, as he prepares for a boxing match. This early documentary also features a voice-over narrator (albeit, a third-person narrator), and Cartier no doubt served as an inspiration for *Killer's Kiss*'s Davy.

2. An interesting point to make here also is that *Killer's Kiss*'s soundtrack was completely redubbed after principal photography ended, and much of the dialogue is out of sync with the character's lips. This production note is extremely significant, as the technical problems probably led Kubrick to rely even more heavily on the voice-over narration as an authoritative storytelling device.

3. Mario Falsetto makes a similar argument about this scene, noting that "the most interesting element in the sequence is the disparity between the visuals (a dance) and Gloria's accompanying narrative" (85). However, Falsetto reads the effect here differently, arguing that "despite the apparent disjunction between film image and voice-over, a metaphorical relationship is established between the intensity of the dance and the dramatic power of her narration, which involves the suicide of her sister and Gloria's subsequent guilt" (86). *Stanley Kubrick: A Narrative and Stylistic Analysis*, 2nd ed. (Westport, Conn.: Praeger, 2001).

4. Dana Polan, "Materiality and Sociality in *Killer's Kiss*," in *Perspectives on Stanley Kubrick*, ed. Mario Falsetto (New York: Hall, 1996), 98.

5. Alexander Walker, Sybil Taylor, and Ulrich Ruchti, *Stanley Kubrick, Director: A Visual Analysis* (New York: Norton, 1999), 54–55.

6. Gene Phillips states that *The Killing* was "Kubrick's first important film." *Stanley Kubrick: A Film Odyssey* (New York: Popular Library, 1975), 31. Walker points out that the film was the "first on which Kubrick was proud to have his name." *A Visual Analysis*, 17.

7. Walker, Taylor, and Ruchti, *A Visual Analysis*, 69.

8. Here, I am compelled to point out that while Kubrick may not have written the lines as such himself, he more than likely did have the right to delete it, if he saw fit. I

remind the reader that I regard Kubrick to be—more precisely—a supervising editor, more so than the author, of the final version of a film. And though Kubrick was dissatisfied with his experience while making *Spartacus*, there actually exists little evidence suggesting the filmmaker, for all his feuding with stars, was denied significant creative control over the film, particularly in relation to postproduction decisions—chiefly, sound and film editing. In fact, one of the only times the film's star and producer, Kirk Douglas, became upset was when, as Vincent LoBrutto notes, reaction shots of the dying Spartacus were initially cut from the film's finale, played only as a joke by Kubrick himself on the star (191–192). *Stanley Kubrick: A Biography* (New York: Fine, 1997). More likely, Kubrick rejected *Spartacus* because he lacked *complete* control over the project, which is much different from *significant* control. As the filmmaker himself told Gene Phillips, "Of course, I directed the actors, composed the shots, and edited the picture. But *Spartacus* remains the only film over which I did not have absolute control." *A Film Odyssey*, 78. For this reason, as Phillips also points out, the film "deserves more scrutiny as a Kubrick film than it has received in the past" from critics (78). Such critics include Alexander Walker, who accepts Kubrick's insistence on being only a "hired hand" on the production of *Spartacus* and thus follows the director's lead by disregarding the film from the Kubrick canon. *A Visual Analysis*, 44.

   9. I realize here that Kubrick could not have possibly controlled the length of such a star-studded film as *Spartacus*, which not only featured a more complicated and epic story line but also demanded a great deal of screen time for so many prominent actors. I would, however, point out that every film prior to *Spartacus* was around an hour and a half long, while after *Spartacus*, only one Kubrick film, *Dr. Strangelove*, was under two hours. The implication here, I think, is that—while Kubrick could not control it—the expanded narrative canvas of *Spartacus* ultimately may have been something that appealed to him.

   10. Leonard Leff and Jerold L. Simmons, in *The Dame in the Kimono*, 2nd ed. (Lexington: University of Kentucky Press, 2001), dedicate an entire chapter to *Lolita*'s censorship history but make no reference to this adaptation decision. No evidence apparently exists that the chronological order of the scene was done for censorship purposes, though such concern may have played a part nonetheless. According to Kubrick biographer John Baxter, "Nabokov had written such a scene, but its placement at the start of the film was Kubrick's idea. It put Quilty—and [Peter] Sellers—at the heart of the story, which became more of a tale of rivalry between two men than, as in the book, of Lolita and Humbert's mutual seduction." *Stanley Kubrick: A Biography* (New York: Carroll & Graf, 1997), 157. Also addressing partially censorship issues, Greg Jenkins, meanwhile, speculates that "the film's unorthodox opening creates a curiosity about Humbert's motivation in committing murder [. . . and] adds a layering of the respectable murder mystery to the more objectionable sexual romp." *Stanley Kubrick and the Art of Adaptation* (Jefferson, N.C.: McFarland, 1997), 36.

   11. In *Inside a Film Artist's Maze* (Bloomington: Indiana University Press, 2000), Thomas Allen Nelson makes a similar point about this detachment, saying that both the discursive shift and the image of Humbert's "enslavement to Lolita (pedicure)" allow Kubrick to "establish . . . a third person detachment from the subjective (first-person) narration" (74).

   12. In his book on narratology, Seymour Chatman actually discusses Humbert's narra-

tive reliability as well, though he is writing in reference to Vladimir Nabokov's literary source. He too argues that Humbert, "whatever his character, is, in my view, reliable. For all his sarcasm about characters and events . . . we feel that he is doing his best to tell us what in fact happened." *Story and Discourse: Narrative Structure in Fiction and Film* (Ithaca, N.Y.: Cornell University Press, 1978), 234.

13. Although this scene is followed up by a shot of Humbert relaxing in the bathtub, seemingly celebrating the loss of his wife, *Lolita*'s discourse does not present a mark of authority that would ask the audience to agree with his contentment.

14. By objectivity here, I mean that no one character has a clear monopoly on imposing meaning onto the discourse in *Lolita*'s first scene. No character uses voice-over, nor does the film rely on any extraneous modes or layers of storytelling (music, montage, and so on) beyond the filmic image.

15. Nelson also draws a parallel between Humbert's line and Kubrick's first film. In a footnote to his second edition, he writes, "When James Mason as Humbert in *Lolita* pretends to be going to Hollywood to make a film about existentialism, which, he ironically tells us, was a 'hot thing' at the time, Kubrick may have been commenting on his own early, misguided ambitions." *Inside a Film Artist's Maze*, 22.

It is also important to point out that Humbert's dialogue here is taken verbatim from Nabokov's original, highly celebrated novel *Lolita* (New York: Everyman's Library, 1992), 220, originally published in 1955. Still, it is not entirely insignificant to point out that—as in the opening voice-over in *Spartacus*—Kubrick decided not to remove it either from the source material or from Nabokov's own screenplay adaptation.

16. Stanley Kubrick, "Words and Movies," *Sight and Sound* 30 (Winter 1960/1961): 14.

17. Kubrick, "Words and Movies," 14.

18. Kubrick, "Words and Movies," 14.

19. Kubrick, "Words and Movies," 14.

· *4* ·

He'll See the Big Board: Narration and the Magic of Words in *Dr. Strangelove*

> When I was researching *Dr. Strangelove* I found that the people in the think tanks happily chatted away about the most somber topic, buoyed up by what must have been pride and satisfaction in their professional expertise; and this seemed to completely overcome any sense of personal involvement in the possible destruction of their world. Perhaps it has something to do with the *magic of words*. If you can talk brilliantly about a problem, it can create the consoling illusion that it has been mastered.
>
> —Stanley Kubrick, 1966[1]

*M*oving away from earlier films such as *Killer's Kiss* and *Spartacus*, we now move into a period where films seem less interested in telling a story with a dependence on "the magic of words." Many people, not just film critics, will no doubt remember the silent looks of Bill Harford in *Eyes Wide Shut*, Leonard "Pyle" Lawrence in *Full Metal Jacket*, and Jack Torrance in *The Shining*. Many will recall those empty faces that imply a sense of not being able to talk with certainty or authority about the events unfolding around them, or that imply a complete lack of "any sense of personal involvement" with the world. These characters perhaps came to realize that words could manipulate and control others' perception and understanding of a situation, but they could not necessarily change the situation or solve the problem they sought to tackle. Implicitly evoked in this discussion of course is the issue of talking as an act of storytelling—the ways in which the magic of words can or cannot give meaning to events. A central, overt instance of such storytelling in film is the voice-over narration—a first- or third-person presence who speaks over the film's soundtrack but not directly in the scene itself. This filmic device can have a powerful impact on how events in a film are received by audiences—humorously, somberly, ironically, and so forth. Seemingly aware of the abusive power inherent in the magic of words, Kubrick's later films use the voice-over sparingly, and when they do (*A Clockwork Orange, Barry Lyndon, Full Metal Jacket*), one senses a clear disconnect between the reality of the story world experienced and the reality imagined by the narrator.

In addition, the idea of a rupture in verbal authority as a form of storytelling at this point in Kubrick's career is not incompatible with the moment—articulated in the quote that begins this chapter—when the filmmaker first suggested that "it has something to do with the *magic of words.* If you can talk brilliantly about a problem, it can create the consoling illusion that it has been mastered." In particular, *Dr. Strangelove* remains a fascinating case study for the use of voice-over in film as an act of storytelling (within the larger act of storytelling—the film's narrative itself). *Dr. Strangelove* also stands as a crucial turning point in Kubrick's films from the talkative nature of earlier pictures to those blank and silent looks in his later ones. The film features not only an explicit third-person voice-over narration that opens the film but also implicit first-person narrators. What remains particularly fascinating are the ways in which the narrative frames certain characters' words and speeches in *Dr. Strangelove* as analogous to a cinematic voice-over. For example, characters speak out through intercoms to other characters in ways that evoke the aural feeling and narrative power of the voice-over. The possibilities of the voice-over—both its power and its fallibility—run throughout *Dr. Strangelove*, even in scenes where it is not directly present. In this chapter, I argue that *Dr. Strangelove* foregrounds acts of storytelling only in so much as they undermine the power of storytelling—undermining an older faith in voice-over narration and the magic of words. By shifting attempts at verbal authority from a third-person narrator to contradictory first-person narrators (as discussed later in the chapter), the film foregrounds human interaction not as a series of misunderstandings but as an aggressive clashing of conflicting narrative constructions—efforts to force no less than the reality of the entire world through a simple, reassuring map (such as the Big Board) centered on preemption, aggression, and patriotism.

If it was not explicit to this point, let me note what should be self-evident: Kubrick's films long had a preoccupation with war—the most dramatic, visceral, and certainly violent form of historical, cultural, and social engagement. His first film, *Fear and Desire*, serves as a serious and melodramatic representation of an allegorical conflict in a nameless forest. *Paths of Glory*, meanwhile, uses a somber tone to critique French military institutions during World War I. Yet in 1964's *Dr. Strangelove*, a Kubrick film actually tackles the topic with complete irreverence. I point out this fairly apparent obsession mostly to emphasize that even while war was always on Kubrick's mind, war and *comedy* was not. And I suspect that the shift to satire in *Strangelove* was perhaps the final cinematic rebuttal to taking life "too serious" (though, of course, *2001* could beg the question of whether or not his films regressed a bit in that philosophical respect; but—at least with depictions of war—even *Barry Lyndon* and *Full Metal Jacket* had a sense of humor, or, as in the former, one of irony). For instance, Sterling Hayden and Peter Sellers give performances in *Strangelove* that give the effect of mocking earlier Kubrick performances. The quiet, controlling certainty of *The Killing*'s mastermind, Johnny Clay, gives way to the quiet, controlling insanity of the paranoid and homicidal General Jack D. Ripper, while Sellers takes his figurative multiple roles from *Lolita* (playing a character impersonating someone else) and makes such farce literal, playing three different and autonomous roles in *Dr. Strangelove*.

Yet such humorous touches (among many others) serve only as a starting point for the same sort of social criticism about war and humanity attempted in the more overtly serious *Fear and Desire* and *Paths of Glory*, which posit profound philosophical assertions on the nature and cost of war. In contrast to those intensities, *Dr. Strangelove*, meanwhile, opens with a third-person narrator as well. However, I argue that this voice serves as the first instance of an unreliable voice-over narrator in a Stanley Kubrick film, and this breakdown in verbal authority precedes the emergence of more, equally unreliable, narrators over the course of the film. This chapter concerns the explicit and implicit forms of narration in *Dr. Strangelove* and how these speakers reveal narrative not merely as an act of storytelling but as an attempt at attaining power over others—an avenue for imposing meaning and order on events and other people. Early Kubrick voice-overs demonstrate the power of narration over the respective film's story events, but *Dr. Strangelove* attempts to subvert this traditional attribute of the voice-over narration—the authoritative magic of words. *Dr. Strangelove*'s narrators—as in other Kubrickian antiwar films—have a vision of "the unchanging shapes of fear and doubt and death," to quote *Fear and Desire*'s dramatic opening, and an assumed form of narrative and thematic mapping of the story world. Yet *Dr. Strangelove* shows each perception to be incomplete, even inaccurate, and thus calls direct attention to both the authoritative aims and, simultaneously, the fallibility of narrative construction. Rethinking the magic of words is one of many fascinating possibilities for examining how narrators and narrations can attempt, with varying degrees of success, to orient audiences to events through an act of storytelling.

The opening montage of *Dr. Strangelove* shows a B-52 bomber attached to a refueling plane in midair. In addition to the inherent sexual imagery depicted and continued throughout the film,[2] the metaphor also serves as a visual reminder of basic attachment and human interaction—the ability for people to connect and communicate with others, beyond just the surface of their own imagined assumptions of who others are and how those others think and behave. Such a metaphor is significant at the very beginning of the film, for this moment of physical contact will essentially prove to be the last example of mutual and productive interaction—(of a symbolic synthesis of narratives)—over the course of *Dr. Strangelove*. More pointedly, the inability of people to communicate effectively and touch base with one another will prove to be the exact reason for humanity's destruction in the film. It is the irreconcilability of competing countries of the mind that makes nuclear war unavoidable in *Dr. Strangelove*. As scholars such as Mario Falsetto and Alexander Walker note,[3] *Dr. Strangelove* revolves around three distinctly separate and isolated locations—Burpelson Air Force Base, the B-52 cockpit, and the War Room. What I would add, however, is that each set is also dominated by a distorting storyteller, competing for a kind of narrative supremacy over perceptions of the Cold War, but each inevitably working toward nuclear holocaust. While Kubrick allows each setting its own story thread, the threads do not—as in *The Killing*, *Paths of Glory*, and *Spartacus*—connect or overlap. Events within the air base, the cockpit, and the War Room remain confined to themselves.

Moreover, each setting has, as a reference point, only simulated and nonmimetic representations of the other settings, thereby further distancing themselves from one another and complicating any act of communication. These simulations again serve as a metaphor for the act of storytelling—the secondhand recounting and repeating of an event, rather than the event itself. The cockpit can perceive and engage with the air base and, later, the War Room only as a series of numbers in code on its control panel; Group Captain Mandrake (Sellers) has only a civilian radio signal as a representation of the outer world, while the War Room reduces the entire outside existence to a telephone and a series of "Big Boards"—giant maps suggesting that an objective narrative of the world, of reality, can be contained within these oversimplified, human-constructed frames. Important here is that the idea of storytelling is implicitly evoked in these moments of *Dr. Strangelove*, even in places in the film where no one is telling a story per se. They are physical reminders (such as the Big Board) of attempts at representing and transmitting information and events. As I have alluded to before, the Big Board is a central instance of mapping in Kubrick's body of work—not just for the obvious reason that it is literally a map but also because it offers us the closest, most direct glimpse we have of a territory approximating what is an otherwise unembodied country of the mind.

General Turgidson's belief in the infallibility, in the direct, mimetic potential of the Big Board in and of itself, allows us to rethink the image in the War Room as something nearing the country of the mind; he can understand events only through their ordering on the Big Board, to such an extent that one wonders if he can even imagine any world beyond the giant map. When other characters in the War Room suggest that there might still be a renegade American plane over Russia, ready to drop the bomb (which we as the audience know is true), Turgidson initially refers to the Big Board's version of events as proof that such a situation is not possible. There is no plane on the Board or in his version of the story; therefore, he dictates, there is no dangerous plane still out there. Even prior to these scenes, his apartment, dominated wall to wall with mirrors, clearly illustrates that Turgidson is interested in himself and himself only. When he imagines the world, he really sees only what he wants to see. The mirrors, meanwhile, also evoke the logic of the maze by creating alienating, disorienting surfaces that further conceal and remove the outside world. Earlier, when the Russian ambassador is about to enter the War Room, Turgidson's specific concern is that "he'll see everything. . . . He'll see the Big Board!" Such is the nature of Turgidson's perception of reality and of his attempts at storytelling. He is highly concerned with protecting and concealing from the Soviets the narrative he has personally grafted onto *Dr. Strangelove*'s story events through the Big Board, even though the map is hardly an accurate reflection of what actually happens.

　　Living in his own fantasy narrative, Turgidson has broken off all real contact with other human beings and with the outside world. We see this self-absorption in part illustrated by his dismissive phone conversation with his "personal secretary" and by his preference for military studies about "World Targets in Megadeaths." *Dr. Strangelove* suggests that the potential of storytelling is a reassurance to Turgidson, allowing him (as with the mirrors) to see things as he would like to see them. It is also a tool for him, allowing him to control other characters' interpretation of events. He manipulates the Big Board to reinforce his assumptions about the world, while encouraging others to do so as well. In the War Room, he not only sees others as statistics and figures on a strategic map, rather than as flesh-and-blood human beings, but also prefers massive war to peace—a personal desire that (beyond his control) becomes a reality played out on Earth. Like those giant maps amid the darkness of the War Room, Turgidson prefers the black-and-white simplicity of his desire for total, violent conflict to the messy realities and subtle nuisances of human interaction. He refuses to accept a version of events that conflicts with his own story of how the world is headed toward nuclear holocaust. He confines himself instead to the comforting narrative he projects onto the Big Board, a surface extension of his own war- and destruction-obsessed desires. In other words, he is a storyteller alienated from the world he first sought to give meaning to and instead is now living within his own twisted labyrinth of a story.

Moreover, his dialogue—evoking a voice-over—frames the War Room's discussion and echoes throughout the chamber as a disembodied voice, as though attempting to control and manipulate the other leaders' interpretation of events. As he presents his five points about the current situation, Turgidson's plan of preemption is rejected by President Merkin Muffley (Sellers again); however, his assessment of the situation's conclusion proves, in retrospect, to be no less accurate than others' perceptions. His narrating of a story, of an unalterable course toward nuclear conflict, seems as closely aligned to events as anyone else's is. This occurs despite President Muffley's futile attempt to gain control of the situation through his own act of storytelling—namely, that he won't start a nuclear war and go down in history as a mass murderer. In his own counteract, Turgidson is the first one to articulate the inevitability of nuclear war and, later on, is the first person to predict the Russians' inability to shoot down the final B-52 bomber. His stories do sometimes prove to be eerily prescient. The War Room and its Big Boards thus suggest Turgidson's, and Dr. Strangelove's (Sellers in his third part), inherent desire for a story of all-out war and "megadeaths," even while they understand little of the reasons or motivations behind what happens.

Like every previous Kubrick film (with the exception of *Lolita*), this Cold War satire also opens with a narrator. Yet the opening voice-over in *Dr. Strangelove*—like the performances of Hayden and Sellers—also seems to mock the self-importance and overt seriousness of earlier voice-overs. Opening the narrative, this third-person narrator attempts to initially establish a story where the events of the film are already placed under a cloud of mystery and danger. He states the following over a wide establishing shot of clouds covering a mountain range:

> For more than a year, ominous rumors had been privately circulating among high-level Western leaders that the Soviet Union had been at work on what was darkly hinted to be the ultimate weapon: a doomsday device. Intelligence sources traced the site of the top-secret Russian project to the perpetually fog-shrouded wasteland below the Arctic Peaks of the Zhokov Islands. What they were building or why it was located in a remote, desolate place, no one could say.

This voice-over narration seems to subvert the authority of other opening voice-overs in *Fear and Desire* and *Paths of Glory*, ones that somberly declare the moral and thematic importance of events that later unfold. These earlier antiwar films begin with third-person narrators offering not only plot exposition but also attempts at profound philosophical statements about the cost of war (this pretension is also embedded in the openings of *Spartacus* and, to a lesser extent, *The Killing*). But, in *Dr. Strangelove*, the subject of the voice-over—the unrepresented "doomsday device"—is shrouded in fog, figuratively and literally. In this sense, the country of the mind has become so overwhelmingly dense and impenetrable that "no one could say" anything about what is, narratively speaking, the centerpiece of the film. Here, we have a Kubrickian voice-over narration that indirectly admits it cannot *say* much of anything about events soon to unfold. And, when viewed through the lens of these preceding Kubrick movies, *Dr. Strangelove*'s manipulation of the voice-over becomes all the more compelling, as the film perhaps suggests to us Kubrick's shifting thoughts on the act of storytelling.

The voice-over narration in *Dr. Strangelove* ironically misdirects the audience in several ways, telling a story that does not adequately account for what later occurs in the film. For one, the grave tone of the narration contradicts the comic nature of the rest of the film. For another, this opening implies that the Russians will be at fault for the nuclear war about to unfold, when in fact such action will be initiated by the Communist-hating General Ripper. Finally, this voice-over narration does not indicate anything that either Strangelove or the Russian premier will not discuss themselves in greater detail later in the film, thus foregrounding this act of storytelling as being, at the very least, redundant to the movement of events in the story itself. This same third-person narrator, meanwhile, returns a few minutes later for the second and final time, again with more narrative exposition rather than attempts at thematic development (common in earlier voice-overs):

> In order to guard against surprise nuclear attack, America's Strategic Air Command maintains a large force of B-52 bombers airborne 24 hours a day. Each B-52 can deliver a nuclear bomb load of 50 megatons, equal to 16 times the total explosive force of all the bombs and shells used by all the armies in World War II. Based in America, the Airborne Alert Force is deployed from the Persian Gulf to the Arctic Ocean. But they have one geographical factor in common. They are all two hours from their targets inside Russia.

Much of this largely expository information is again repeated by characters later in the film. Thus, I would argue that these particular instances of voice-over narration compel us to sense the first example of a wholly *unauthoritative* voice-over narrator in a Kubrick film. But this revelation is not so much in the sense that he passes along necessarily wrong information in the process of his storytelling. Rather, I argue this point in regard to the fact that what the narrator says is completely extraneous to *Dr. Strangelove*'s story, while also showing little awareness of most events within the film. Every bit of information the narrator states becomes either redundant or unnecessary as the narrative progresses. Indeed, as I mentioned previously, the highly comic nature of *Dr. Strangelove* undercuts any attempt at credibility or authority that such a serious voice, in subject matter and in tone, attempts to set. Falsetto posits *The Killing* as an early instance of an unreliable narrator,[4] mostly by attempting to point out temporal inconsistencies in the course of the narrative. While I find this criticism valid to a point, such a pretentious and didactic voice-over—however sloppy in its temporal order—is consistent with other Kubrick films released before and after *The Killing*. I am instead more inclined to argue that the shift away from the magic of words really began eight years later with *Dr. Strangelove*'s particularly irrelevant voice-over.

Dr. Strangelove's third-person narrator gives way, meanwhile, to other characters, such as Turgidson, who also serve as storytellers. These characters narrate in the sense that they attempt—through disembodied broadcasts and announcements—to frame the meaning and importance of events within the film. In the other main settings of *Dr. Strangelove*, the B-52 cockpit and Burpelson Air Force Base, two characters each give speeches over an intercom to subordinates within their respective filmic spaces. In the B-52, Major Kong (Slim Pickens) addresses his men:

> Now, look, boys. I ain't much of a hand at making speeches, but I got a fair idea that something doggone important's going on back there. I've got a fair idea of the kind of personal emotions that some of you fellows may be thinking. Heck, I reckon you wouldn't be human beings if you didn't have pretty strong personal feelings about nuclear combat. I want you to remember one thing—the folks back home are counting on you. And, by golly, we ain't about to let them down. Tell you something else—if this thing turns out to be half as important as I figure it just might be, I'd say that you're all in line for some important promotions and personal citations when this thing's over with. That goes for every last one of you, regardless of your race, color or your creed. Now let's get this thing on the hump. We got some flying to do.

With the intercom turning his speech into a voice-over for the entire cockpit, Kong justifies the actions they are about to take by way of a story suggesting the grave importance at hand as well as the recognition and glory he believes await them afterward. During Kong's speech, quiet soundtrack music plays in the background, featuring a chorus of male voices humming "When Johnny Comes Marching Home." This musical selection allows the narrative structure to reinforce his patriotic words while also foregrounding his delivery as instead being an artificial act of storytelling (while also subtly hinting at the irony of it being a Civil War tune). The use of music here further establishes the B-52 as a set subjected to Kong's attempts at narration, separate from the other spaces in the film. Moreover, Kong dictates the agenda of the characters—a trait often associated with voice-over narrations, such as the efficiently omniscient voice overseeing events in *The Killing*.

Thomas Allen Nelson astutely points out how Kong, complete with cowboy hat, "acts out [his own] private drama in an Old West showdown with civilization."[5] I would add that General Ripper and Turgidson also play out similar private dramas. They control their respective sets and influence the other characters. In this way, then, Kong attempts to control his story line, even while he is under certain orders from General Ripper, the third implicit narrator. Ripper delivers to the air base soldiers a rallying speech similar to Kong's attempts at narrating:

> Your Commie has no regard for human life, not even his own. For this reason, men, I want to impress upon you the need for extreme watchfulness. The individual may come individually or he may come in strength. He may even come in the uniform of our own troops. But, however he comes, we must stop him. We must not allow him to gain entrance to this base.

Ripper's speech is more clearly limited and unauthoritative than Kong's is. Yet they both attempt to give order and meaning to events. And through their respective lack of contact, *Dr. Strangelove* reveals their individual failures as narrative authorities. Just as important, Kong too is a limited storyteller in this context, as the audience is aware of the misinformation under which he operates—Ripper is insane with paranoia, and the Russians have not already attacked. Kong's very words betray a lack of intelligence that undermines his narrative authority. For example, he claims to know what emotions his fellow crewmen may be "thinking," as opposed to the more appropriate "feeling."[6] He also needlessly repeats "race" and "color" in the same sequence, as though he does not quite understand exactly what he is talking about. Meanwhile, Ripper's rants against the "Commie" and his infiltration tactics vaguely resemble a narrative of right-wing propaganda as much as they do anything else. Yet Ripper clearly attempts absolute narrative order and control over the events within his environment. For example, he confiscates all the radios on the base, as though (in a nod to the voice-over and the radio in *The Killing*, perhaps) they suggest to him avenues for competing narrators (who will of course contradict his version of events). In *Dr. Strangelove*, Ripper strives for complete narrative authority, in part by initially dictating the following to his subordinates:

Now, I am going to give you three simple rules. First, trust no one, whatever his uniform or rank, unless he is known to you personally. Secondly, anyone or anything that approaches within 200 yards of the perimeter is to be fired upon. Third, if in doubt, shoot first and ask questions afterwards. I would sooner accept a few casualties through accident than lose the entire base and its personnel through carelessness. Any variations on these rules must come from me personally.

Having isolated the soldiers completely within his world, Ripper outlines what he thinks should and will unfold in the narrative. Ripper's long-windedness, meanwhile, only further emphasizes the fundamental emptiness of his words. His is a story removed from the world itself as he projects upon his soldiers his own narrative of the events about to unfold (i.e., the American soldier is really a Communist in disguise). He does this without any acknowledgment of the fact that he himself is the one who began this war—not the Communists he believes made him impotent. In a tale relayed to Mandrake halfway through the film, the imagined effect of water fluoridation on his sexual abilities perfectly typifies the egregious extent and determined drive of Ripper's storytelling abilities to overcompensate for experiences he cannot otherwise clearly come to terms with.

Although Ripper displays real potential for the power of storytelling to control and influence others, he also ends up saying very little of substance. This revelation illustrates how quickly acts of narration can become disconnected from those events they hoped to narrate over. And this hollowness is thus reinforced by his subsequent verbal descent into military and patriotic clichés. Ripper here echoes Kong's nationalistic jargon, words that nonetheless carry the potential to greatly influence those listening:

> Now, men, in conclusion, I would like to say that in the two years that it has been my privilege to be your commanding officer, I have always expected the best from you and you have never given me anything less than that. Today, the nation is counting on us. We are not going to let them down. Good luck to you all.

Ripper essentially misleads with every word uttered over the intercom and becomes Burpelson Air Force Base's implicit, unreliable narrator. Through Kong's and Ripper's figurative voice-overs, *Dr. Strangelove* calls attention to the danger of any one mind attempting to impose exclusive understanding on the world of the film. The presence of competing subjective narrators collectively illustrates the individual inability of each to control *all* the events occurring. Their narrative constructions crack under the weight of all that they seek to narrate. They can at best barely control some of the events occurring within their own limited settings, and not with positive results. Beyond even the third-person narrator who opens the film, all the first-person "narrators" in *Dr. Strangelove* (Kong, Ripper, Turgidson, and Strangelove) reveal a compelling lack of narrative control and authority within the film. They are each playing out their own stories, imposing their own narrative order on the other characters around them. Yet Kong, Ripper, and Turgidson, if nothing else, each lack some capacity that prevents their complete reliability and authority as storytellers. The gung ho Kong does not know the truth behind the orders, Ripper lacks sanity, and Turgidson does not possess any kind of human compassion or social awareness. Just as important, each character cannot alter reasons for or the inevitability of nuclear war. Although they all play some limited role, the enormity of the devastation that ultimately happens lies beyond the reach of their immediate grasp.

Similar to Turgidson's Big Board in the War Room, the B-52 cockpit and the air base suggest narrative canvasses realized by Kong's and Ripper's respective attempts at storytelling. The intercom/voice-over narrations here mark out each character's territory, not unlike the (often) disembodied narrators in earlier Kubrick films. The Burpelson Air Force Base plays host to the beginning of nuclear war and of armed conflict between ground soldiers, just as Ripper had in some sense envisioned. Kong meanwhile uses his B-52 bomber as a way to play out his own high-noon scenario with the "Roo-skies." Important here also is the fact that both Kong and Ripper (and, to a lesser extent, Turgidson) do not actually have any contact with the outside world, as though they are indeed *trapped* within the stories they've told others and they themselves have come to believe. They are literally imprisoned in situations manifesting their own narrative assumptions. They attempt to impose narrative order not only on their immediate surroundings but on the surrounding world as well. Kong verbally assumes that the Russians have already launched a massive nuclear strike on America. Ripper tells his men an elaborate story whereby the Russians have already invaded the domestic front, have poisoned the water to make men impotent, and are now posing as American soldiers on their way to the air base. Turgidson calls the Russian premier a "degenerate, atheistic Commie," even though quite probably he has never met the man. In fact, Turgidson is so self-absorbed that he cannot even initially say the insult to the Russian ambassador face to face. He instead whispers the comment as an aside to another American in the War Room as though conscious in some way of how shaky his story might be.

As each of these stories moves collectively toward its part in *Dr. Strangelove*'s unavoidable conclusion, the impossibility of genuine human interaction and communication, and the impossibility of direct experience with moments and events, in the world of the film becomes more and more apparent. Ripper sits silently at his desk late in the film and passively stares out with a blank look. Foreshadowing the faces of many later Kubrickian characters mentioned in chapter 1 and returned to in subsequent chapters, Ripper gives up on the ability of the magic of words to change anything. Ripper's face here is another facade, another Kubrick facade—it presents us nothing but the surface. Deep inside, he cannot understand anything of the experience he senses, or of the experience he in part helped create. He does not possess any internalized meaning. He can only await death, accept it in some small way. And thus we begin to see the emergence of a radically different form of Kubrickian storytelling—not narration, but silence. Put another way, silence—nothingness—becomes the new form of narration. This narrative effect (or chaotic affect) becomes especially important in subsequent films. In the early 1960s *Sight & Sound* article "Words and Movies" (written shortly before the preproduction on *Dr. Strangelove*), Kubrick notes:

> Often, at one point, the writer expects a silent look to get across what it would take a rebus puzzle to explain, and in the next moment the actor is given a long speech to convey something that is quite apparent in the situation and for which a brief look would be sufficient. Writers tend to approach the creation of drama too much in terms of words, failing to realise that the greatest force they have is mood and feeling they can produce in the audience through the actor.[7]

Dr. Strangelove gives us, I think, the first instance of that "brief look," which will be so crucial in Kubrick's later films. This is especially important because, as in the previous quote, the look is placed in contrast to words. This look—in a manner of speaking—*says* more than words. In sharp contrast to his earlier dictations over the intercom and to Mandrake, Ripper does not offer a long-winded speech in this moment of the film to explain what he thinks has happened or will happen. His look will "be sufficient." He has already given us enough long speeches in *Dr. Strangelove*, by telling us stories about his impotence and impending Russian invasions—nothing has been changed for the better through talking. All he can give us is the look—and silence. His face thus means nothing, but it creates in us a sense of narrative failure. He cannot change anything, least of all through more words.

Likewise, the narrative of *Dr. Strangelove* cannot actively alter the course of events set in motion. Ripper can instead only sit back and await the impending, speechless violence (and yes, we can only laugh in horror). In this moment, the entire film becomes an unfulfilling realization of Ripper's attempts at narrative construction as he presumably envisions all the destruction his stories of impotence and deception will wreak on the world. Such are some of the themes of *Dr. Strangelove* and of the dark side of storytelling—where honest human communication and attempts to narrate a tale still directly relating to the world, and thus that can enact some level of social and political change, are simply not possible. As Kong famously rides the H-bomb off the bomber and down to its target, the film highlights the innate sounds of Kong's wild screaming and the rushing winds over any grand composed musical score or coherent verbal description. The naturalistic emphasis here seems to point away from verbal or explicit narrating of any kind. *The event is the event.* There appears to be no further desire for the fractured kinds of storytelling that have brought *Dr. Strangelove*'s world to this point. Like Ripper and his blank stare, Kong is thus liberated from the *magic of words.* And, as with the suitcase bursting open at the end of *The Killing* or with the executions in *Paths of Glory*, the audience confronts only the diegetic sounds of the story world. Yet in *Dr. Strangelove*, Kong is completely alone, with no appreciation of the true devastation he is about to unleash. Instead of offering understanding or a story that still connects to the world outside Kong, this moment in the film merely serves (cowboy hat–waving and all) as the culmination of a fantasy confrontation with an enemy he has no understanding or awareness of at all, except as an abstract enemy in his own personal Cold War epic.

    Dr. Strangelove offers the first overt Kubrickian account of the potential cultural and social tensions inherent in acts of storytelling—not everyone sees things the same way. We see here most clearly how the description and retelling of events can become quickly disconnected from the events themselves. The film specifically allows us to rethink such a concept from a cinematic point of view by utilizing and playing with the potential of voice-over narration. The redundant and superfluous third-person narrator precedes and foreshadows characters within the film who serve as unofficial first-person narrators imposing meaning on military movement and national intentions. Here *Dr. Strangelove* reveals the inability of storytelling either to unify and order events within and beyond the film's three isolated settings or to prevent nuclear conflict. Both the third-person narrator and the implicit first-person narrators—General Turgidson, General Ripper, Major Kong, Dr. Strangelove—suggest a breakdown in the ability of narrating to actually tell a story with the same expository and thematic clarity that the respective third-person narrators of *Fear and Desire* and *Paths of Glory* previously offer. The stories constructed within *Dr. Strangelove* by various narrators openly contradict each other. And these ruptures between storytelling and events first point toward an increasing awareness of the fractured and incongruous narrations that will later highlight *A Clockwork Orange, Barry Lyndon,* and *Full Metal*

Jacket. These more distant and ironic Kubrick films thus will give rise to blank faces and voiceless voice-overs only hinted at in *Dr. Strangelove.*

NOTES

1. As quoted in Alexander Walker, Sybil Taylor, and Ulrich Ruchti, *Stanley Kubrick, Director: A Visual Analysis* (New York: Norton, 1999), 184.

2. Thomas Allen Nelson, among others, argues that such imagery suggests "copulation." *Kubrick: Inside a Film Artist's Maze,* 2nd ed. (Bloomington: Indiana University Press, 2000), 95. Walker notes that "the image anticipates the sexually based human motivation [Ripper's impotence] for the coming destruction." *A Visual Analysis,* 121.

3. For example, Walker points out how the film contains "three highly localized settings . . . sealed off from the others" (*A Visual Analysis,* 116), while Mario Falsetto adds that "none of the film's characters has much of a sense of what is occurring in the other spaces." *Stanley Kubrick: A Narrative and Stylistic Analysis,* 2nd ed. (Westport, Conn.: Praeger, 2001), 43.

4. Falsetto, *Narrative and Stylistic Analysis,* 5.

5. Nelson, *Inside a Film Artist's Maze,* 90.

6. By articulating the seemingly paradoxical idea of "emotions that some of you fellows may be thinking," Kong does also introduce another possibility. One could make the argument here that Kubrick is very subtly introducing what I argue dominates the filmmaker's later films—the thinking feeling, or the feeling that thinks, independent of human cognition. This phrase is, for example, one way to describe the Kubrickian look—a sense that narrates narrative ambiguity—that will emerge later in the film on Ripper's blank face. But I fear this is probably reading a bit too much into Kong's speech in *Dr. Strangelove.* But, all the same, it's pretty to think so.

7. Stanley Kubrick, "Words and Movies," *Sight and Sound* 30 (Winter 1960/1961): 14.

· 5 ·

I Can Feel It: Sounds, Intensities, and Subjectivities in *2001*

It's not a message that I ever intended to convey in words. *2001* is a nonverbal experience; out of two hours and 19 minutes of film, there are only a little less than 40 minutes of dialog. I tried to create a visual experience, one that bypasses verbalized pigeonholing and directly penetrates the subconscious with an emotional and philosophical content. . . . I intended the film to be an intensely subjective experience that reaches the viewer at an inner level of consciousness, just as music does; to "explain" a Beethoven symphony would be to emasculate it by erecting an artificial barrier between conception and appreciation.

—Stanley Kubrick, 1968[1]

$\mathcal{A}$s I alluded to in the first chapter, there seems to be a shift in narrative authority and narrative failure in *Dr. Strangelove*. And there are other moments here that affectively suggest to me that something does change in the body of Kubrick's work around the time of *Dr. Strangelove* and *2001*. Whether or not Kubrick (and—in parallel—his films) was still coming to terms with the mind and its ability to give order and meaning to the world, there is a sense of greater misgivings about the mind and about cognition. For example, in 1966, two years after the release of *Dr. Strangelove* and well on his way to the experience of *2001*, Stanley Kubrick offered his thoughts that the atomic bomb and its detonation had become—as a spectacle—a "complete abstraction" for people:

> By now the [atomic] bomb has almost no reality and has become a complete abstraction, represented by a few newsreel shots of mushroom clouds. . . . People react primarily to direct experience and not to abstractions; it is very rare to find anyone who can become emotionally involved with an abstraction. The longer the bomb is around without anything happening, the better job that

77

people can do in psychologically denying its existence. It has become as abstract as the fact that we are all going to die someday, which we usually do an excellent job of denying.[2]

Society, he argues, could no longer appreciate or understand the true horror of the weapon's capabilities because people had spent the last twenty years or so being bombarded with facades—watching grainy footage of mushroom cloud after mushroom cloud rising above the horizon without any sense of the experience itself. Again, I do not read Kubrick's quotes and his biography with the quixotic intent of uncovering the true "intentions" of his films. Then again, there is no logical reason why Kubrick's thoughts about life and his films should be regarded as automatically synonymous with intention in the first place. Kubrick does remain at the center here, but I am thinking about Kubrick as—among other things—a historical figure for change, integrated into and externalized from his own work as a filmmaker. In other words, I read Kubrick's own quotes as the mark of his own experiences with his films and as the mark of his own adaptation in moving forward as a director. Kubrick cannot control his films in an absolute rhetorical sense, then or now, but he did no doubt engage with them. And, he may have been *affected by his films* as much as he affected them. So, I'm wondering if he felt—as a moviegoer, as a revisionist—the oppression and restriction of the flat abstractions in *Fear and Desire*, the abstractions and the magic of words throughout most of his earlier films, *sensed the possibilities emerging outside the lingering emphasis on cognition*, and thus perhaps helped facilitate the evolution of a new sensory type of cinematic experience.

Naturally, Kubrick's observations here constitute more than idle chatter with *The New Yorker* reporter Jeremy Bernstein. The final montage of his then recently released satire, *Dr. Strangelove*, repeats similar images of nuclear explosions, not merely to signify the literal end of the world but also to challenge audiences to acknowledge how their only narrative understanding of this catastrophic event had come through a mediating representation of filmic storytelling—an appearance. Whether or not Kubrick *meant* all this is tangential—he experienced it to the point of discussion. And, indeed, it remains in the experience of *Dr. Strangelove*, whose final montage creates an effect similar to that of his interview with *The New Yorker*. Because most global audiences perceived the atomic bomb through film and not through direct, personal experience of any kind, the film medium, according to Kubrick, was capable of quickly desensitizing society to the actual bomb's potential impact—allowing them experience only with the cognitive act of "montagic" narration and cinematic representation. *Dr. Strangelove*'s method of layering the atomic bomb's representation through montage upon additional similar representations suggests the cultural perception of the event as being another facade—a discursive copy (fiction film) of a discursive copy (newsreel footage), seeming to mask and negate the authority of its horrific origin. At that moment, Kubrick seemed to think that people would respond affectively to "direct experience" and not to these "abstractions"—the conscious *cognitive exterior* of the bomb's presentation instead of the bomb itself.

Again, I do not mean to impose a reading of intention on Kubrick or his films. I am instead positing how a new sense is at play there—something preconscious that engaged Kubrick then, and his films now, as much as they similarly engage us. By invoking biography, I posit Kubrick here as a historical figure, experiencing his films along with (and before) us, as much as he is the muse that willed his films and their "meanings" into being. In fact, as I will attempt to argue later in this chapter, *2001* ultimately doesn't *mean* anything. Or, its meaning refers to the absence of explicit meaning. I am tempted to suggest that Kubrick is perhaps responding in this interview to his early works—say, the cognitive abstractions of *Fear and Desire* and *Killer's Kiss*—as much as he is foreshadowing or decreeing the aural and visual experiences of subsequent films. There seems to be a sense that the failure of *Dr. Strangelove*'s verbal mastery pushes toward an emphasis on the experiences of the body and toward the *feel* of *2001*. In *Dr. Strangelove*, it is the process of narrating, of reading Turgidson's Big Board, of the bomb's own abstraction, that takes precedence over the particular events of the story world—where direct, physical experience for them is denied, and several different, often isolated, people's assumptions about what is unfolding never quite align themselves. One could also speculate that Strangelove himself becomes so wrapped up in his own thoughts and visions precisely because—being in a wheelchair, possessing a fascistic arm—he literally has lost all control of his body and has no ability to react to his senses. In this way, Strangelove's inability to control his own body directly suggests the failure of his mind and of his words. He literally cannot control anything; he can only talk. While many early Kubrick films foreground the importance of this process of cognitively mapping the experience through language, *Dr. Strangelove* is the first of these films that most clearly emphasizes the rupture between what the mind envisions and thus represents and what is actually occurring to the senses, within a body of work whose films increasingly lose track of what *is* actually occurring in narrative. Attempts at narrative control—at claiming any kind of understanding of the story world—bring us from the happy ending of the reunited lovers in *Killer's Kiss* to the frozen isolation of the failed marriage in *The Shining*.

If I may go further still into Kubrick's biography yet again—in the 1960s, between the completion of *Dr. Strangelove* and preproduction on *2001*—

interesting changes occurred not only in Kubrick's professional life but in his personal one as well. During this time, biographer Vincent LoBrutto notes, the filmmaker "took a quantum leap in his career as a film director . . . about to change the way he conceived and made movies by fusing his life and art to gain absolute creative control."[3] For one, Kubrick moved his entire base of operations from New York to England, a place where he would reside for the remainder of his life. After the disappointing experience of helming the big-budget spectacle *Spartacus*, Kubrick vowed never again to allow the Holly-wood studio system to watch directly over his shoulder during the course of filming a movie. Subsequently, he shot his next two films, *Lolita* and *Dr. Strangelove*, in England, even though these films are set in America. How-ever, Kubrick still resided in a Manhattan penthouse apartment during this period; only after *Dr. Strangelove*, no doubt smitten with the independence afforded by shooting across the Atlantic, did he move his entire family, his entire life, over to England. Preproduction on *2001* began at Boreham Wood's MGM Studios, just outside London, as far from Hollywood studio control as Kubrick could achieve. His family, meanwhile, resided in a large apartment in London's Dorchester Hotel; by the time the film was com-pleted, Kubrick would move everyone to a large, even more isolated estate in Hertfordshire, on the outskirts of England. This environment, previously denied him within the frantic settings of Manhattan, further encouraged Kubrick to "produc[e] movies under conditions he dictated."[4]

During this period, Kubrick's physical appearance began to shift as well. Up through *Dr. Strangelove*, Kubrick resembled a 1950s New York intellec-tual, with a clean-cut appearance and a reliance on sharp-looking suits. Start-ing during the production of *2001*, however, his look became increasingly scruffy and eccentric. LoBrutto astutely summarizes this sudden physical alteration:

> By 1964, Stanley Kubrick's appearance was beginning to transform. With each year his eyes became more intense and deeply lined, and his eyebrows formed even higher arches. His hair, once kept barber-trimmed, was growing longer. The clean definition of the former taper haircut had shaggy wisps tumbling over his ears and back collar. The top was no longer parted neatly to the side; it was uncombed and beginning to thin. As this new project [*2001*] germi-nated he grew a beard. It was full and unmanicured, giving Kubrick the aura of a Talmudic scholar. The glen plaid business suits and white shirts he had worn at age nineteen at the urging of the senior photographic staff of *Look* [his first job as news photographer] were gone.[5]

When Kubrick spoke of "direct experience" with *The New Yorker*'s Jer-emy Bernstein, the interview came during this same transformation period—

directly between the release of *Dr. Strangelove* in 1964 and of *2001: A Space Odyssey* four years later. This is also one of several interviews and articles at the same time in which Kubrick suggested another transformation—a new kind of storytelling. His earlier films had dealt formally with what Kubrick referred to as "abstractions," to some degree or another—something the filmmaker now strongly believed audiences could not relate to. Kubrick condensed his entire first film to an abstraction; taking place during a war without depth or context, *Fear and Desire* reduced itself to mere allegory. Even *Dr. Strangelove*, in all its brilliance, tackled the narrative device of abstractions in its own way, perhaps most prominently with Turgidson's Big Board—an abstract, artificial representation of very real conflicts. In fact, even the film's final montage of nuclear explosions served only to heighten the idea of the bomb as a cultural abstraction rather than reinforce its reality as a deadly weapon of mass destruction. Yet the interview with Bernstein suggested Kubrick was moving away from the sarcasm and success he had achieved with the humorous excesses of *Dr. Strangelove*; instead, he evinced a greater interest in the kind of cinematic direct experience that resists those abstractions.

Perhaps—though, of course, we can never know for sure—the greatest abstraction of all for Kubrick was ultimately the verbal one. Words can only approximate, not reproduce, human experience, and his later films often highlight their futility as a means of expression. During the much-circulated 1968 interview with Eric Nordern, Stanley Kubrick famously described the narrative construction of *2001* and its intended audience response as that of "a visual experience, one that bypasses verbalized pigeonholing and directly penetrates the subconscious with an emotional and philosophical content." Though explicitly discussing *2001*, Kubrick essentially detailed a formal type of narrative construction—emphasizing images over words—that it seems to me he employed for the rest of his cinematic career. In other words, I see in Kubrick's interview one way in which to rethink the *affect* of his films. Each of his subsequent films—on a very broad level—affected "nonverbal experience[s]," trying to bypass "verbalized pigeonholing" and *directly* penetrate the "subconscious with an emotional and philosophical content." I find this quote—on its own—to be an extraordinary way of approaching Kubrick's films. There is an element of what may once have been called "intention" at play in the *Playboy* and *New Yorker* interviews. And how much do these bits of personal observations add to understanding Kubrick's films? Perhaps very little, and I'm not trying to create a definitive biographical or memorial reading of his films. Put another way, Kubrick echoes the effect in which his films attempt to circumvent an "artificial barrier" of human cognition in favor of an affective reception of his films. This chapter, meanwhile, is my affective reading of Kubrick's sci-fi production. It is an attempt to articulate what I

sense aurally in *2001*. However, it is not purely subjective. I also wish to articulate what I believe exists in the film itself, beyond my own (unavoidable)
instance of verbalized pigeonholing. It is also an approximation of what I
believe is there, in the experience of *2001*.

I find myself drawn to this turning point, the *historical* moment somewhere in the mid-1960s, between *Dr. Strangelove* and *2001*, when something
clearly shifted; something engages me in this period, even before I begin to
articulate it. In larger part, I am drawn by the affect of the film, by the sound
in the film, and simultaneously by the *absence* of sound in the film. I wish to
show not only how I receive *2001* in the context of Kubrick's career but also
how there may be something there in the experience to justify a different kind
of authorial reading. Certainly there is something about *2001*—especially its
ambiguity (a stark counterpoint to Kubrick's earlier films)—that compels
people to return again and again to the film. Luis M. Garcia Mainar states
simply that "*2001* is also an open-ended narrative [. . . that] refuses to be
highly communicative about its real meaning."[6] Thomas Allen Nelson adds
that the Star Child's eyes in *2001*'s famous final shot look "directly into the
camera, like a dehumanized monolith mutely imploring the audience to pon-
der its mystery."[7] Similarly, Alexander Walker acknowledges both pessimistic
and optimistic interpretations of the ending, though he clearly prefers the
latter, eloquently arguing that Kubrick "leaves the film open-ended, yet oddly
comforting in the way that dream imagery can be to an awakened sleeper
gratified by the echoes and associations lingering in his conscious mind."[8]
Indeed what provokes me (and, I suspect, others) into writing about Kubrick
and *2001* again are these "echoes and associations lingering" in the conscious
mind after the initial, affective moment of viewing. There is not an opposition at play here, however. Affect is not set *against* cognition (or vice versa).
Affect unfolds new modes of understanding in the mind, in a way that is
somehow initiated by the sensations of the body—not only what I feel but
also what I see and hear. What I am trying to articulate is not the "formal"
elements of Kubrick's films but rather how the experience of Kubrick's
films affectively compels me to rethink and write at a cognitive level about
his films.

2001 is still written about not because it is a good film or a well-made
film (in fact, just as many people find it immensely boring) but because it
contains an affective power that causes us to will an understanding of it. And
perhaps even its supposed boredom for some contains its own affective powers (think of the deliberately and belligerently slow experimental films of
Andy Warhol, for example). Critics and scholars write about Kubrick's films
because something nonverbal compels them to—something nonverbal in the
films themselves. Even though the artificial readings of his films are inade-

quate to the experience of the film itself, they are nonetheless induced by the films. It is something nonverbal that I am attempting to articulate here. Using the intensities and subjectivities of *2001*, I am trying to imagine here a *pre-conscious* Cinema of Stanley Kubrick.

What Kubrick once said about abstractions and direct experience is not the "right" way or the "better" way to see *2001*. Certainly it would be foolish to commit here the same mistake of verbally pigeonholing the film. Rather, the quote—like this project—is a materialization of what I have always already felt (much) earlier when watching those films. The interest in Kubrick's "intensely subjective experiences" and in, separately, *2001*'s "open-ended" "mystery" is meant to be sensed rather than read. That is, for me, the films before *2001* all *feel and sound* different from the ones that followed. There is the shift in emphasis from voice-over narration (indeed the shift away from most dominant nondiegetic sounds), accompanied by the shift in emphasis from word to image. Kubrick's interview with Bernstein is but another suspended moment—where a fleeting feeling remains for us—that heightens our awareness of the possibilities for an affective reception to the work existing in the films at an "inner level of consciousness." And, I am tempted to add, maybe at the inner level of *preconsciousness*, at the level of sight and sound.

If talk is the defining characteristic of Kubrick's prior film, *Dr. Strange-love*, then *2001*'s defining characteristic is silence, or at least sounds that are mostly marginal, ambient. But precisely because of the film's silence, sound is extraordinarily important to *2001*—the ways in which sound engages the audience affectively on an inner level prior to our own artificial, cognitive bar-riers, erected after that first moment of intensity. By relying on Kubrick's use of the word *artificial*, I am referring to how our minds come to terms with the physical experience of film viewing in a way that cannot help but always already be a simulation, a representation, of what I thought I saw (and heard) at the preconscious level. For example, the emphasis on talking in *Dr. Strangelove* seems to suggest that "artificial barrier [of] appreciation," where characters attempt to explain away experience through words, even while they cannot discursively prevent nuclear war.

Then we have the shift in biography from New York to England, the shift in production attitudes, the shift in appearance. Again, what does it mean? It probably does not mean anything, but I cannot ignore the effect of all these radical changes in and around Kubrick's work at this time. I do not claim to know with any clarity of vision what any of this *means*, and perhaps this is the point where auteurists often run into trouble. We can get a sense of something in the films and history of Stanley Kubrick—a change perhaps? But we cannot quite explain it through the magic of words. This point on the trail is maybe the best place at which to stop for a moment and restate one of the central assumptions of this book—"Stanley Kubrick" is unrepresentable at the critical level, even while he is always already there as an effect.

This particular chapter is an attempt to rethink the importance of words and voice-over narration in the emergence of an affective cinema in *2001*, by way of their stunning absence in this long-honored "nonverbal" film, and to reconsider new possibilities for violence and destruction underlining the inherent awe and ambiguity of its narrative content. In spite of the remarkably different structures, styles, and tones of *Dr. Strangelove* and *2001*, nuclear wasteland imagery nonetheless connects the end of Kubrick's H-bomb satire with the beginning of his equally effective follow-up. At the end of *Dr. Strangelove*, a string of nuclear weapons, led by the Russian doomsday machine, apparently obliterates all life on Earth. Watching the two films back to back, one senses that the empty landscape of *2001* recalls the complete devastation of life at the end of the former film.

Symbolically emerging from the nuclear destruction of *Dr. Strangelove*, *2001* then opens with an extended "Dawn of Man" sequence, featuring pre-intelligence apes in an unnamed desert—a postnuclear future, I would say, as much as a preevolution past. Yet despite this symbolic link, *2001* hardly signifies an implicit sequel to its Kubrickian predecessor; instead, the latter film creates a blank slate for a revised narrative structure—both figuratively and literally—when looking out across the empty, smooth desert. If *Dr. Strangelove* indicated, as Nelson argues, "the last orgasm of language in an explosion of bombastic clichés, overwrought euphemisms, and a strangulating jargon,"[9] then the endless montage of nuclear explosions in the earlier film's finale represents the inevitable impotence of effective verbal communication for both voice-over narration and the films' characters.

Provocative landscapes were clearly of importance in the openings of Kubrick's films. Yet whereas fog covers the forests of *Fear and Desire*, the British countryside of *Lolita*, and the high mountains in *Dr. Strangelove*, there is little to impede our view of the barren, sun-drenched landscape in *2001*. As I noted before, it is not difficult to argue that fog in these opening images creates the effect of a dominant narrative authority (which clouds our own vision). In this context, I think the desolate, exposed desert that opens *2001* may well prove to be the first of many instances where the film will resist attempts at blocking or frustrating our vision of events in the story world as they occur through artificial means. *2001* may not open with fog because there is little overtly narrative effort at framing story events through language. As I have outlined in the previous chapters, for six straight earlier films, the films directed by Stanley Kubrick displayed a great dependency on what the filmmaker himself referred to as "the *magic of words*," especially voice-over, as a narrative tool. In the ashes of *Dr. Strangelove*, however, the filmmaker's productions engage for us a revised thematic and narrative structure of feeling that privileges nonverbal over verbal modes of communication. In the postapocalyptic aftermath of *Dr. Strangelove*, 2001 privileges diegetic over nondiegetic content while resisting claims to narrative authority. The ending of *2001*, meanwhile, returns to a similar critique of narrative order as a fundamentally violent activity much like that at the end of *Dr. Strangelove*, as the Star Child symbolically appropriates the narrative structure with *Also Sprach Zarathustra* and begins plans for obliterating Earth.

Indeed, the production history of *2001* supports this tentative assertion about resistance to narrative authority. Like *Fear and Desire*, early cuts of *2001* originally featured a third-person narrator imposing a meaning on the events of the film, and those forcing a prescribed appreciation of them as well. Echoing the opening moments of every Kubrick film up to this point—especially *The Killing*, *Paths of Glory*, *Spartacus*, and even *Dr. Strangelove*—the following narration supposedly first accompanied the "Dawn of Man" sequence that opens the film:

> The remorseless drought had lasted now for ten million years, and would not end for another million. The reign of the terrible lizards had long since passed, but here on the continent which would one day be known as Africa, the battle for survival had reached a new climax of ferocity, and the victor was not yet in sight. In this dry and barren land, only the small or the swift or the fierce could flourish, or even hope to exist. The man apes of the field had none of these attributes, and they were on the long, pathetic road to racial extinction.[10]

While not thematically directive in the way that previous voice-overs had been, this third-person narrator does contextualize the story in a manner reminiscent of the openings of *The Killing*, *Paths of Glory*, and *Spartacus* and, moreover, suggests a return to the forms of narrative authority used to frame earlier films. In this sense, the critique of language posited in *Dr. Strangelove* would have been negated by Kubrick's wordy follow-up. Later, during this same opening sequence in *2001*, Kubrick also initially inserted the following narrated description of one of the apes:

> As he looks out now upon the hostile world, there is already something in his gaze beyond the capacity of any apes. In those dark, deep-set eyes is a dawning

awareness—the first intimations of an intelligence that would not fulfill itself for another four million years.

By this point, *2001* already would have undermined the critique of language posited in *Dr. Strangelove* and consistent with the deceptive power of words, having every detail spelled out to the audience. And there are additionally interesting cues here, beyond the direct assertion of narrative authority, whose subsequent omission itself may be telling. As I noted before, the reference to the subject's relationship to "the hostile world" is—whether consciously or not—a direct echo of Kubrick's own verbal description of *Fear and Desire*. Also, the narrator's decision to describe the ape's "gaze," to describe what occurs *beneath* that "gaze," is particularly interesting in light of the emergence of the Kubrickian look, the look of a face that refuses to unequivocally dictate to us what is going on inside the mind. The faces we see in Kubrick's subsequent films may or may not possess a "dawning awareness," but if they do, it is an awareness we sense, not an awareness we are explicitly told about. Though images and sounds can be equally deceptive, words more closely approximate overt attempts at narrative order in the story world. It is not that the sounds and images aren't necessarily deceptive in *2001* so much as the experiences of these images and sounds would be consciously distorted further by the voice-over narration—our experiences filtered through someone else's. After the Monolith first appears, the narrator then was to explain the following, in words that threatened to push any sense of narrative subtlety to the breaking point:

> They [the apes] have no conscious memory of what they had seen; but that night, as he sits brooding at the entrance of his lair, his ears attuned to the noises of the world around him, Moon-Watcher feels the first twinges of a new and potent emotion—the urge to kill. He has taken the first step toward humanity.

In discussing *2001*, Walker aptly refers to these passages as "verbal commentary couched in a pseudo-Genesis style."[11] They fail to add anything more than what the images and sounds already clearly dramatize, or what little commentary they do add invariably would undermine the experience of the films. They also echo the abstract, pretentious overexplanation that marred the openings of *Fear and Desire*, *Spartacus*, and even *The Killing*. More important, the voice-over's subsequent exclusion from *2001* suggests that a shift may have indeed occurred, as I sensed it did (beginning in *Lolita* and *Dr. Strangelove*), from voice-over narration as the dominant stylistic element in early films to being increasingly distanced and ironic in subsequent films (*A Clockwork Orange*, *Barry Lyndon*):

Kubrick eventually removed an enormous amount of the screenplay's original narrative scaffolding (a documentary prologue about aliens, a voice-over commentary, Alex North's epic score), scaffolding that at the outset was an integral part of the project, and without the support of which he doubtless could not have constructed this singular film.[12]

Michel Chion's *Kubrick's Cinema Odyssey* (2001) is an extraordinary look at *2001*, and there is more yet to be said about the film's de-emphasis on words. Visual aspects of *2001* also illustrate a new resistance to explicit verbal meaning and narrative authority—moments of extended takes and of blank-faced characters with little to say. Much of *2001* consists of long, extended shots strung together, such as the two space travel sequences—first, when the Pan-Am ship approaches the space station, and then when Heywood Floyd (William Sylvester) travels to the Moon. Similarly, Kubrick constructs the film's much-discussed "Star Gate" finale by piecing together various extended takes of images depicting the galaxy. All these sequences essentially feature long take after long take.

Yet *2001* uses the extended take during the film's quieter moments as well. For example, extended shots produce the scene where Floyd speaks with his daughter on the video phone; the conversation where Dave Bowman (Keir Dullea) and Frank Poole (Gary Lockwood) discuss HAL's fate, with HAL himself centered in the background; and the famous shot where the stewardess walks "up" the wall, into the cockpit, during Floyd's trip to the Moon (a shot that foreshadows a similar take later in the film when Bowman and Poole walk down a rotating corridor and out of the ship's pod bay). Meanwhile, the film uses the Jupiter ship's centrifuge as a stage for several long takes. When Poole runs around the circular room for exercise, *2001* edits together four separate extended takes of the crewman running. The first shot frames Poole from a distance, while the subsequent shots follow methodically behind him. Later, when Bowman enters the centrifuge, an extended shot captures the entire room, framing both Poole and Bowman performing different tasks in different sections within the same shot. This particular shot also echoes a later take where the same two men again perform different technical duties within the same frame, despite their spatial distance. Each of these extended takes, which resist ascribing overt and explicit meaning to the events of the story through cutting and montage (as seen in *The Killing* or *Spartacus*), represents an attempt to downplay any form of authoritative subjectivity—any inhabitant presence of verbalized pigeonholing—in *2001*. Whereas the voice-over narration would *describe* the experiences to the audience, the long takes here allow something of a direct experience with the story world itself to emerge. However, this is not to say that these images of long takes are necessarily objective (though they are, in a Bazinian sort of way)—rather, not unlike in the opening murder sequence of *Lolita*, I simply do not sense an overt, artificial, or cognitive lens distorting our experience of *2001*.

In *2001*, there is a distinct failure by characters to understand experience or to engage with others. Thus, we see characters retreat to the look accordingly. For example, Bowman retreats into a fixed, voiceless stare when he realizes both HAL's awareness of his and Poole's plans for the computer's fate and HAL's violent intentions toward him. Unable to control the computer, Bowman's psychological internalization as he contemplates his options (if any) coincides with HAL physically shutting him out of the spaceship. Verbal meaning breaks down as the computer's evolving plan of murder undermines Bowman's earlier assumption of events—namely, that he could undermine HAL's authority without the computer catching on to his plans. Every shot of HAL, meanwhile, essentially captures this blank look, as the self-absorbed computer perhaps best typifies a character in *2001* incapable of thinking outside its own mind and engaging with others. The film's final image, the Star Child, similarly offers such a look. With newfound powers at his disposal, the Star Child stares out at the galaxy but really only ponders, as the film ends, his limitless options as a new life form. As I will later show in my discussion of the film's conclusion, I believe it can begin to be sensed that the Star Child is interested only in himself, not in communicating or evolving with others. Here, this character's face, along with HAL and Bowman, provides *2001* with a preview of a new Kubrickian narrative authority—one that no longer overtly manipulates the perception of events and their meaning, like the deleted third-person narration. The face points us toward a voiceless voice-over.

Yet while many, including Kubrick and Walker, focus on *2001* as a visual experience, the film's sound plays every bit as much a role as the images do. Foreshadowed by moments during the finales of *The Killing*, *Paths of Glory*, and *Dr. Strangelove*, diegetic sound becomes especially important in *2001*. Yet while a few critics have previously noted the use of sound,[13] what I would add is the striking degree to which *2001* *repeats* these sounds over and over, as though heightening and intensifying an audience's awareness of their presence—these sounds, not unlike the blank faces, having now supplanted voice-over narration as a dominant cinematic mode of storytelling in this new film. While Kubrick indeed deleted the film's planned voice-over, such a decision does not suggest a distrust of, or even lack of interest in, sound as a narrative device. The omission instead highlights a shift from the early emphasis on nondiegetic sound (music and third-person voice-overs) to a later one on ambient sound, in the breakdown of previous verbal meaning.

As though constantly reminding audiences of the failure of words (including those that would have opened the film originally), diegetic sounds abound in the absence of a dominant narrative authority throughout *2001*. During the "Dawn of Man" sequence, the film opens with an extended series of shots establishing the barren desert landscape in which the apes live, accompanied by ambient sounds—winds, birds, grasshoppers, and so forth. Once the film introduces the apes, this trend continues. The apes produce only incoherent, grunting noises and chaotic, violent screams, which the film's soundtrack emphasizes over other sounds. When the Monolith appears, however, an unseen chorus of voices takes over the natural sounds, seemingly nondiegetic in its story space. They may emanate simply as inaudible voices from the film's soundtrack—György Ligeti's *Requiem*. Yet they evoke for me much more—alien voices, watching the apes, and thus diegetic in origin. These voices appear on the film's soundtrack only at moments when the Monolith arrives, the foreign beacon meant to provoke another level of experience. Their incomprehensibility, meanwhile, only further plays against an earlier, audible, voice-over narration. With these new voices—the sounds of an alien presence and the impending violence as the apes become more aware of their destructive powers—a new type of nonverbal narrative authority seems to emerge. I get here the sense that the neat and clean order of voice-over narration has been replaced with the chaos of these inaudible voices. These softer sounds and images suggest the impending chaos and violence later in the film when apes and humans will shift aggressively to another plane of existence. They contrast sharply with the much more pronounced and overstated voice-over narration originally planned.

During the next sequence in *2001*, taking place during the title year, a group of scientists encounter another Monolith on the Moon. This is the second Monolith in the film, after the one discovered by the apes on Earth. Diegetic sound again plays a crucial role, manifesting itself only slightly differently. As Floyd travels through space on his way to the space station and then the Clavius Moon Base, the soundtrack fills with Strauss's "Blue Danube Waltz." As with the alien voices, the music may suggest at first a nondiegetic entity, something not in the story world proper. However, the score also evokes the sounds of elevator music, reminiscent of the monotony and repetitiousness of space travel. In this case, "The Blue Danube Waltz" stands as nondiegetic sound performing an essentially diegetic function—background noise clutter, only slightly less chaotic than the alien voices. When the scientists visit the Monolith, meanwhile, alien voices again make the ambient noise, followed by a loud, shrieking beacon sound as the Monolith sends out a signal to the other Monolith near Jupiter. Here, *2001* foregoes the subtlety of some other noises found in the film and thrusts diegetic sound directly into the ears of audiences, who perhaps align themselves with the film's characters by also fighting off the urge to block out the bombastic noise. This is, I feel, a representative instance for the entire film—neither the characters nor the audience have any sense of *meaning* during this initial experience; rather, they have only the *affect* of sound.

Subsequently, over the course of *2001*, diegetic sound becomes a more and more aggressive element. Whereas the naturalistic sounds in the early "Dawn of Man" sequence blended calmly into the background, by the time the narrative shifts to Jupiter in the film's second half, the sounds of the story world play an even more prominent role, particularly through the repeated use of both the film's ambient sound and the dialogue between characters. During the film's Jupiter mission, the audience hears various sounds of breathing in space suits, such as the scenes where Bowman and Poole, respectively, go outside the ship to repair the AE-35 satellite. The sounds of vibrating air ducts inside the ship also populate these sequences. When Bowman prepares to blow the door off the space pod, meanwhile, *2001* repeats two distinct beeping sounds as time counts down before the explosion. After the explosion, Bowman rushes out into the space duct; at this point, Kubrick eliminates all sound from the film, as though confronting audiences with the ultimate experience of space—silence. The diegetic sound of space, the sound of the story world itself, is silence. Similarly, the film employs a silent soundtrack when HAL attacks Poole and sends his body hurtling out into space. Computer alert sounds, such as the ones heard before the pod door explosion, dominate over a solid minute of the film when HAL disconnects the life functions of the three hibernating crew members, accompanied by monitors flashing first "Computer Malfunction," then "Life Functions Critical," and finally, "Life Functions Terminated." The film repeats each of these sounds and thereby implicitly brings into relief the failure of *Dr. Strangelove*'s and *Fear and Desire*'s earlier reliance on words within the new, emerging nonverbal (preverbal) cinema of *2001*.

Of all the sequences in *2001*, however, one scene in particular best highlights the multilayered use of diegetic sound—HAL's "death" scene. Beginning with Bowman's heavy breathing, the sci-fi film layers one level of diegetic sound onto another. Once inside HAL's "Memory Logic Center," the audience again hears sounds of the ship's air duct, even while Bowman's hyperventilating increases as he begins to anticipate and ensure HAL's imminent demise. Yet the most prominent diegetic sounds in this remarkable sequence derive from HAL itself. As the computer quietly panics over Bowman's actions, HAL attempts to talk the fellow crewmember out of his actions—like the character of Strangelove, HAL has no usable body left, only the (failing) agency of words. Specifically, HAL repeats itself in a vain attempt to save its own life (punctuated with long pauses):

Dave, stop. . . . Stop, will you? . . . Stop, Dave. . . . Will you stop, Dave? . . . Stop, Dave. . . . I'm afraid. . . . I'm afraid, Dave. . . . Dave, my mind is going. . . . I can feel it. . . . I can feel it. . . . My mind is going. . . . There is no question about it. . . . I can feel it. . . . I can feel it. . . . I can feel it. . . . I'm . . . afraid.

HAL's monologue, delivered to a determined Bowman, most pointedly and even tragically emphasizes the failure of words. HAL repeats such key phrases as "stop," "I'm afraid," "my mind is going," and especially, "I can feel it," making the viewer especially aware of the computer's specific word choices. The audience is also especially aware of HAL's implicit attempts, through the act of narrating its own death, to control our understanding of the scene. HAL does not control the scene per se, of course, because it cannot stop Bowman from killing it. But it can and does attempt to frame a way of perceiving its experience through language. Yet the computer's words may or may not approximate the truth of the matter. Can HAL, for example, be afraid, or can it feel its mind going? This is not a rhetorical question, and its ambiguity only further forces us to confront the failure of its words. To be sure, HAL cannot manipulate the events through its narration. And that's what HAL's actions are—a cry for help, perhaps, but also a failed narration. Its voice is powerless. Even when HAL reverts back to its original programming as a result of Bowman's actions, the song it sings for him starts out with "Daisy . . . Daisy"—another empty verbal repetition, whose ineffectiveness is even more highlighted for the viewer because of the hollowness of the words. It is doubtful that what HAL says here means anything—it struggles and even fails to put into words what it is experiencing. It may "feel" something, but what can we (or it) *say* of feelings?

Early scenes, moreover, foreshadow the dying HAL's repetitious delivery and again highlight the emphasis, paradoxically, on sound repetition and on the failure of words in *2001*—that is, the more the words are repeated, the less relevance and connection they possess to their origin. When HAL first detects a malfunction in the AE-35 satellite, he interrupts Bowman— "Just a moment. . . . Just a moment." When Mission Control informs the crew members of HAL's likely mistake on the matter, they too emphasize repetition—"We should advise you, however, that our preliminary findings indicate that your onboard Niner-Triple-Zero computer is in error predicting the fault. *I say again*, in error predicting the fault." Later in the film, characters repeat much of the dialogue involving HAL. Bowman and Poole combined say, "Rotate the pod, please, HAL," five times. Likewise, Bowman says, "Open the pod bay doors, please, HAL," four times. When HAL shuts Bowman out of the ship, meanwhile, the human crew member says, "Do you read me, HAL?" seven times and simply, "HAL?" four times, in a largely futile attempt to contact the computer. In each case, the repetition seems to suggest that communication has broken down. The speakers do not achieve their desired effects on others. Added to the other repeated sounds throughout *2001*, these dialogue excerpts further highlight diegetic sounds while also illustrating the failure of language that must be fruitlessly repeated (much like Bill Harford's constant repeating of other people's words said to him in *Eyes Wide Shut*).

As with all films, however, nondiegetic sounds exist as well. Appearing periodically throughout the film, *Also Sprach Zarathustra* stands out as a prominent example of nondiegetic sound in *2001*. The score here is nondiegetic because it does not derive from the world of the story—the space, the ships, the planets, and so forth. It exists only for the audience. One possible explanation for *Zarathustra*'s purpose rests in the only two prominent scenes where the music plays (after the film's opening, where this sound has literally replaced the opening voice-over narration). These two moments are (1) the ape's recognition of the bone's possible use as a weapon and (2) the film's finale, where Strauss's music plays over the image of the Star Child staring back at the screen. The classical music here does not become a part of the diegesis, but it does amplify for audiences the importance of events *within* the diegesis. I would argue that both of these moments in *2001* powerfully convey humanity's capacity for destruction. The ape scene precedes a violent and primal act of murder during the "Dawn of Man" opening. The film's final shot possesses greater ambiguity. However, I would argue that neither the Star Child nor his implications are nearly as ambiguous as argued by others, such as those—Mainar, Nelson, Walker—I noted earlier.

Arthur C. Clarke's literary explanation of this moment, if not certainly a definitive mapping, at least suggests an *opening* for a reorientation to earlier assumptions about the film. His novel was importantly written concurrently with the film's production, not before or after. While literary adaptations are always problematic in terms of identifying what the novel means versus what the film means, *2001* is a tentative exception here. Indeed, *2001* may be unique among "adaptations" because the film isn't an adaptation of the novel any more than vice versa. They were conceived and they existed (and still do) co-temporaneously. Clarke and Kubrick worked on their respective versions of *2001* together, and thus one no doubt influenced the other. In other words, what occurs in the film isn't just an adaptation of the novel but possibly something that coexists with its literary counterpart. Clarke describes the story's final moments of *2001* with the Star Child—having shed the earlier existence as Bowman—unleashing nuclear bombs on Earth and obliterating all human life. This is a remarkably pessimistic ending, condemning humankind's selfishness and replacing it with an equally self-absorbed "higher" life form. And this ending haunts its cinematic counterpart. The literary version of *2001* allows us tentatively to think about the cinematic experience of *2001* in slightly different ways. While it is yet another text, another cognitive level to erect when trying to understand the film, I would argue that it does help us approximate the preconscious affect of the film. In other words, I may hear in *2001* what Clarke describes in the novel—as in earlier moments of the film, *Zarathustra* evokes the possibilities of destruction more so than wondrous new opportunities. We may *see* the wide-eyed Star Child at the end of *2001*, but I *hear* an ape learning how to kill with a bone. The use of this sound, as formulated previously, further reinforces the emergence of inevitable violence stemming from an empowered subjectivity that—no longer relying on words—imposes its will through atomic destruction. After all, "the urge to kill," *2001*'s opening narrator originally articulated, was "the first step toward humanity." Why would the next step of humanity be any different?

Kubrick's later films repeatedly suggest that if words fail to change actions or perceptions (and they always do), then physical violence will be tried next (in this respect, a film about domestic abuse [*The Shining*] was probably inevitable for Kubrick). Importantly, the Star Child's intentions would seem to approximate the previous ape's violent behavior. And the affective memory of that sound—hearing that music again—may similarly suggest to me that the Star Child has equally violent ambitions, even without explicitly going back to Clarke's book. The filmmaker himself also saw great potential violence in humanity's transitions from ape to human to Star Child. When interviewed by the *New York Times'* William Kloman, Kubrick noted, "Man's whole brain has developed from the use of the weapon-tool. It's the evolutionary watershed of natural selection. . . . It's a simply observable fact that all of man's technology grew out of his discovery of the weapon-tool."[14] According to several sources, Kubrick removed this original literary ending, depicting nuclear destruction of the Earth, only because he feared the perception that he was simply copying the successful finale of his previous film. For example, biographer LoBrutto notes that the detonation of nuclear bombs by the Star Child "was in the shooting script, but eventually Kubrick felt he had done that particular idea already for the ending of *Dr. Strangelove*."[15] Though I resist any unconditional statement of intention or meaning in one of the most famously ambiguous conclusions in the history of cinema, several different factors—not only the literary source—affectively suggest to me that the climax of *2001* may not be as ambiguous, or at least, optimistic, as previously assumed. Not the least of these reasons—formally speaking—is that the ending sonically parallels the apes' discovery of the bone-as-weapon earlier in the film. I use Clarke not as an explanation of *2001*; I think instead that his novel helps me articulate the ways I thought I experienced *2001*.

In an early article on the film, Robert Burgoyne notes the formal symmetry of the opening and closing moments of *2001*. In a way, the film returns to its beginning—the destination of the film in the end is a return to the self. All Bowman finds at the end of his quest is himself aging rapidly, himself watching himself, and then being reborn as another form of (self-)consciousness. In this respect, I would argue that the Star Child is the pinnacle of evolved (or devolved) subjectivity—the most perfectly realized manifestation of the mind (and thus consumed with the mass obliteration of what it condescendingly sees as primitive consciousnesses, which it selfishly does not want to understand or work with; there might be a reason the Star Child literally looks like a big baby). "In *2001: A Space Odyssey*," Burgoyne writes, "the subject is discovered to be the object of the quest. The scopic impulse comes full circle in Kubrick's treatment and finds its ultimate object and terminal point in the self."[16] In another way of thinking, Bowman returns to the maze of the mind here in the Memory Room, looking out but seeing nothing but himself (just like the limitations of vision in Turgidson's apartment). Whereas Burgoyne suggests a Lacanian ending to the film—where the subject realizes and materializes its own apprehension of the gaze—we might also be able to say that Bowman fails to outrun his own mind. Instead of moving outside himself— into a world of direct experience and interaction—Bowman can only retreat further into his own thoughts. Returning with the final scene in mind to *2001*'s opening moments, which also feature *Zarathustra*, it is entirely conceivable that Kubrick really opens his sci-fi epic with a declaration that the film is a tale of destruction, not of hope and wonder—where attempts to impose too much verbal meaning on events lead only, as in *Dr. Strangelove*, to obliteration. As the Star Child, Bowman will turn to destruction because attempts at constructive communication have failed. And thus—not unlike Ripper—Bowman finds comfort in retreating into his own mind and in imposing his own will on the human race.

Moreover, the other appearance of Strauss's score, when the one ape in the "Dawn of Man" sequence discovers the violent potential of the bone, reinforces the link between retreating into the self and destruction—higher understanding only means advanced ways of killing. In various ways, *Zarathustra*, as nondiegetic sound, signifies an authoritative presence in the film—the classical piece may alert us to the emergence of a dominant narrative authority—an attack on a nonverbal cinematic experience that rejects abstractions, scaffolding, and narrative assumptions. When the narrative moves inside HAL, revealing its point of view as it reads Bowman's and Poole's respective lips, the narrative move almost explicitly indicates the violence ahead, as the audience first realizes the deviousness and destructive potential of HAL's behavior. Indeed, HAL represents *2001*'s most destructive presence (not including the Star Child, whose actions remain fundamentally ambiguous, or at least, outside the narrative proper); accordingly, the film assumes the computer's point of view most often, such as when the film literally moves inside its view of events in the space ship (its "lip-reading," as one example). HAL, the only character in *2001* completely self-absorbed, thus often pulls the film inside its own mind as well—perhaps the one character powerful enough to recapture some sense of narrative authority. Its subjectivity dominates the narrative to such an extent that HAL regularly appropriates the narrative, imposing its own limited order on events within the story world, even while it is ultimately unable to verbally save itself.

In *2001*, the structural nonverbal experience (diegetic sound, extended takes) opens out to a kind of thematic nonverbal experience—the breakdown in explicit narrative meaning—and this affectively propels me to rethink the larger issues in the film. *2001* may not be ambiguous and filled with multiple meanings, as much as it actively tries to resist all meaning. If meaning is relational, then the failure for anyone to connect in *2001* would seem to suggest that meaning isn't ultimately generated in any way within the film itself. For a brief moment in *2001*, when Bowman kills HAL, a genuine unmediated moment of connection exists between the two characters, a connection that exists affectively without the additional layers of cognition or narrative scaffolding. Of course, I can speak only for myself, but I sense human experience is meant to thrive without many words because HAL can feel its own death, or *imagine* it is feeling its own death, much more than it can describe it to us. And Bowman can likewise feel HAL's death. But it is a moment that cannot be explained; it can only be experienced. Despite his overriding need for survival, Bowman feels sympathy for the computer as HAL meets its demise. His sweat and hyperventilation indicate the primal power of Bowman's experience in these moments; they finally indicate his humanity, previously lost amid the dehumanized world that fostered him. The world Bowman knows communicates through time-delayed, prerecorded video messages, and he can interact with hibernating coworkers only by drawing their pictures; in other words, they can communicate only through abstract representations. For that one brief moment when Bowman feels HAL's suffering, he may become human; unfortunately, this same character, by the film's end, again reverts to a sterile, dehumanized entity, capable of worldly destruction without a second thought, having gained—like the ape in the film's first moments—empowerment through killing, the ability to craft the behavior of others. Ultimately, like *Dr. Strangelove*, I feel *2001* tells the story of a human race refusing to move beyond its own self-interests, its own reassuring addiction to words and artificial barriers, and assumed narratives of shallow politeness—so much so, in fact, that humanity ends up producing a machine, in HAL, capable of reproducing its creators' own egotistical selfishness and denial of their own fallibility and subjective instability, even to the point of murder. Yet for a while, *2001* privileges the breakdown of the magic of words over the story world. Consequently, the film implicitly creates in me the need for social interaction—the intensely, multiply, intersubjective (and thus nonsubjective) affective sense of experience—over the isolated, asocial human mind and its singular destructive attempts at meaning and understanding. In other *words* (I fear to say), experience in *2001* is heightened, realized, only at the moment of contact, rather than at the moment of dictation.

NOTES

1. As quoted in Eric Nordern, "*Playboy* Interview: Stanley Kubrick (1968)," in *Stanley Kubrick Interviews*, ed. Gene D. Phillips (Jackson: University Press of Mississippi, 2001), 48.

2. Jeremy Bernstein, "How about a Little Game?" *The New Yorker*, 12 November 1966, 80.

3. Vincent LoBrutto, *Stanley Kubrick: A Biography* (New York: Fine, 1997), 257.

4. LoBrutto, *A Biography*, 319. I am indebted to LoBrutto's work in general for giving me a sense of Kubrick's biographical life—not a dominant aspect, but not an avoidable one either, in any self-proclaimed auteur study.

5. LoBrutto, *A Biography*, 258.

6. Luis M. Garcia Mainar, *Narrative and Stylistic Patterns in the Films of Stanley Kubrick* (Rochester, N.Y.: Camden House, 1999), 156.

7. Thomas Allen Nelson, *Kubrick: Inside a Film Artist's Maze*, 2nd ed. (Bloomington: Indiana University Press, 2000), 135.

8. Alexander Walker, Sybil Taylor, and Ulrich Ruchti, *Stanley Kubrick, Director: A Visual Analysis* (New York: Norton, 1999), 192–93.

9. Nelson, *Inside a Film Artist's Maze*, 116.

10. The deleted lines of voice-over narration are quoted in an essay by Frederick I. Ordway, *2001*'s scientific and technical consultant, titled "Perhaps, I'm Just Projecting My Own Concern about It," which includes the advice he gave to Kubrick after viewing a first cut of the film. This essay appears in the Jerome Agel–edited book *The Making of Kubrick's 2001* (New York: Signet, 1970), 193–98. Ordway actually wanted the "splendid" voice-over narration reinserted because "the audience not only has a right but a need to know" what the meaning is of the "Dawn of Man" sequence (195). It is hard not to think of government think tanks and policy, and Kubrick's amusement at their insistence on "the magic of words," when reading through the insistent advice of *2001*'s technical consultant.

11. Walker, Taylor, and Ruchti, *A Visual Analysis*, 180.

12. Michel Chion, *Kubrick's Cinema Odyssey*, trans. Claudia Gorbman (London: British Film Institute, 2001), 1.

13. Most recently, Chion wrote, in *Kubrick's Cinema Odyssey*, about how "sonically speaking, *2001* is a stripped down film. . . . its ambient sound is simple, consisting of insect noises in the prehistoric section and varying degrees of air hiss and engine rumble in the spacecraft" (97–98).

14. William Kloman, "In 2001, Will Love Be a Seven-Letter Word?" *New York Times*, 14 April 1968, D15.

15. LoBrutto, *A Biography*, 275. Walker also acknowledges this editorial decision by Kubrick; however, he adds that "the best argument against [the final scene] is that it would have clashed with the whole structure of a film that had scrupulously avoided neat narrative payoffs." *A Visual Analysis*, 192.

16. Robert Burgoyne, "Narrative Overture and Closure in *2001: A Space Odyssey*," *Enclitic* 5 (Fall/Spring 1981/1982): 179.

·6·

A Kubrickian Look: Narrating in a Voiceless Voice-Over

I'm not being grouchy. I just wanna finish my work.

—Jack Torrance, *The Shining*

$\mathscr{F}$or Geoffrey Cocks, the style of *2001* and subsequent Kubrick films "reflects a postmodern appreciation of the volatility and ambiguity of language, the plurality of meaning, and the diversity of experience and point of view. But it was also a method by which Kubrick could bring his own musings and meanings to the screen to stimulate and interact with impressions and insights generated by viewers—or 'readers'—of his films. It was for this reason that Kubrick would never explain his films."[1] Many critics, only most recently Cocks, as well as Kubrick himself in various interviews, focus on how the filmmaker's later works ask audiences to construct their own meanings and interpretations of his films. Certainly, we (myself included) cannot *not* think of interpretations and meanings—more precisely, we cannot not think around or outside interpretations and meanings when we consciously think about films we experience. Yet my own argument here is to attempt to do precisely that. If we accept that Kubrick's later films refuse to telegraph particular meaning or meanings to us, then perhaps we should not think in (older) postmodern ways of thinking—namely, that we fall into a state of relativism, where everyone brings their own interpretations to the film, or that our respective interpretations are simply contextual. There may be another way to think—if *2001* (as one example) resists interpretation, then it may itself be a film *not about* interpretation. It may be a film about *not being about anything*. It may be pushing toward what's *outside* interpretation—toward that which is not interpretative in and of itself—even while it might engage or affect interpretation. Or to approach it in a different way, there may be a particular but inexplicable reason why Jack Torrance as writer can

99

never "finish his work" in *The Shining*, and to attempt to do so is to become "grouchy" and, eventually, to be trapped, frozen forever in the maze of the mind.

In the next two chapters, I hope to show how Kubrick's post-*2001* films—while never moving outside their own aborted attempts at interpretation and narrative—compel us to try to (un)think these interpretative acts. Though I have my own theories (outlined in the previous chapter), it ultimately does little good to resist the chaos and ambiguity of *2001*. It is the experience—indefinable as it may be—that matters. But to note only the ambiguity, the absence of narrative meaning, in so many of his films is to miss all those instances in which characters (such as HAL and Bowman) try so hard to resist that inevitable narrative chaos as well as to fail to confront how *visually* those characters deal with the chaos. When I watch Kubrick's films, I experience a heightening awareness of the ambiguity, but what impacts me the most is not the conscious knowledge of an absent meaning (how can one be aware of what is not, by itself, there?) so much as the feeling in which these films—at the *pre*conscious level of sight and sound—compel me to sense that uncertainty. We cannot sense an affect of chaos except as an effect of narrative (just as we cannot consider narrative except by chaos). We experience one because of the other. In this sense, Stanley Kubrick's films foreground the narrative desire to resist that diegetic ambiguity as much as they foreground the ambiguity in and of itself. The sense of ambiguity in *The Shining* begins as a particular resistance to Jack's narrative ambitions. There is not so much a dialectic at play here as a constructive *antinomy*—Kubrick's films embrace chaos only through narrative, and narrative through chaos. These seeming contradictions serve well as groundwork for reapproaching the later films of Stanley Kubrick.

While so many of his films embrace narrative ambiguity and diegetic chaos, we also clearly have an emphasis on voice-over narration (even in later works), the mark of a character's attempt to show us a way through the story, throughout so many of his productions. So, how can we align such a conflict? Of course, we needn't automatically reconcile the two, if ever, except to say that they *appear* to always already coexist. The heightened emphasis on such clear, thorough narrative exposition serves in no small part to only strengthen our awareness of that which the characters cannot understand or make sense of. In *The Shining*, Jack Torrance goes to The Overlook Hotel to write his novel, to tell a great American story, but he does not ultimately succeed at anything except losing his mind and his own grasp of his situation, thus morphing into a cold-blooded killer. Originally, Jack expects to go to the Overlook to write his novel and get a little peace and quiet. However, his earlier aspiration to a narrative of authorial productivity quickly becomes undermined as the film's plot evolves. A blank expression on his face emerges as his storytelling power fades. Just under an hour into the film, after Jack's first fight with his wife and after the first snowstorm hits, he stares blankly out the window during a long, slow zoom-in to a close-up on his face (in direct contrast to his hyperactive, ball-bouncing activities a few scenes earlier). The coldness and whiteness of the snow reflect off his face, and the audience begins to sense for the first time his withdrawal from the world around him. The impact of Jack's changes on his family becomes more directly apparent during another sequence when Jack sits on the side of his bed, staring off into space as his son approaches to talk to him. He is so withdrawn from the world that it takes a moment before Jack even realizes Danny has entered the room; he then holds his son and attempts a superficial comforting of Danny, who realizes something is wrong with his father. Jack still seems to be trapped in that look, his own sense of the situation, even as he talks to Danny (who himself often retreats to moments of "shining," affecting a similar look). A rupture has clearly occurred between the two of them and their respective understandings of the world. This is most pointedly highlighted when the boy asks a sedated yet nonetheless surprised Jack if he would ever physically hurt members of his own family. And importantly, it is here that we too in the audience begin to lose track of the story.

We do not begin to experience Jack's loss of reality until we also begin to see him fail to write his novel. In this sense, the manuscript in *The Shining* supplants the Kubrickian voice-over—both are what the characters in his films *want* to say and *want* to believe, with only passing glances at the world they actually encounter. And both fail to achieve their effect. "All work and no play . . ." becomes as meaningless as the verbal repetitions in *2001*. Of course, this is also the point in that experience when such linguistic and narrative assumptions dissipate and fail these characters—it is at this point that we begin to sense the inevitable disorder, and it is at this point where we as an audience are provoked by another sense. Kubrick's characters reveal a great fondness for narrating, and I believe there is also a way we can begin to quantify, additionally, a new kind of *voiceless* voice-over in his films—a way in which we and our senses are still guided, but by sight instead of sound, and to chaos rather than to narrative.

For me, the most lasting image in *The Shining* is Nicholson's face—it's a facade; it sits, frozen, throughout the film, both attracting and repelling my vision. It is, in fact, that which first and most clearly compelled me to the present research. His blank face materializes increasingly in proportion to the waning of his authorial powers. This shift is most strikingly realized in one of the film's last images; after Jack has failed to kill his family, he is trapped in the hotel's outdoor maze and freezes to death—literally frozen in a look for eternity, trapped forever. He may even be frozen within his own faulty vision of the world, of which we may catch a glimpse in the film's final shot—Jack attending an Overlook Hotel party in a black-and-white photo from the 1920s.[2] That event may have actually happened, or it could just be the only place, cognitive or otherwise, where Jack possesses a sense of place and time. As with the opening of *Fear and Desire*, this alternate existence is a narrative suspended "outside history," contrasting sharply with the experiences of a freed Wendy (Shelley Duvall) and Danny.

This final narrative turn suggests that—as with previous films—unified narrative order can exist only within a dream (or through brute force). Like Jack, who cannot complete his novel, the solitary, asocial, and alienated subjectivities in Kubrick's films offer only a failed, fractured narrative authority, one ultimately incapable of ascribing meaning to events. His look marks a heightened awareness of the limits of the character's narrative understanding, the ability to look but the inability to see. The face, that facade, looks at nothing, but *to look* is itself the key; while it offers me nothing but a feeling, that nothingness is itself a sense of what the film offers narratively. Through our senses, this face narrates narrative ambiguity. I propose here the possibility of Kubrickian protagonists narrating not only in a voice-over but also in a voiceless voice-over—a *look* to invite us to an ambiguity we can otherwise never understand, a look that marks and intensifies for the audience the narrative possibilities for sustaining narrative ambiguity. As I have shown earlier, and will further elaborate on here, his characters love to narrate; but when they can no longer do so, it is the silence, and their blank faces, that fills in for us the narrative void.

In my earlier chapters on Kubrick's prior films, I focused on the use of voice-over narration; this chapter, meanwhile, attempts to more explicitly document the point at which the country of the mind begins to dissipate and fade, when the narrators and narrations begin to sense they can no longer quantify and qualify the experiences with which they engage in a way they had mastered in films such as *Fear and Desire*. And through this fractured narration emerges the feeling of chaos. We can think of Kubrick's films through the way experience is sensed—both received and given meaning to, both felt and understood. To truly appreciate the competing notions of chaos and narrative, and of the voiceless voice-over, it is crucial to first reconsider how the more traditional voice-over narration reveals itself in Kubrick's later films. I hope to then move closer to an appreciation of the possibilities for diegetic chaos outside the scope of this older type of "filmic authority."[3] On the surface of Kubrick's Vietnam film, *Full Metal Jacket*, Matthew Modine's character, nicknamed "Joker," would seem to fulfill the role of narrator. He is someone, like Jack at the beginning of *The Shining*, who thinks he under-stands his surroundings. Largely silenced as a character in a dehumanizing military environment, his thoughts periodically intensify as a voice-over nar-ration when he speaks about moments and events unfolding in the film. In this sense, Joker's voice-over is an attempt to tell his story and the story of his fellow recruits. It is also an attempt to resist the ambiguity of his world—to refuse to succumb to the chaos of his experiences. As in previous Kubrick films, the voice-over narration in *Full Metal Jacket*—whether sincere (*Fear and Desire, Killer's Kiss*) or ironic (*A Clockwork Orange, Barry Lyndon*)—is ubiquitous, if not always dominant. Whatever one wishes to say about Kubrick's intentions or the meanings of such usage, it is clearly an important cinematic device that unifies his work. And though the sentences and ideas within them often seem less than memorable and even irrelevant when set against the awesome intensity of the other aural and visual stimuli in these films, the very sound of those words plays upon my senses continually, affect-ively engaging me to remap a line of thought throughout his body of work.

Usually, the voice-over narration opens the Kubrickian narrative, marks it in part as the effect of this particular filmmaker, while dictating over the first few images what it assumes we will (or should) experience in the course of the film. In *Full Metal Jacket*, however, Joker's voice-over does not appear until the third scene, after the montage of shaved heads and, importantly, the powerful, noted introduction of Gunnery Sergeant Hartman (R. Lee Ermey). Both these moments dehumanize Joker, certainly, and, equally important for me, they immediately undermine any privileged position as speaker that he may aspire to later. In fact, Hartman's delivery to the new recruits, telling them how they will speak ("Sir, yes, sir!") and what they will be called by name ("Joker," "Cowboy," "Gomer Pyle," and so forth) immediately suggests, even before we hear his voice, that Joker has very little authority as a speaker. But it is a limited authority lost on him initially. Joker's words are evocative of the openings of *Fear and Desire* or *Paths of Glory*, where each narrator attempts to situate events of the particular antiwar film geographically. "Parris Island, South Carolina," he tells us, "the United States Marine Corps Recruit Depot. An eight-week college for the phony-tough and the crazy brave." His words are not particularly interesting or dramatic, and his observation about "the phony-tough and the crazy brave" seems as obvious and didactic as the "unchanging shapes of fear and doubt and death" in *Fear and Desire* or the "disease of slavery" in *Spartacus*, to return to only two instances of such the-matically prescriptive voice-over narration. In his voice-over, Joker seems naively arrogant—even rather pretentious—about the situation he is in. Whether conscious of it or not, his voice-over is itself the mark of a "phony-tough."

Yet lest it seem as though I am overgeneralizing, there are also many ways in which his voice-over differs from those other third-person narrations. For one, Joker's voice must compete with another, less explicit, "narrator" in *Full Metal Jacket*. Certainly, his soft, wimpy voice seems especially impotent when set as a counterpoint to Hartman's infamous verbal abuse as the drill sergeant in the preceding and following scenes. And this is to say nothing of the fact that he is attempting to share his thoughts with us over a sequence in which the men march in unison with Hartman, who is simultaneously telling them what to sing—"Oh, give me some . . . Good for you and good for me . . . Up in the morning to the rising sun." His attempts to establish his own independent, authoritative voice, to critique the military institution of which he is a part, are ironically cut off by the directions of his superior officer. His words, as Tony Williams notes, "are unindividualistic, banal and uninspired."[4] He cannot differentiate himself from others and cannot say anything particularly original or insightful. His voice affects us, but it also pushes us away. He attempts to guide us, but we sense he speaks initially with no authority and—perhaps more important—with no experience. It is only after Hartman is killed that Joker can speak without the influence or intimidation of the former's words—and by then, the trauma of that episode has no doubt shaken his narrative confidence, anyway. Joker is an aspiring journalist, as we learn later in the film, and thus is clearly the most likely candidate to transfer information and news to the audience. Yet, in case it has not been clearly stated enough, let me emphasize now that, to me, he is not a very good narrator.

Thus, these words do not leave as much of an impact as earlier films of which I previously wrote, even while they are highly evocative—on a content and thematic level—of such prior efforts. They even *sound* like those earlier voice-overs—confident and straight, yet bland; assertive and direct, but droning. Editorializing about the phony-tough and the crazy brave suggests, for example, the opening of *Paths of Glory*, where that third-person narrator comments on the fact that "successful attacks [in the trench warfare of WWI] were measured in hundreds of yards and paid for in lives by hundreds of thousands." Yet these omniscient narrators in earlier works open the films and thus can establish the scene more clearly and with much greater authority than Joker can trailing meekly in the wake of Hartman. The voice-overs of those earlier movies may not ultimately offer anything more enlightening about the content or the themes of the films that we will eventually experience ourselves—they too might be little more than dictated didacticism. Nonetheless, their authority is not challenged in the way that Joker's is. They are not cut off by characters talking within the diegetic space of the film (nor are they ignored, not unlike the tuned-out narrator in the middle of *Barry*

Lyndon, for instance). In *Fear and Desire, Killer's Kiss, The Killing, Paths of Glory*, and *Spartacus*, each narrator opens the film and frames the importance and meaning of events with as much discursive and thematic authority as can be expected in a typical Hollywood narrative film.[5] When I watch each of these films begin, they sound remarkably similar to me.

Reconsider, again, the opening moments of *Killer's Kiss*. While pacing up and down the train station waiting area, Davy perhaps offers us a fascinating opportunity to look at the earlier first-person Kubrickian narrator. He also serves—like Jack—as a blank-expression narrator attempting to envision the world and, as in *Fear and Desire, Paths of Glory*, and so forth, impose order upon it. One big difference, however, is that Davy has not yet been denied his voice, his control over the text. He talks about events, and we aren't compelled to believe he has lost his sense of the situation. Even while we see his expressionless face on the screen—frozen not unlike Jack's—we can still *hear* his thoughts: "It's crazy how you can get yourself in a mess sometimes. . . ." Contrasted with Jack and Joker, Davy is an authoritative narrator here, through whom the audience can make sense of the film. Thus, Davy is allowed to "finish" his narrative work in *Killer's Kiss*. We don't feel the sense of detachment we feel with Joker's tepid voice-over or with the voiceless Jack. And Davy's authority is not threatened—literally and verbally—as Joker's is by Hartman. Moreover, Davy really believes in the power of the spoken word—not settling for, or resigning himself to, the silence that permeates Kubrick's later films. And yet, though he may not realize it, his difficulties with stating exactly what "it" is in that opening voice-over narration may suggest an emerging sense of the affect of chaos, perhaps foreshadowing the eventual Kubrickian descent into voicelessness.

If the voice-over had been deleted from these first moments in *Killer's Kiss*, Davy's face might well align itself with the look that haunts Jack (and Ripper), as though perhaps—Davy at that point having lost the romantic partner and seemingly defeated—the world thus makes sense, in those films, only inside their own heads. But we go inside Davy's head in *Killer's Kiss*, and importantly, he leads us back out of the maze. On the other hand, the denial of Jack's voice—literally and as writer—provides us with a much greater sense of ambiguity than what we encounter in Kubrick's second film. And I suspect we can think of the later uses of the face in this same way—a figuration for characters, such as Jack, who wish to tell a story of their experience, tell it the way they remember or want to remember it, and thus reground themselves to events within the world. But these later films do not have the happy ending that *Killer's Kiss* does. The separated lovers don't reunite in later Kubrick films, such as *The Shining* or *Barry Lyndon* (the exception here might be *Eyes Wide Shut*, but even that marriage is far from stable at the film's end). And thus characters have no further claim to the agency or power of narrating and narration because they cannot reconcile their respective visions of the world with their experiences of it.

The opening of *Lolita* and the character of General Jack D. Ripper in *Dr. Strangelove*, meanwhile, both offer a transition to this now silenced story-teller. *Lolita* denies Humbert Humbert his own voice through a voice-over until after the crucial climax of the film has already and prematurely been played out, thus challenging our willingness to align with his murderous point of view (not unlike the verbal abuse of Hartman's preempting the voice-over of Joker). Meanwhile, Ripper—first dependent upon his loudspeaker—eventually finds himself with nothing left to say in *Dr. Strangelove*, having already begun nuclear war and then forced to contemplate his next life, if any, having squandered the experiences of the first one. Something is shifting here in the use of voice-over. The voices are losing their prominence and their power. These sequences, along with the largely voice-overless middle third of *A Clockwork Orange*, reconsider the absence of voice-over narration as it relates to a form of narrative authority. And they foreground a strikingly consistent image of the face throughout the films directed by Kubrick, seemingly presenting a suddenly voiceless voice-over.

There is a shift in narration *there*, and certainly Joker is not the same type of narrator as Davy. And *Full Metal Jacket* does not sound the same as those pre-*2001* films when it begins. We don't hear the droning, bland voice-over narration explaining everything. We hear popular music (Johnny Wright's "Hello, Vietnam") instead. In fact, it does not sound like the beginning of any other Kubrick film, save perhaps the subtle sarcasm of the "tenderness" that opens *Dr. Strangelove*. *Full Metal Jacket*, however, *does* sound like a typical Vietnam film, in the way it uses a contemporary, popular sound. But it disrupts my sense of a Kubrick film. And Joker is not a narrator in the sense that those earlier narrators are. As should be clear by now, earlier Kubrick films sound and feel different for me from his later ones, even while they both force me to consider the boundary between narrative and chaos. The later use of color is an obvious enough one, but it should not be discounted, either. It *does* affect our senses. There are also the longer takes in the later films—the long, slow zooms of *2001*, *Barry Lyndon*, *The Shining*, and *Eyes Wide Shut* contrast with the constant cutting of *Killer's Kiss*, *The Killing*, and *Dr. Strangelove*. The mood music of films before *2001* clashes with the silence of those films that follow the sci-fi epic. The sincerity of the voice-over narrators in *Fear and Desire*, *Paths of Glory*, and *Spartacus* clashes with the irony of those in *A Clockwork Orange* and *Barry Lyndon*. And so, we may have pause to think that the *form* of narration has also shifted.

Maybe Joker in *Full Metal Jacket*, the narrator in *Barry Lyndon*, and even

Alex in *A Clockwork Orange* do not really narrate in the (later) Kubrickian sense of the word. They talk but do not guide; they dictate but do not deliver the experiences in the form that our senses do. Perhaps their words are verbal interruptions, distracting us from the *feel* of the films. What if Joker isn't really the narrator in *Full Metal Jacket*, in any useful or constructive sense? His voice-over narration is not really a dominating presence, even though the device appears throughout the film, while also, to an extent, closing it (which, for whatever it's worth, *doesn't* happen in most Kubrick films). Thomas Allen Nelson writes that "Joker's character and his occasional voice-overs increasingly are used to explain or clarify both *what* we see and hear and *how* Kubrick wants us to see and hear. His two brief voice-overs . . . are mostly expository rather than personal."[6]

It may be that Kubrick wanted the audience to see and hear a certain way, so he deployed Joker accordingly. I would argue that if we are meant to align so closely with Joker and his vision of the world, then it is only to make the jarring ambiguity, and his deafening silence, all the more provocative when it occurs (such as Pyle's murder/suicide and Joker's own killing of the sniper near the end). If Joker is meant to be a point of audience identification, then it is only insomuch as we are carried out to, and then abandoned at, the limits of his weak narrative understanding, with little in place to fill the void. His words seem distant and banal, as other critics such as Williams note, and—at the very least—extraneous to the narrative movement of the film. His voice hardly leaves a strong trace on the viewer. Yet what does dominate the film and leave an indelible imprint on those who see *Full Metal Jacket*? Aurally, it is Hartman's voice that lingers in our ears and in our minds. But it might not be a voice at all, or even a sound, that catches the attention of myself and others and guides the attentive viewer of Kubrick's films.

Even beyond the sound of the voice-over, Kubrick's films clearly possess the ability to affect their audiences in ways we don't usually consider. People are welcome to question the validity of the auteur—a particular film's production history, themes, and intentions all rest in the unrepresentable spaces outside the images and sounds of the film itself. We may sense them, but we can never mimetically reproduce them. But critics of the auteur do so at their own peril, for what seems even sturdier as a form of criticism (to me) is to consider the ways a certain group of films impacts the senses of separated individuals in a consistent, provocative way. The consistent effect of Kubrick's films is why, I think, so many want to write about him. When thinking of Kubrick films as an experience, as an expression, there are distinctive ways in which they sound and look. For me, yes, but for others, too. And to reaffirm a sense of Stanley Kubrick's cinematic body is to unavoidably reaffirm the auteur as a form of critical inquiry—more specifically, it is to reperceive the auteur as the mapping of an affective experience through, but also *beyond*, the facades of our own mental, critical constructs. If the auteur is a scholarly myth (and it may yet prove to be), why do so many receive the effects of the auteur in much the same fashion?

While the earlier chapters in this book were preoccupied with sounds in Kubrick's films, it is to vision that I now turn. As a means to reconsider the affect of Kubrick in general, and the possibilities of a different kind of narration in *Full Metal Jacket*, I start with Michel Ciment's observations, about *Eyes Wide Shut* in particular but that open up a larger glimpse into all of Kubrick's later films:

> More than forty-five years passed and thirteen films before the word 'eye' appeared in the title of one of Kubrick's films. Yet it is the key to this visionary film-maker's work. Take a look at the intense, dark, piercing, almost hypnotic gaze, beneath the heavy eyebrows of the director. Recall the eye of Bowman in 'Beyond the Infinite,' of the astral foetus at the end of *2001*, Alex at the beginning of *A Clockwork Orange*, Danny and his father in *The Shining*, Gomer Pyle before murdering his sergeant in *Full Metal Jacket*.[7]

For some, like Ciment, Vincent D'Onofrio's character, Leonard Lawrence, aka "Pyle," captures the attention of the spectator and emerges as one of the most potent—if not *the* most potent—visual images lingering from the experience of *Full Metal Jacket*. Intriguingly, Ciment also extends this "gaze" to the filmmaker himself and to startling moments within other Kubrickian films, such as *2001*, *A Clockwork Orange*, and *The Shining*. Yet such an affective response is by no means isolated among past Kubrick scholars. Consider, as another example, Alexander Walker's thoughts on Kubrick's most powerful visual stimuli, appropriately in a chapter on *Full Metal Jacket*:

> Faces are what register most memorably, first and last, as Kubrick's most hallucinatory creations. The Star-Child gazes benignly down on earth from its angelic bubble in *2001*. Alex, the Devil's child, looks mankind in the eye and grins with satanic relish at the future shock he is about to deliver in *A Clockwork Orange*. . . . Faces are up-front, too, in *Full Metal Jacket*.[8]

Such an effect on the vision of critics is well noted, suggesting to me that there is something in the realm of the body, of *pre*consciousness, with which we sense Kubrick as an auteur, regardless of whether or not we subsequently choose to try to understand it, to verbalize or analyze it. Finally, look at the reception of Michel Chion, author of two outstanding Kubrick books, who further notes very simply how the filmmaker "had long been trying to capture something on a face that was undergoing a transformation from within, a face that was changing."[9] I do not know if Kubrick was trying to capture something, or if there was anything "within" that look to be revealed, but I do know that Chion was affected in the way that Walker, Ciment, and I previously were while experiencing the films of Stanley Kubrick. I cannot speak for them, but I sensed it even before I read their work—that is only to say that I think this affect exists in the experience of the films themselves, even before the first subsequent moment of critical inquiry. In their recent respective studies of Kubrick's films, Walker, Ciment, and Chion also collectively sense this dominant stylistic and visual trait in his works—which they then attempt to quantify as "the intense, dark, piercing, almost hypnotic gaze" or as "faces" that were "undergoing a transformation from within." Indeed, looking back over Kubrick's body of work does reveal this strikingly consistent visual image, from General Ripper in *Dr. Strangelove* right up until Bill Harford in *Eyes Wide Shut*. There is something *there*.

And while Walker, Ciment, and Chion have all briefly mentioned the affect of this important visual stimuli in Kubrick's cinema, none have thus proceeded to fully explore how they view the thematic implications of this face or develop its importance to the process of narrating in Kubrick's films. Throughout his later films, Kubrick regularly inserts off-center shots of his various characters gazing out either in a moment of thought or (more likely) in the absence of thought; they stare blankly. All this provokes for me a distinctive *look* to Kubrick's films—looking to a look; the *Kubrickian look*. This look is a sense in two meanings of the word—an affective response *from* his films and a narrative logic *to* his films. What we see from here, but what is also already there. It compels us to a narrative void in the films, but does so narratively (it also compels us to the auteur, to Kubrick's films as a legitimately constituted body of work). I wish to argue that, in these frames, the look points us to a complete denial by one solitary, asocial character of the ability to ascribe meaning to events and direct experience with others—a failed narrator. Something like the hypothetical experience of watching *Killer's Kiss* without Davy's voice-over. This Kubrickian look approximates the resignation of a narrative authority once wielded with overriding power through the country of the mind in *Fear and Desire* and *Killer's Kiss*. There is nothing for these characters to look at, or look for, because they have abandoned understanding the outer world around them—it is only looking for the sake of looking.

So what if, in some respects, *Full Metal Jacket's* true narrator is not Joker, but rather Pyle, the marine recruit who slowly loses his mind in boot camp and ends up killing his drill sergeant and then committing suicide? Perhaps Pyle is the primary narrator, not because he actually attempts to impose meaning on events within the story, but because his blank expression embodies the film's inability to tell its story in a way that Joker does not seem initially to understand. As one representative example, Pyle effects the look. After constant physical and verbal abuse—at lineup, during obstacle courses, while marching or jogging, and so forth—at the hands of both his drill sergeant and eventually his fellow marines (with the occasional exception of Joker, who attempts to help him), we begin to see Pyle absorbed within his own mind, finding external comfort only in his rifle. Shortly after being beaten by fellow recruits while trying to sleep in bed, Pyle begins to exhibit the experience of a Kubrickian look; as with characters in *Barry Lyndon* and *The Shining*, the camera zooms slowly in on Pyle's face as he stares blankly out during roll call. The fact that he does not join in with his fellow soldiers as they scream in unison with the drill sergeant indicates just how far detached he has become from the narrative surrounding him. This scene is then followed up with a similar sequence where the drill sergeant talks about infamous people—Charles Whitman and Lee Harvey Oswald—who had learned from the Marines how to kill with rifles. Pyle also stares emptily, detached from his fellow marines, as the sergeant talks about how those men "showed what one motivated marine and his rifle can do! And before all you ladies leave my island, you will all be able to do the same thing!" Though the drill sergeant is perhaps symbolically imposing meaning on him (and his fellow soldiers), it is a moment lost on him. The clearest example, however, comes during the scene where Pyle shoots the drill sergeant and then blows his own head off in the barracks bathroom—a sequence yet again preceded by Pyle's blank, introverted stares when Joker, on fire watch, stumbles into him sitting on a toilet, playing with a gun clip. Having failed to come to any understanding of the world that has abused him, Pyle must use violence as a last resort while also turning the gun on himself, unable to live with the world he has experienced and just irrevocably twisted.

When I first watched films such as these (especially *The Shining*, which first affectively compelled me to write about the films of Stanley Kubrick, though I wouldn't realize it until years later), it was not the words I heard that drew me in—it was these faces I saw. It was only later, as I worked my way back through his earlier films prior to *2001*, that I began to hear the "magic of words" and their attempts to dictate to me some kind of dramatic event—a dramatic possibility that was more sensuously and stunningly rendered in these blank stares that I experienced. I have chosen to call this affect the Kubrickian look because it makes the most sense, an experience of narrative ambiguity intensified by the face of a withdrawn character. I too am affected by the power of those faces—they stare through me, marking the films' chaos and coldness that they too feel—but I am compelled further, compelled back to narrative. These faces are signs of narrative—by paradoxically suggesting the point at which narrative fails, at which previous assumptions fail, just like Pyle's vision of the world—but they are themselves *nonetheless narrative.* They communicate to us and show for us a story of narrative ambiguity. Their mute expressions narrate for us the extent to which meaning can be grasped. They use narrative to resist narrative. The voice-over narration, while crucial, is not the only unifying feature in Kubrick's later films. But it is *there*, and I think there is a connection between the voice-over and these faces. Narration is not just a crucial device in Kubrick's films; more pointedly, I would really love to argue—as I implied with the Jameson quote in the first chapter—that narration is a crucial *theme* in Kubrick's films. Narrative, in its simplest form, is the act of imposing linear meaning and causality on events that might not otherwise be linked in such a manner, if at all. And it is this act of narrative construction that consumes Kubrick's characters and Kubrick's films, even when—or *precisely* when—narrative construction fails and we no longer believe in an abstract idea such as the "phony-tough and the crazy brave." These stereotypes, for example, may or may not be true, but—in any case—they do little justice to the experience of *Full Metal Jacket*, or to the experience of Joker. That words do not do justice to the situation of combat and war, however, is *not* a conclusion that appears to be lost on the face of Pyle.

And what is left to be said about the experience of Alex? Better yet, what can Alex still say (or not) about himself? What can he say to us? The most fascinating aspect of Alex (Malcolm McDowell) in *A Clockwork Orange* that remains to be illuminated is found not so much in the irony of what he does say but in how and when Alex doesn't talk. Listening back across the film, I suspect that in an odd way, the failure of words affects him, too. Alex's face at the beginning of *A Clockwork Orange* not only serves as a visual link to the last image of its Kubrickian predecessor (the Star Child at the end of *2001*) but also represents another moment of the Kubrickian look. Yet here (as opposed to the framing of Ripper in *Dr. Strangelove*), Alex stares *directly* into the camera. I'm inclined to believe the connection is not a coincidence, as Alex's mind, instead of passively accepting his fate, directly assaults the audience, visually and aurally, in *A Clockwork Orange*. More important, the film's narrative aligns with Alex and Alex alone in the type of authoritative and violent way that no other Kubrickian character ever matches in terms of aggression, anger, or destruction. Subsequently, Kubrick's ninth film stands as the filmmaker's most deliberately subjective cinematic work—not only as a cinematic abstraction in and of itself but also as a cinematic abstraction (in direct contrast to *Fear and Desire*'s pretensions) seemingly aware of its own abstractions. Continuing from the Star Child at the conclusion of *2001*, *A Clockwork Orange* foregrounds the extreme possibilities of the mind in its purest, uncontested, and most selfishly violent form. From a narrative standpoint, the film privileges first-person voice-over as the primary narration tool.[10] Technically, the film makes ample use of editing, rather than less obtrusive long takes, throughout much of the film, highlighting the artificiality of film as a cognitive storytelling device. Moreover, *A Clockwork Orange* uses expressionistic sets to heighten its own thematic self-awareness and subjectivity.[11] Finally, in regard to sound, the film employs both classical music and Walter Carlos's synthetic, electronic score as its dominant soundtrack, rather than ambient and diegetic sound—a direct counterpoint to the nonverbal cinema of *2001*. At one point early in the film, when returning to his parents' home in municipal flatblock 18a Linear North, Alex strolls through the lobby, quietly whistling the same tune as the nondiegetic music playing on the film's soundtrack, which clearly illustrates how deeply connected, even in the quieter moments, Alex is to the narrative structure. Each of these filmic devices highlights *A Clockwork Orange*'s expressionistic nature, revolving around a character, Alex, who is consumed within a mental state that focuses on Beethoven and on idiosyncratic language and who obsesses with violence and sexual gratification. *A Clockwork Orange*'s structural emphasis on subjective images reflects the self-importance of its main character, discursively reinforcing his unrestrained violent and sexual desires. In short, *A Clockwork Orange* is Kubrick's most overtly extreme cinematic critique of claims to narrative authority and its asocial and even violent nature. It gives us an ironic counterpoint to the absence of narrative meaning and failed narration—it shows the extent to which subjectivity can thrive when unchallenged by competing experiences. Yet even this is a bit more complicated because *A Clockwork Orange*, meanwhile, also clearly disrupts Alex's authority in the middle of the film. Not unlike the effect of Jack's incomplete novel, Alex does illustrate moments of the Kubrickian look as a manifestation of the voiceless voice-over—emerging as his own voice-over begins fading in the middle third of the film.

One of the things that intrigues me about *A Clockwork Orange* is not how we experience Alex's subjectivity per se but how we experience the cracks in this otherwise overwhelming, even suffocating, cognitive facade. The film follows Alex along his path of self-absorption until approximately forty minutes into the film, at the beginning of the second act, when his deviant behavior catches up with him; the police arrest him and place him in jail for fourteen years after Alex beats a woman to death with a phallus-shaped statue. My project here is most concerned with this less self-conscious middle third of the narrative—the sequences of *A Clockwork Orange* that highlight

Alex's brief conversion from a violently dominant narrator to a central character who becomes more of a slate for other people's narratives and agendas, such as the fellow droogs, the homeless people, and, most prominently, even the government itself. During Alex's incarceration, authorities immediately challenge the young man's comfort zone—they force him to speak in a certain way (or not speak at all), force him to listen to sermons and to read the Bible, and most important, force him to watch violent and pornographic material until he becomes physically sick. From saying too much as a narrator early in *A Clockwork Orange*, Alex suddenly cannot say much at all.

The government forces the self-absorbed Alex to engage with the world outside him—a narrative counter to his own—denying him the thematic and structural comforts of his own subjectivity, earlier illustrated most clearly by his voice-over and by the visual representation of his own thoughts and desires. An even more curious transformation, however, also occurs during these passages—as Alex becomes more aware of his environment and of other people, the narrative de-emphasizes the rhetorical tools privileged in the first forty minutes; Kubrick strips away these extra layers of storytelling—Alex's voice-over becomes less prominent (even nonexistent)—and the film employs fewer montages and favors longer takes over excessive cuts. The sets, transformed from elaborately decorated houses, apartments, and shops to utilitarian and sparse prison locations, become less expressionistic and more realistic. In sharp contrast to when Alex is whistling (not so) innocently in his apartment lobby, an alignment between diegetic and nondiegetic sound again occurs when Georgie and Dim, now police officers, drag Alex out into the forest, submerge his head under water, and proceed to beat him with a billy club. The original diegetic sound of each beating is matched and then magnified by a nondiegetic echo. In other words, not only has *A Clockwork Orange* abandoned Alex's personal point of view, but the narrative structure is now working against him.

Most notably—in a sonic parallel to much of *2001*—diegetic sound takes over the soundtrack during this middle sequence in the film. The quiet of the jail rooms, the dialogue of the characters interacting with Alex, the sounds of violence and pain emanating from the films forced upon Alex for viewing—all these sounds supplant Alex's preferred modes of experience. Even in relation to sound, the film turns from a focus upon Alex's subjective point of view to a more objective representation of Alex's surroundings—that is, no overt mediation through the country of Alex's mind (which reaches its most perfect point in the "Beethoven/Jesus Statues" montage early in the film, and then again in the "I was cured, all right" finale). The climax of this use of sound, however, comes when one of his former victims, Mr. Alexander (Patrick Magee), locks Alex in a room and forces him to listen to Beethoven, played at extremely loud levels on speakers, which makes Alex—after his "treatment"—both physically sick and eventually suicidal. Here, a once comforting sound is now used within the story as a weapon against Alex. Not unlike the sounds of the beating by Dim and Georgie, the narrative now is turned actively against him, abandoning Alex without protection within the harsh realities of the story world. This narrative decision also reinforces the idea that people's concept of interaction (at least, the kind that *A Clockwork Orange*'s society asks the main character to engage in) is fundamentally violent, thereby inadvertently encouraging Alex's and the film's eventual retreat back into the comfort of his own subjectivity.

Indeed, *A Clockwork Orange* shows the destructiveness of Alex's subjectivity, yet it paradoxically shows, as *Dr. Strangelove* previously had, the ultimate inability of members of society to communicate productively with each other. When other characters finally confront Alex and force him to acknowledge their presences and assumptions, the behavior is equally violent. After Alex murders the cat woman, his "postcorrective advisor," Mr. Deltoid, comes to see him; yet rather than try to actively communicate with his pupil, Mr. Deltoid merely mocks Alex and then spits in his face. Later, when Alex attempts an act of kindness, by giving money to the homeless man he once beat up, the older man repays the generosity by getting other homeless people to help him beat Alex up in revenge. Such are the paradoxical social narratives and behaviors of people within *A Clockwork Orange*'s story world. Alex's subjectivity and social deviance are criticized and punished yet ultimately matched by the equally asocial lack of compassion displayed by the surrounding members of society. Moreover, the scene in the prison auditorium, where Alex must put on a performance for the politicians to show he has been "cured," speaks to this fundamental social contradiction—the treatment forces Alex into direct human contact (when he is beaten up by the anonymous, clearly annoyed stranger) while at the same time denies him any direct human contact of his own (both by not being able to fight back and by denying him sexual relations with the topless woman meant to arouse his desires). This double bind highlights the breakdown in narrative continuity and the absence of centered, fixed meaning in the story—a dominant country of the mind to replace the power of Alex's narrative authority, seen in the beginning. Society in *A Clockwork Orange* does not seem to know what its narrative of appropriate and accepted behavior should be, thus planting the seed for Alex's reemergence.

This more objective second act (where *A Clockwork Orange*'s narrative explicitly resists Alex's point of view), meanwhile, climaxes first in this staged narrative for government officials, where Alex's attempts at human interaction become a literal physical and psychological weapon the institution uses against him. When confronted with the possibilities of physical violence or sexual intercourse, feelings of physical pain consume Alex. From being interested only in his own desires as a form of narrative mapping, Alex has been completely transformed into a person painfully aware of and manipulated by his surroundings—much more conscious of how his body reacts instead of just what his mind desires. This middle sequence also climaxes in a far more intimate moment as well. After Alex's government-imposed "transformation," he returns home to his family, only to find his role there figuratively and literally overtaken by another—a lessee named Joe. When Alex expects his family to take him in without hesitation, Joe quickly confronts him—"So, you're back, eh? You're back to make life a misery for your lovely parents once more, is that it?" Previously oblivious to the damage he once inflicted, Alex must now accept the consequences of his earlier behavior toward his family. Later in the scene, Alex responds to the rejection, as well as to his treatment at the hands of society—"I've suffered and I've suffered and I've suffered, and everybody wants me to go on suffering." Here, he briefly tries to reestablish his own narrative, telling them what he's experienced and how that should change their behavior toward him. Unmoved, Joe observes, "You've made others suffer. It's only right that you should suffer proper." In Alex's previously self-absorbed state, he had been ignorant to the suffering of others, an awareness of which now overtakes him. The film refuses stylistically to support his point of view, to adopt his narrative understanding of the world (in this case, that his parents will take him back unconditionally), but instead compels him to confront the perspectives of others.

Just after this "homecoming" scene, the most striking example of the Kubrickian look in *A Clockwork Orange* appears; however, this sequence is significantly different from the look that opens the film. As Alex walks along the Thames, he contemplates his fate—alienated from society and from his family. This scene also directly foreshadows a moment in *Barry Lyndon*, where Barry is also caught in a similar gaze, when he stands on a bridge, staring out in contemplation at a river. As I noted previously in the chapter on *Fear and Desire*, the films' respective protagonists here both have been completely shut out by the society that surrounds them—both received, as *Barry Lyndon*'s third-person narrator puts it, "with . . . coldness and resentment." In *A Clockwork Orange*, Alex stops and stares at a spot within the river. The film frame captures Alex in a moment of contemplation, yet, unlike at the beginning of the film, he is not staring directly at the camera. This reflective moment—as the one in the next Kubrick film does—illustrates just how far *A Clockwork Orange* has moved from the narrative of its main protagonist. Here, the camera focuses on a seemingly insignificant spot in the river— presumably what Alex is looking at—just beneath a bridge. The effect is to show the audience that, as is typical to the Kubrickian look, Alex really is not looking at anything; he is caught in a moment of complete introspection, of silence—his narrations having failed him—a process of self-evaluation that he will not be able to sustain through the end of the film. In this moment, he realizes how little he understands of the world and his role in it. Most important, Alex's face here has truly become a mantle for the Kubrickian look—the silent narrator, denied his earlier first-person narration. Yet instead of attempting to actively engage further with his surroundings as a way to ascertain new narrative meaning (his subsequent beating at the hands of homeless people does not help here), Alex begins to retreat back to his own subjectivity, pointing the way to the film's finale, where he will embrace his violent and sexual desires again.

Interestingly, even the sequences where Alex is forced to watch violent and pornographic material illustrate the concept of the Kubrickian look. Although clearly not an instance of the look per se—for the simple reason that Alex is forced out of his own mind violently and into direct visual and aural confrontation of the ugly consequences of his actions and desires—the very fact that the doctors must literally pry his eyelids open with small clamps, and must hold them open so that Alex cannot avert his eyes (or his mind) from the narratives playing out before him, effectively illustrates the extreme extent to which Kubrick's characters have become so self-absorbed. Their respective narratives would seem to suggest that Ripper, Kong, Turgidson, and others would all be served well by such a treatment as this—one that forces them to see outside their own "islands" and faulty narratives covering the surrounding world (would Turgidson be so excited about "megadeaths" if he was forced to watch hours of graphic physical violence, or hours of images showing what the bomb can do to the flesh?).

The final instance of the Kubrickian look in *A Clockwork Orange* occurs in the last objective shot of the story world. As he sits in the hospital, recovering from his near-suicidal fall and surrounded by the media, anxiously capturing his picture with the Minister of the Interior, Alex stares off into the distance. This shot is then followed by the last shot of the film—a subjective shot of Alex's fantasy, as he ravages a girl in a pseudo-wedding setting, in front of a large, applauding crowd. Only in his fantasy—behind the look—can Alex's narratives truly play out as he wishes. All that has changed with Alex, from the beginning of the film to the end, is that society is now more supportive of his desires, the narrative he has chosen to live, than ever before. By having the people and various media types approach Alex directly, surround him, and take his picture repeatedly, *A Clockwork Orange* clearly acknowledges that its narrative structure, like the cameramen, is unabashedly interested in Alex's story again. The rolling in of the large speakers (playing

Beethoven) in this scene symbolically suggests that the film's soundtrack is once again interested in playing only Alex's musical tastes as well, rather than the diegetic sounds that populated most of the second act of the film. Alex has reclaimed his voice-over—"cured" of his silence—his comfort zone of isolated, asocial subjectivity. And, just as important, he has reclaimed the film's structure as well. The playing of "Singin' in the Rain" over the film's closing credits, a clear reference to the film's early gang rape scene, also reminds the audience, as though any further proof was needed, that Alex really has not changed from his self-absorbed and violent ways, and his narrative understanding of the world has been restored as the film's main story.

The fractured tensions between the look and narration continue in *Barry Lyndon*, though we never quite come close to aligning ourselves with any one point of view as we do with Alex in *A Clockwork Orange*—least of all, with the perspective of the third-person narrator. Though the film is heavy on talking—like *Dr. Strangelove*—little is actually said in *Barry Lyndon*. "Beyond the level of story, that rudimentary urge to tell a tale," writes Nelson, "the narrator has little or nothing to say. Significantly, he does not comment on most of what we *see* and *hear*. He has no access to the cinematic order of images and sounds of which his narration is but a small part."[12] The ironic detachment of the narrator, meanwhile, is matched by the cold detachment of the film's characters, and their blank facades tell us as much—probably more—about "what we *see* and *hear*" as the narrator does. As in *The Shining*, in *Barry Lyndon* we have a failed love affair, and perhaps another way of signifying the failure to understand and qualify experience. After the film's intermission, Redmond Barry (Ryan O'Neal) marries the recently widowed Lady Lyndon (Marisa Berenson) as he continues his assent through the social ranks. However, shortly after the ceremony, they are seen sitting in the back of a carriage, essentially ignoring each other. Both Redmond, now Barry Lyndon, and Lady Lyndon stare out their respective windows, with no communication between them. The image frames both the newlyweds caught in a dual look, having withdrawn from their immediate surroundings. This sequence, meanwhile, foreshadows the eventual disintegration of their marriage over the course of the film. Also important in this scene, however, is that Lady Lyndon attempts, after a few moments, to connect with Barry by looking over at him and waving away the smoke from the pipe he smokes, only to be completely shut out by her husband. This moment foreshadows both Barry's general withdrawal from the outer diegetic world in *Barry Lyndon* and the more general social withdrawal of men from their spouses in Kubrick's later films (particularly *The Shining* and *Eyes Wide Shut*). Eventually, she asks him to not smoke for a while, only to have smoke literally blown in her face. Barry simply has no interest in speaking to her. Much later in the film, Barry is again caught in a moment of the look, after the scene in which he fights with an older Bullingdon, as he stands on a bridge, staring out in contemplation at the river—an image that directly recalls the moment when Alex gazed out over the Thames River in *A Clockwork Orange*. Barry's continued shutting out by society, meanwhile, is accompanied by another moment of the look, as he sits at the accounting table and contemplates his mounting debts.

Barry Lyndon's withdrawal from his family into a state of alienation also impacts his wife and stepson, especially early in the second half of the film. A few scenes after the earlier carriage sequence, *Barry Lyndon* captures Lady Lyndon and young Lord Bullingdon in a similar dual look, as they sit quietly in their home, seemingly indifferent to the new baby, lying in the nearby crib, they are supposedly watching. The coldness in Lady Lyndon's stare is matched by another shot later, when she sits in the tub as an attendant reads to her. Apparently, completely unaware of the woman, the lady rests absolutely still; she too has lost almost all contact with the outer diegetic world. Intriguing here is that Lady Lyndon gives us the only female version of the Kubrickian look in his films. When Barry enters the room to apologize for his behavior of late, meanwhile, she seemingly accepts his apology, though she (like Barry in the carriage scene) says nothing in return, as though indicating that perhaps a true moment of connection between the two people has not yet occurred.

The love the two spouses bestow on their young son, Bryan, proves to be a temporary respite from this lack of affection, but once the young Lyndon has died from complications resulting from a horsing accident, the mutual withdrawal from one another continues, again marked by the Kubrickian look. As Lady Lyndon prays in the church, her blank expression suggests direct contact with neither religion nor anything else beyond her own mind. The tragedy of Bryan's death and her subsequent mourning has detached her mentally from the surrounding diegesis (this image is then shortly followed up—as moments of the Kubrickian look often are—by a violent outburst, this time by a hysterical Lady, flailing around in pain during a failed suicide attempt in her bedroom). After her recovery, and the film's dueling finale, *Barry Lyndon* then closes with Lady Lyndon in a moment of the look, possibly stopping to momentarily contemplate her now ex-husband—once again Redmond Barry. At this point, he is just a name on a debit slip and a memory in her mind, having been excised from the experience of the Lyndons' life.

I opened this chapter with a discussion of the voice-over narration in *Full Metal Jacket* because the failure of Joker's initial inability to narrate leads us directly to the question of narrative fallibility, which in turns leads me to the most visually provocative and aurally silent character in the film, Pyle. And this in turn leads me—like Walker, Chion, and Ciment—to those other faces that so strongly populate Kubrick's films. And I am drawn to those other characters in Kubrick's later films, the failed narrators whose inability to narrate is not negated but in fact highlighted and intensified by the blankness of their faces. Kubrick's later films repeatedly employ a distanced, ironic voice-over narrator, as other scholars have noted.[13] These narrators—such as Joker (his very name suggests an inability to narrate honestly)—seem to some degree or another removed from the experience of the stories that unfold, just like the third-person (hardly omniscient) narrator in *Barry Lyndon*. Conversely, these faces, these looks not unlike the one on Pyle's face, appear more in tune with the coldness, the narrative failure, of the films. What if the true embodiment of the Kubrickian narrator is not the talker but the one with the blank look, the one resigned in silence—the one transparently incapable of telling the story? As I have noted, the evolution of the Kubrickian voice-over has been charted before. Luis M. Garcia Mainar, for example, has argued that "voice-over narration in Kubrick's films evolves from an element that shows the mastery of the text by itself . . . to a more detached, ironic relationship of narrator to text that hints at the growing feeling in the later films that reality cannot be controlled and that the text is unable to present it to us in a clear, reassuring way."[14] Mainar's reading of Kubrick's body of work is not necessarily inaccurate, though it is my feeling that these looks—more so than the voice-overs—seem to better hint at the emerging possibility "that reality cannot be controlled" or that the human mind cannot represent the meaning and motives of events in Kubrick's later films or tell the story the way it had in films such as *Fear and Desire* and *Killer's Kiss*. I am tempted to argue that the descendants of the early voice-over are not so much the ironic narrators in *A Clockwork Orange* or *Barry Lyndon*, which seem like rhetorical red herrings—that is to say, devices deflecting the illusion of verbal mastery over the text and prolonging the inevitable sense of chaos. Evolving from the first Kubrick films to the later ones, the true descendant of voice-overs may instead be the Kubrickian look, the voiceless voice-over, those blank faces that guide us to the surrendering of any claims to narrative authority over the text.

If it seems excessive to offer the thought that those looks are the faces of failed narrators, consider the plot of so many of those films. Alex in *A Clockwork Orange* retreats behind the look in the middle portion of the film after he is arrested and his ideas and assumptions about the world have collapsed. For a period of time in the film, his voice-over no longer seems of much use, as these new experiences in prison overwhelm the ability to make sense of them. In *Eyes Wide Shut*, Bill Harford stares in silence when he periodically realizes he does not know his wife or his marriage—or even any of the events in the film at all—as well as he thought he did. The death of the prostitute, the disappearance of his friend Nick Nightingale—they do not mean, or might not mean, what he assumed they had. Or consider, most clearly, *The Shining* as an instance of the failed narrator. Jack Torrance—a novelist and storyteller—retreats progressively more to a look as his writer's block overtakes him. When we watch for the look in *The Shining*, it essentially aligns with moments of "shining"—times when characters appear to tap into some kind of spiritual existence beyond the physical world, often represented in this film by images of violence. Montages of shining suggest an alternative narrative—a contradictory way of perceiving the experiences of the world. Early in *The Shining*, Danny stares blankly into the bathroom mirror. This scene is followed by a montage of images—blood gushing from the Overlook Hotel's main elevator, the twin girls who were murdered by their father in the hotel ten years earlier, and Danny himself screaming (a scene that shows up much later in the film when Dick Hallorann is killed by Jack with an axe). Similarly, Hallorann, the hotel's chef, also "shines," such as when he sits on his bed at home in Florida and begins to envision the impending violence at the Overlook. His sense of a look precedes another montage of both room 237—one location of violence throughout the film— and Danny himself, caught with a similar blank expression. In a later scene, Danny retreats yet again as he lies on his bed, staring directly into the camera, while his parents fight in the next room and his father yells angrily at his wife, Wendy, for suggesting that they leave the hotel. The inherent social violence of this scene is reinforced by another image of blood gushing from the elevator, almost as though this image serves as Danny's narrative sense of the violence penetrating his family. A similar dynamic occurs again during another confrontation between Wendy and Jack—cut with images of Danny shining as he sits on his bed and images of blood running from the elevator and flooding the hallway—where she eventually hits her husband on the head with a baseball bat. In each instance, the images could be a spiritual manifestation, or they could be simply the voiceless narrative projection of a boy watching his family disintegrate. In either case, these expressionistic images—as with the ones in *A Clockwork Orange*—seem to approximate an attempt at reimposing order on an increasingly chaotic world, or to narrate through the voiceless voice-over. The final narrative turns in both *A Clockwork Orange* and *The Shining*—where characters retreat to something approximating the country of their own minds—suggest that narrative order can exist only within a dream, a realm of extreme subjectivity whose ability to impose exclusive meaning on events exists out of the reach of singular human perception (Alex, Jack, and so forth). Like Jack, who cannot complete his novel, solitary, asocial, and alienated subjectivities offer only a failed, fractured narrative authority, one incapable of ascribing meaning to events experienced within the story world. We find ourselves far removed from the thematic and narrative certainty that frames the events of *Fear and Desire* and *Killer's Kiss*.

Perhaps, at the end of *Full Metal Jacket*, Joker ultimately understands this, too, even though he cannot help but narrate one final time. After he kills the female sniper, he looks down in silence—echoing Pyle (so to speak)—realizing, maybe, that words don't do justice to that moment. Perhaps he is finally ready to supplant the authority of Pyle and emerge—like Bill—as a voiceless voice-over, noting that the most efficient and honest narration is silence. But, of course, he returns to his voice-over, but I can't help but feel that something there has changed. "I am so happy that I am alive, in one piece and short," Joker says in a passage that could easily relate to Bill as well. In *Eyes Wide Shut*, Bill is also lucky to be alive (just read the newspaper headline—a ruse, I think—in the café scene). And Bill, too, might realize that he is "in a world of shit, yes. But I am alive and not afraid." Again, this doesn't apply to the end of *Full Metal Jacket* as much as it does to *Eyes Wide Shut*, where there seems to be courage for Bill in confronting and confessing his indiscretions to his wife. As for Joker, I sense he knows that less is more, and the chaos will always be there. Notice that Joker notes twice that he is "alive"—he understands experiences remain, and he will remain an experience.

Nelson adds here that Joker finally does "confront and acknowledge his fear of death, and thereby save[s] himself from the greater fear of losing his humanity."[15] This may well be; one cannot deny Joker's slowly emerging humanity at the end of the film, as a contrast to Pyle and to the dehumanized and assimilated killing machine Hartman had hoped to build in the film's opening sequences. Yet one cannot also deny that—in the end—Joker is a little less sure of himself, too. He emerges from behind the look just long enough to share his fleeting thoughts one final time, but aware perhaps that they might not mean anything. He does not pretend any longer to understand the world around him—it is "shit," of course, but that does little to explain or clarify events in a thorough, substantive manner. Moreover, I sense he does not want to create any greater (and probably arbitrary) understanding of it. He says just enough to illustrate that he knows it's all chaos, a chaos that cannot be otherwise explained. His narrative assumption is no more profound than the belief that he's just grateful to be alive. Thinking about the evolution of Joker's narration (and of Kubrick's sense of storytelling), to speak of the "phony-tough" and the "crazy brave," accomplishes nothing constructive at a time when he is still engaging a world he has only truly begun, not to understand, but to *experience*.

NOTES

1. Geoffrey Cocks, *The Wolf at the Door: Stanley Kubrick, History, and the Holocaust* (New York: Peter Lang, 2004), 6.

2. Fredric Jameson draws a thematic link between Jack's frozen gaze and the eyes of the Star Child in his chapter "Historicism in *The Shining*," while also addressing the issues raised by the final enigmatic hotel photograph. "The great maze in which the possessed Nicholson is finally trapped," he writes, "and in which his mortal body is frozen to death, casts a glancing sideblow at the meretricious climax of Stephen King's novel in the destruction by fire of the great hotel itself, but more insistently rewrites the embryonic face of the Star Child about to be born into the immobile open-eyed face of Nicholson frosted in sub-zero weather, for which, at length, a period photograph of his upper-class avatar in the bygone surroundings of a leisure era is substituted." *Signatures of the Visible* (New York: Routledge, 1992), 98.

3. Mario Falsetto's term for the narrative power of voice-over narration in Kubrick's films, which I alluded to in earlier chapters. *Stanley Kubrick: A Narrative and Stylistic Analysis*, 2nd ed. (Westport, Conn.: Praeger, 2001), 5.

4. Tony Williams, "Narrative Patterns and Mythic Trajectories in Mid-1980s Vietnam Movies," in *Inventing Vietnam: The War in Film and Television*, ed. Michael Anderegg (Philadelphia: Temple University Press, 1991), 125.

5. I realize that not all of these films were made in Hollywood or with Hollywood money. My point is instead that they seem to more or less follow straightforward Hollywood storytelling conventions that no doubt served as a template, with little experimentation or digression. Even the complicated temporal structure of *The Killing* comes within the generic boundaries of a standard noir or heist formula.

6. Thomas Allen Nelson, *Kubrick: Inside a Film Artist's Maze*, 2nd ed. (Bloomington: Indiana University Press, 2000), 243.

7. Michel Ciment, *Kubrick: The Definitive Edition*, trans. Gilbert Adair (New York: Faber and Faber, 2001), 259.

8. Alexander Walker, Sybil Taylor, and Ulrich Ruchti, *Stanley Kubrick, Director: A Visual Analysis* (New York: Norton, 1999), 318.

9. Michel Chion, *Eyes Wide Shut*, trans. Trista Selous (London: British Film Institute, 2002), 31.

10. Unlike my past discussion of Kubrick's films, I will not spend much time on the use of voice-over narration in *A Clockwork Orange*, for the very simple reason that this device has already been examined in detail. Nelson argues that "the [source] novel's first-person's narration provided Kubrick with a psychological and narrative focus even more subjective and nightmarish than the one in Nabokov's *Lolita*." *Inside a Film Artist's Maze*,

142. Falsetto, meanwhile, points out Alex's "ironic, distanced commentary." *Narrative and Stylistic Analysis*, 90.

Most Kubrick scholars have noted, in some way or another, the unreliability of later voice-over narrators, such as Alex in *A Clockwork Orange* and the third-person narrator in *Barry Lyndon*, and thus I will not spend a great deal of time explicating them. As one example, Michael Klein talks about the occasional "ironic perspective" taken by the voice-over narrator in *Barry Lyndon*. "Narrative and Discourse in Kubrick's Modern Tragedy," in *The English Novel and the Movies*, ed. Michael Klein and Gillian Parker (New York: Ungar, 1981), 99. Nelson, for another, discusses how *A Clockwork Orange* "employs a limited first-person narrator—an ironic persona." *Inside a Film Artist's Maze*, 138. I, meanwhile, return yet again to this later use of the device, not with the intention of exploring ironic and limited voice-over narrators in and of themselves, but instead to establish them, as Mainar does, as a direct contrast to earlier voice-overs in pre-*2001* films and to distinguish them from instances of the look. In particular, I attempt to argue that the ironic voice-overs are, in a sense, supplanted in their narrative function by the voiceless voice-over.

11. Nelson discusses the use of expressionistic sets, which, he also adds, "suggest symmetry and doubling (Korova Milkbar, a mirrored hallway with a chessboard floor, a mirror bathroom)." *Inside a Film Artist's Maze*, 145.

12. Nelson, *Inside a Film Artist's Maze*, 172.

13. As with *A Clockwork Orange*, the voice-over narrator in *Barry Lyndon* is an ironic commentator—in direct contrast to the straightforward narrators in films such as *Fear and Desire*, *Killer's Kiss*, *The Killing*, *Paths of Glory*, and *Spartacus*. However, as with *A Clockwork Orange*, I will not devote much space to this subject, as critics have explored this region previously in great detail. In *Inside a Film Artist's Maze*, for example, Nelson highlights "[William Makepeace] Thackeray's use of the limited narrator" in the original literary source material (167) and the film narrator's "ironic and sympathetic reflections on the rise and fall of *Barry Lyndon*" (170). Falsetto makes the distinction that "although one may not be justified in calling the voice-over in *Barry Lyndon* limited, one can still reasonably question its authority." *Narrative and Stylistic Analysis*, 99. Most notably, Klein—as previously alluded to—devotes an entire article ("Narrative and Discourse in Kubrick's Modern Tragedy") to the discursive tools used in *Barry Lyndon*, including the voice-over narration, which he sees as both a source of "necessary information to bridge gaps between shifts of time or place and thus to ensure hypotactic continuity" (98–99), as well as that of an "ironic perspective" (99).

14. Luis M. Garcia Mainar, *Narrative and Stylistic Patterns in the Films of Stanley Kubrick* (Rochester, N.Y.: Camden House, 1999), 58.

15. Nelson, *Inside a Film Artist's Maze*, 259.

· 7 ·

Their Eyes Were Wide Shut:
Bill Harford as Failed Narrator

> If you go back and look at the contemporary reactions to any Kubrick picture (except the earliest ones), you'll see that all his films were initially misunderstood. Then, after five or ten years, came the realization that *2001* or *Barry Lyndon* or *The Shining* was like nothing else before or since.
>
> —Martin Scorsese[1]

*M*artin Scorsese's preface to the latest edition of Michel Ciment's noted study on Kubrick nails not just the initial reception of the filmmaker's works but also the subsequent reactions to his films. Not unlike how several other scholars have previously noted,[2] Scorsese points out that "if you go back and look at the contemporary reactions to any Kubrick picture (except the earliest ones), you'll see that all his films were initially misunderstood." While perhaps an overgeneralization, the basic thrust of Scorsese's assertion holds true. And, indeed, initial reviews of *Eyes Wide Shut* were not kind overall, even though Kubrick himself was quoted as saying he felt the work was his "best film ever."[3] Adding to this reception, A. O. Scott wrote in early 2000:

> Stanley Kubrick's death last spring, followed by the release of *Eyes Wide Shut*, revived a long-running argument among critics and fans about whether Kubrick was one of the most important contemporary filmmakers or merely among the most self-important—an avatar of cinematic perfection or a cold, detached perfectionist. The debate shows no signs of ending any time soon.[4]

Indeed, the debate no doubt continues to this day. Receiving Stanley Kubrick—however one chooses to define him—has never been a simple task, which may perhaps be precisely why he continues to provoke such a response. Though some critics—such as Janet Maslin and Richard Schickel—praised

Eyes Wide Shut, initial criticisms outweighed the praise, labeling Kubrick's "ponderously . . . dated"⁵ final film "overblown" and "unresolved,"⁶ with Toby Young—in an article self-evidently titled "I Wish I Hadn't Seen It"—condemning the work as "a mess, a puzzlingly amateurish film"⁷ (which, interestingly, echoes criticisms—decades earlier—of *Fear and Desire*). Even famous auteurist Andrew Sarris himself chimed in, considering the film "ridiculously though intellectually overhyped for the very marginal entertainment, edification and titillation it provides over its somewhat turgid 159-minute running time."⁸ "Kubrick's swan song," adds Richard Alleva, "turns out to be a squawk."⁹ Perhaps the initial reaction was complicated by the recent passing of the director, which brought on the expected celebration of his whole body of work, a weight on *Eyes Wide Shut* that would not have been otherwise foregrounded in the general public's consciousness. The film's "somber beauty is deepened by our knowledge that this is Kubrick's final film."¹⁰ Indeed, as Joseph Cunneen presumes, "there was no way that *Eyes Wide Shut* could have lived up to its buildup. Unfortunately, instead of being the dazzling climax of the late Stanley Kubrick's justly celebrated career . . . it turns out to be a pretentious bore."¹¹ Echoes Sarris, in a more apt observation, the film "did not live up to all its advance hoopla . . . but then what could, short of the Second Coming?" When *Eyes Wide Shut* was first released, the film carried not only the expectations of a famous filmmaker coming off a twelve-year hiatus but also the recent revival and attention paid to his most famous films. Subsequently, people seemed to mourn not only the passing of Kubrick but also possibly the even earlier passing of his talents. Whatever the strengths of the film (and I believe they are certainly far from negligible), it is not difficult to see how, unavoidably perhaps, *Eyes Wide Shut* was seemingly crushed under the immense critical weight of earlier Kubrick films and even of Kubrick himself, as that cinematic entity that collectively transcended the value of individual artistic achievements.

However, as Scorsese notes, it has become commonplace for Kubrick films to be appreciated after their original debut, and, indeed, many critics and colleagues subsequently came to the defense of Kubrick and his last film. "You've probably read by now that Stanley Kubrick's final film *Eyes Wide Shut* is a terrible let-down—neither a definitive farewell statement nor the out-and-out art-bonkbuster promised by so many seasons of media gossip," wrote Jonathan Romney. "The mood is akin to erotic disappointment, which is quite fitting, for that is essentially the film's subject."¹² Moreover, several critics suggested the same possibility—previous criticisms had evaluated *Eyes Wide Shut* not according to the film itself but according to the film's admittedly misleading publicity campaign. "The critics denounced the film for not living up to the claims its publicists had made for it,"¹³ wrote Lee Siegel.

Adds Tim Kreider, "critical disappointment with *Eyes Wide Shut* was almost unanimous, and the complaint was always the same: not sexy."[14] Writing with a great deal of critical and temporal distance, Mario Falsetto looks back and suggests that "the audiences that came to see what many thought would be the most sexually explicit film of the summer, were instead confronted with a magisterial, feverish dream movie."[15]

Many critics have since embraced *Eyes Wide Shut*, and the film seems quickly on its way to being regarded as one of Kubrick's finest films. Thomas Allen Nelson regards the movie as Kubrick's most "personal" film.[16] "Kubrick," Alexander Walker adds, "has often been accused, though never convicted, of an incapacity to reveal the 'warm, human stresses' in his subject matter because of a flaw in his own sympathies. This valedictory production gives the lie to that."[17] Perhaps Michel Chion offers the most pointed defense of the film: "*Eyes Wide Shut* is Kubrick's last and, in my view, one of his three greatest films, alongside *2001: A Space Odyssey* (1968) and *Barry Lyndon* (1975)."[18] For my own part, I will add only that the decision to use *Eyes Wide Shut* in so many ways here—both as culmination and response to earlier Kubrick films, but also as a fascinating story in its own right, one of destructive male subjectivity and the fragility of a modern marriage—was not an arbitrary one. In some ways, *Eyes Wide Shut* is partly that which propels the journey back to uncover earlier films such as *Fear and Desire*. I was mesmerized the first time I saw it, even at a time when I had not yet fully appreciated Kubrick's genius and his craft. Sure, I could pay lip service to *2001* and *A Clockwork Orange*—what Midwestern film geek in those days couldn't do that? But this last film created a different experience for me. I wasn't just being told that the film was brilliant. I was already sensing it, at a time when some didn't even know what to make of it at all. For *Eyes Wide Shut* pushes itself into consciousness. *Eyes Wide Shut* is a deeply moving film.

Such a statement is excessive, of course, but it is still on point. What is moving about the film, to me, is precisely its refusal to move us. Like many of Kubrick's films, its narrative coldness is the site of its greatest thematic warmth. *Eyes Wide Shut* does not give us an ideal predigested experience—it challenges us to see and embrace the ambiguity of experience itself, with the desire that we can see its anger, its pain, its confusion, its tragedy, *its hope*, for ourselves. And, moreover, I would argue that initial negative critical and audience reactions directly result from this daunting quality—Kubrick's and *Eyes Wide Shut*'s resistance to the narrative authority promised through the country of the mind and its narrator. That may sound just like more jargon at this point, but there are very real consequences for not opening up one's self to the experience of the film, expecting instead that its intended effects will be easily transmitted. To expect the film to tells its own story transparently, with pat summaries and easy conclusions, is to refuse to allow the haunting quality of the film to overtake you. What is moving in *Eyes Wide Shut* is the story of a man who cannot reduce his life to a simple, reassuring narrative. It foregrounds a man unable to understand his life and experiences; yet just as important, it also offers a glimmer of hope. It offers a sense of someone who—over the course of two and a half hours—comes to understand his own discursive inadequacies, exposing himself to the ambiguities and possibilities of experience.

∿

You're not even looking.

—Alice Harford

I think I'm going to have to go and show my face.

—Bill Harford

Similar to the main male protagonist in *The Shining*, Bill Harford (Tom Cruise) retreats to blank stares consistently throughout *Eyes Wide Shut*, and as with the earlier film, this look parallels his withdrawal from his wife, Alice (Nicole Kidman). The very first exchange of dialogue in *Eyes Wide Shut* establishes the concerns of the film—the possibility of divergent personal narratives—and the slowly decaying relationship between the spouses. As they prepare to attend a friend's party, Alice asks Bill how she looks. He responds by saying that she looks perfect and that her hair looks great, but, as Alice notes, Bill is not even looking at her. This clearly foreshadows Bill's retreat into his own mind and narrative assumptions, and importantly, his willingness to project a narrative onto his wife without even looking at her. Later, Bill displays a significant degree of ignorance about his wife's fidelity and women's sexual desires in general—a solid early example of Bill as a failed, even foolish storyteller. Alice then confesses to a narrative fantasy of adultery she had the summer earlier as a form of retaliation against his assumptions, a fantasy where she imagined herself with a mysterious and unknown sailor. This unexpected confession jolts Bill into a moment of the look, his previous narrative stunningly undermined by the opposing story of her adulterous thoughts. Yet rather than attempt to talk constructively about the admission with Alice, to reconcile their experiences and competing attempts at narrative understanding, he retreats inside his own mind. Before they can further discuss this rupture, Bill is called away to deal with the unexpected death of a family friend. In a perfect summary of *Eyes Wide Shut*'s visual motif, and of the voiceless voice-over, he must "go and show [his] face."

On the drive to the friend's place, Bill stares contemplatively in the back of a taxi—long, slow zoom-ins on his face serving as bookends to a series of expressionistic, black-and-white images depicting Bill's sense of Alice engaging in sexual contact with the naval officer. Projected as filmic images, just as Danny's emotional interpretation of events had been earlier in *The Shining*, Bill's jealousy is now getting the best of him (an identical sequence, meanwhile, follows later in the film as he rides in the taxi cab to the orgy[19]). The black-and-white images his mind projects not only highlight his marital fears but also illustrate two other crucial aspects of *Eyes Wide Shut*'s depiction of Bill's sense of narrative authority. The use of black-and-white film highlights the artificiality and inaccuracy of the story being presented to the audience. Yet more crucially, the expressionistic images—which also recall the overt presentation of Alex's subjectivity in *A Clockwork Orange*—also illustrate the general inability of Bill's mind to make sense of events within the story world of *Eyes Wide Shut*, a trend that will continue throughout the film. Similar expressionistic images, meanwhile, occur later in the film, accompanied by Bill's blank staring, as he walks down the streets of New York. In both of these sequences, Bill's imagination presents events that did not necessarily occur, so the images bring into relief Bill's failure to perceive and order the events of *Eyes Wide Shut*—his prominence as a failed, voiceless narrator (perhaps the use of black-and-white film in *Eyes Wide Shut* serves as a symbolic reminder of Kubrick's early career and failed aspirations for explicitly profound narrative meaning). Unlike *Killer's Kiss*, we are denied his thoughts aurally. Such an inability is also foreshadowed in the previous scene—where Alice makes her confession—when Bill attempts to construct a narrative of the sexual attitudes of men versus those of women, who "don't think like that," and only ends up looking foolish.

Much of Bill's odyssey through the underworld of New York in *Eyes Wide Shut* is an attempt to reclaim narrative sense amid his newly realized chaos, when there is little to be found. Alice's admission shatters the stability that Bill previously thought he had, and in retaliation, he immerses himself in seedy New York life—essentially looking for an affair—perhaps in an attempt not to gain revenge against his wife but instead to use seduction as just one of many avenues through which he can reassert his narrative powers over the people and events around him (whereas Ripper, HAL, Bowman, Alex, Jack, and Pyle resort to violence in order to impose their will on others, Bill seems willing to use sex). Yet his attempt at constructing a narrative is repeatedly undermined by the narratives of others. After Bill is caught trespassing at the orgy at the Somerton Manor, he is asked to walk into a large room, only to be confronted by hundreds of eyes staring directly at him. In this moment, Bill loses sight of his selfish sexual desires and becomes all too aware of the world around him; the orgy is not a blank slate for his aspiring narrative of seduction; it instead uses Bill as a character for its own production of accusations and sacrifices. This awareness of his place in another's narrative is heightened when he is asked to remove his mask and then his clothes; Bill even repeats the one man's verbal command to remove his clothes, as though highlighting the difficulty that Bill has with relating to other people and sensing their own stories (Bill often repeats what is said to him throughout *Eyes Wide Shut*, as though the self-centered protagonist is continually struggling to understand the thoughts of other people).

Eyes Wide Shut further highlights Bill's inability to narrate as he spends the latter part of the film trying to figure out what happened to both his friend Nick Nightingale (Todd Field), who first told him about the orgy, and to the prostitute, whom he first saved from an overdose early in the film and who then ends up dead after she presumably intervened on his behalf at the orgy, allowing his life to be spared. This mystery proves to be a clear indication of Bill's attempts to reassume the role of narrator, as he arbitrarily tries to piece together the otherwise random events following the experience at the mansion. In his own version of the story, he becomes convinced that Nick was roughed up and sent out of town as a result of the information he passed on to Bill, which is probably more or less accurate. However, he also comes to believe that the woman was killed because she helped him the previous night. He is also convinced that his life is likewise in danger—an assumption that actually contradicts the narrative played out at the orgy, namely that he would be spared because of her sacrifice. This latter assumption—where a paranoid Bill imposes an extended mystery plot onto the events he perceives throughout the film and where he is being chased by killers—proves to be misguided, at best.

The construction of Bill as a failed narrator in *Eyes Wide Shut* is most clearly realized by his late encounter with Victor Ziegler (Sydney Pollack). Outside of the interaction within the intimate sequences of the Harfords' marriage, the most crucial moment of direct experience—of the attempted alignment between competing narratives—comes when Ziegler talks to Bill about what may have really happened the previous night, telling him a story that undermines the one Bill came to believe, the story he himself constructed. In this scene, Ziegler admits that he too was at the mansion and is concerned that Bill may have the "wrong idea" about what happened. Interestingly, it is Ziegler who has a better understanding of story events than Bill, the presumed narrator, figuring out correctly how Bill knew about the orgy and having people follow Bill throughout the day, thus knowing his activities. Ziegler attempts to contradict Bill's assumptions, pointing out that Nick was not killed but instead sent on a plane to Seattle. Bill then responds by trying to make his own sense of the situation, asking if it was the second password, which he did not know, that gave him away to the others in the mansion. Throughout this scene, the audience is repeatedly reminded of the limits and the inaccuracies of Bill's perception—his failure in large part to give meaning to the moments he experienced. And in this scene, these limitations are again intensified by his blank, silent expressions. Ziegler undermines even Bill's most basic assumptions about what he thought he had perceived. Knowing Bill is still visibly agitated, Ziegler offers the following story:

> Suppose I told you that everything that happened to you there—the threats, the girl's warnings, her last-minute intervention—suppose I said all of that was staged. That it was a kind of charade. That it was fake. . . . In plain words, to scare the living shit out of you. To keep you quiet about where you'd been and what you'd seen.

This possibility at once both reinforces the power of narrative construction—by suggesting that events inside the mansion were conscious manipulations, designed and presented as a performance for Bill—and simultaneously undermines its authority. Ziegler's narrative contradicts Bill's previous possible meanings, such as the notion of a suspenseful murder mystery, while also highlighting how human understanding of events—even if *perceived* by a singular subjectivity directly—can be completely inaccurate. Of course, this explanation of what happened at the mansion is not necessarily true either, but Ziegler's suggestion essentially undermines any attempt by Bill to impose exclusive order on events and removes any sense of authority from Bill's point of view. "Maybe," as he aptly summarizes his shortcomings as a narrator, "I'm missing something here."

Even when Bill reminds Ziegler of the death of the prostitute as proof that those events were "real"—that the punishment promised was indeed carried out—and attempts to reestablish his own understanding of events, Ziegler still undermines Bill with his most troubling possibility: chaos. Whereas a film such as *The Shining* posits the look and narrative authorities as mutually struggling to make sense of the story world, *Eyes Wide Shut* takes such a failure one step further by foregrounding the real possibility that no definitive, authoritative order can ever be established. The film also posits a Kubrickian protagonist who may finally—if only vaguely—come to sense this ambiguity, and thus he again retreats to a look. Ziegler argues that the prostitute's death was completely random, or at least that any attempt to impose additional meaning on the event, insofar as Bill is concerned, is futile—not a murder, but simply the result of a drug addict's overdosing one too many times. Ziegler also reminds Bill that she had overdosed the night before, when Bill came to her aid during the Zieglers' party, as though attempting to reorder Bill's *own* perception of events into a new story—she was not murdered; she killed herself. "Listen, Bill," Ziegler reassures him, "nobody killed anybody. Someone died. It happens all the time. But life goes on. It always does until it doesn't." There is here a complete resistance to meaning. "Somebody [just] died"—a random event that "happens all the time."

Ultimately, Ziegler's assessment of experience in *Eyes Wide Shut* is nothing more than the fact that life always goes on "until it doesn't." In other words, he does not obsess with finding logic in the story world, with telling a story, to anywhere near the extent that Bill does. *Eyes Wide Shut* not only foregrounds the absence of narrative meaning as a central subject in the film but also points us to its own story as meaningless *in and of itself.* The event is the event—it cannot be mediated. Things just happen all the time. Again, Ziegler may also be lying, but what is most important is the unresolved ambiguity here, the unresolved tension between competing narrative authorities and the very real possibility that Bill, in his solitary, asocial state, is not just attempting to impose too much meaning on an experience, that there may, in fact, be no definitive narrative to narrate, no clear territory to map, no sense to the sense.

Having been further undermined in his attempt to find order and meaning in the world outside his marriage, Bill once again returns home. Shocked even further by the sight of his orgy mask lying next to Alice—painfully realizing the unavoidability of counternarratives he cannot control—Bill finally breaks down in tears and opens up to his wife. "I'll tell you everything," he confesses, something he should have been prepared to do the night they both got high and Alice told him about her secret sexual desires. This willingness to confess, meanwhile, perhaps points to (without certainly solidifying) the possibility of Bill finally emerging as a relatively effective narrator, recalling to his wife neither his foolish desires nor his faulty assumptions but merely his own limited experiences. Thus, Bill is willing finally to talk with her about "what . . . you think we should do," as though struggling to construct a new narrative together. Alice reasserts her own perceptions—in her most focused counterpoint to Bill's previous attempts at narrative order—that "the reality of one night [both Bill's perception of events and presumably Alice's fantasies], let alone that of a whole lifetime, can never be the whole truth." This last statement negates the significance of many of the film's events, thus reaffirming narrative ambiguity as the primary effect of *Eyes Wide Shut.* Bill, meanwhile, responds by stating that "no dream is ever just a dream," indicating a willingness to listen to Alice's concerns while also voicing his own. Unlike the failed marriages at the heart of *Barry Lyndon* and *The Shining* (where divergent narratives remain isolated in mutual misunderstanding and contempt), Alice and Bill have found some kind of agreed meaning, on some level. Both are "awake now and hopefully for a long time to come." At this point, Bill again attempts to impose narrative order by suggesting they will be happy together "forever," but Alice cautions him not to think in those terms. Alice's warning highlights how the marriage is by no means saved, but the union at least understands the dangerous potential for some—such as *Fear and Desire* and a younger Stanley Kubrick—to take life too seriously, for thinking excessively and placing too much meaning on events, and thus being marooned on islands throughout the country of the mind.

NOTES

1. As quoted in Michel Ciment, *Kubrick: The Definitive Edition*, trans. Gilbert Adair (New York: Faber and Faber, 2000), vii.

2. For example, Mario Falsetto, in his separate edited collection of essays on Kubrick, notes that "the critical standing of a Kubrick film seems to undergo extensive revision over time." *Perspectives on Stanley Kubrick* (New York: Hall, 1996), 3.

3. As quoted in the most recent book-length study of Kubrick: Paul Duncan, *Stanley Kubrick: The Complete Films* (Los Angeles: Taschen, 2003), 184.

4. A. O. Scott, "Opening *Eyes* to a Kubrick Masterpiece," *New York Times*, 16 April 2000, 2.9.

5. J. Hoberman, "I Wake Up Dreaming," *The Village Voice*, 27 July 1999, 59.

6. Joe Morgenstern, "There's Plenty of Sex, But *Eyes Wide Shut* Never Hits a Climax," *Wall Street Journal*, 16 July 1999, A1.

7. Toby Young, "I Wish I Hadn't Seen It," *The Spectator*, 11 September 1999, 48.

8. Andrew Sarris, "*Eyes* Don't Have It: Kubrick's Turgid Finale," *New York Observer*, 26 July 1999, 29.

9. Richard Alleva, "Final Curtain," *Commonweal*, 10 September 1999, 22.

10. Richard Alleva, "Final Curtain," 22.

11. Joseph Cunneen, "Bored *Wide Shut*," *National Catholic Reporter*, 3 September 1999, 19.

12. Johnathan Romney, "Exclusion Zone," *New Statesman*, 13 September 1999, 43.

13. Lee Siegel, "*Eyes Wide Shut*: What the Critics Failed to See in Kubrick's Last Film," *Harper's Magazine* (October 1999), 76. Overall, Siegel's essay works not only as an effective defense of the film but also as a concise and astute summary of its initial criticisms from writers such as Hoberman, Sarris, and David Denby.

14. Tim Kreider, "*Eyes Wide Shut*," *Film Quarterly* 53, no. 3 (Spring 2000): 41.

15. Mario Falsetto, *Stanley Kubrick: A Narrative and Stylistic Analysis*, 2nd ed. (Westport, Conn.: Praeger, 2001), xii.

16. Thomas Allen Nelson, *Kubrick: Inside a Film Artist's Maze*, 2nd ed. (Bloomington: Indiana University Press, 2000), 328.

17.   Alexander Walker, Sybil Taylor, and Ulrich Ruchti, *Stanley Kubrick, Director: A Visual Analysis* (New York: Norton, 1999), 359.

18.   Michel Chion, *Eyes Wide Shut*, trans. Trista Selous (London: British Film Institute, 2002), 9.

19.   Falsetto notes that "these images . . . are interspersed five times throughout the film." *Narrative and Stylistic Analysis*, 17.

· 8 ·

Conclusion: Sensing Stanley Kubrick

And then he's gone. Kubrick himself died just a few weeks after "finishing" *Eyes Wide Shut*. A controversy revolving around the film's orgy sequence and the insertion of digital figures to block certain sexual thrusts for American audiences kept his essence in the spotlight. And upon the film's release, the voices of dissent and support raised themselves in full chorus, proving that, even from beyond the grave, an artist can challenge and rile the masses. Nor did the other moviemakers he influenced forget Kubrick. Steven Spielberg adapted a long-in-development Kubrick project called *AI: Artificial Intelligence* (2001), which, true to the master, defied easy interpretation. And Kubrick's other unfinished projects (from a biopic of Napoleon to a WWII drama called *The Aryan Papers*) remain out there in some form, either to tantalise with their possibilities or to be finished by those who may dare to try. The legacy of Stanley Kubrick remains, as do the many stories surrounding his projects and his life, frustrating all attempts at complete synopsis.

—Keith Uhlich[1]

In any case, *experience continues.*

—Brian Massumi[2]

*J*ust as both Bill and Joker cannot help but be compelled by the affect of death—to attempt to weakly, unsatisfactorily quantify the experience of it in some way—and just as the latter character cannot help but narrate one final time, I cannot help but write my thoughts of the experience of Stanley Kubrick. When Kubrick died, his films still remained (and remain). Kubrick may have died, but in contrast to what Ziegler believes, these films don't just happen all the time. While Kubrick is long gone, the films of Stanley Kubrick are still there. And we have not begun to understand them so much as we have just begun to experience them. His films are there, waiting for viewers and reviewers—and yet for so many of us, that is not enough. This is not to say that Kubrick's films are somehow "better" than someone else's films, or that they are more worthy of study. It is only to say that something draws many of us back still. There is *something* there.

As a final thought on the Kubrick facade, I now hope to move briefly on to how Kubrick is similarly sensed, even beyond his own filmography. In particular, I explicitly wish to extend my discussion, appropriately (even necessarily) enough, beyond Kubrick himself, beyond even the films of Stanley Kubrick. In some ways an arbitrary, even superfluous, form of criticism, the auteur has been cast aside subsequently many times over; and yet it returns. Though our brains rationally tell us that Kubrick cannot be solely "responsible" for the "intentions" behind his films, there is nonetheless a *sense*—an unqualified feeling—implying that the auteur somehow remains. The Cinema of Stanley Kubrick remains. Or, at least, that which is in the films themselves, that which propels us to *Kubrick*, somehow remains, something not just in the mind of the scholar. Nor is there just something in the films. There is something in culture that evokes a *sense of the auteur* beyond the critical facade.

The reception of Kubrick suggests that there is a moment sooner than the reactive act of scholarship—the possibility that the auteur is always already there, beyond the surfaces, compelling the critic to map the traces of this affect. My research on Stanley Kubrick, for example, is not just about my interests and then, secondarily, about Kubrick; it is also about a notoriously reclusive biographical figure who directed a distinct body of work that offered narrative and stylistic patterns even before I (and others) chose to articulate them. I wish only to reiterate that "he" did in fact exist and thus does admittedly facilitate my auteurist readings, though reclaiming "Stanley Kubrick" as a historical figure is not my agenda here.

Instead, my particular project here concerns not just the process of storytelling but also, ultimately, the revelation of that process's own fallibility in the face of the experience. And I accept that my own process of recharting a trail through his films is similarly inadequate to the experience. It is a failure that Kubrick's films eventually embraced, and I am similarly content with my own critical disorientation. Nevertheless, I return to a brief overview of the route I have charted through this cinema. Kubrick's early films reveal a preoccupation with the mind's claim to narrative authority over story events and their prescribed meaning—through the filter of the country of the mind—but his later films expose a shift in emphasis to the resignation that such unified, knowable storytelling is fractured at best. Kubrick's production allows us to rechart the evolution of a form of narrating that increasingly loses a grip on the thematic and narrative certainty of the story it had aspired to tell. *Fear and Desire*, certainly, suffers from no such overt ambiguity, when compared with subsequent mappings. As soon as the third-person narrator positions the story of the film in relation to the country of the mind, the assertion is made that the human mind—the first- and third-person narrators—will clearly delineate the narrative and thematic meaning of the film's events. Struggling to tell an important message about war and humanity, *Fear and Desire* believes in its ability to position all humans as alienated and isolated "islands."

Killer's Kiss moves away from the social concerns and allegories of *Fear and Desire*, understanding the temptation to take life too seriously, yet also crucially preserves the ability for a narrator to remember, understand, and order events as they unfold in flashback. Like Davy in *Killer's Kiss*, the narrators in *The Killing*, *Paths of Glory*, *Spartacus*, and *Lolita* seem equally capable of framing stories about heists and war, often in flashback or hindsight, and narrate parts or all of the story with presumed thematic clarity. However, *Lolita*'s supposed narrative focus, Humbert and his voice-over, is confined to the film's flashback, with the crucial event—the murder of Quilty— remaining outside the range of his narrating power and cognitive mapping. Thus, in contrast to *Fear and Desire* and *Killer's Kiss*, *Lolita* more evidently resists framing story events with the omniscient authority offered by *The Killing*'s third-person narrator, who maintains his presence and influence throughout all events within the film.

Dr. Strangelove offers the first evident Kubrickian account of the failure of narrating. After the redundant and superfluous third-person narrator fades away in favor of characters within the film who serve as unofficial first-person narrators (by imposing meaning on military movement and national intentions), *Dr. Strangelove* reveals the inability of narrating either to unify and order events within and beyond the film's three isolated settings or to prevent nuclear conflict. The illusion of verbal mastery promised by the process of narration thus fails the characters of *Dr. Strangelove*—an implosion that *2001* seems to address by resisting this same rhetorical method. Rising from the barren wasteland symbolically leveled by the spectacular failure of verbal communication in its Kubrickian predecessor, *2001* emerges as a text that meticulously avoids all overt forms of orientation and narration. Aside from the removed third-person narrator and ample use of ambient sound, *2001*'s chief narrator, HAL, projects its voice throughout the Discovery spaceship and attempts to mold events to the computer's needs. But HAL is also the film's most violent character because its inability to narrate—its loss of verbal authority over crewmen—leads to murderous actions as a last, desperate form of imposing its own control.

This stylistic and thematic shift occurs at the same time that Kubrick's films begin to feature prominent examples of the Kubrickian look—the blank-faced manifestation of the failed narrator and voiceless voice-over—namely, General Ripper in *Dr. Strangelove* and HAL in *2001*. Yet Alex in *A Clockwork Orange* presents an even more compelling and suggestive instance of the look and its direct association with the loss of voice and failed narrating. Alex's voice-over dominates the first and third acts of the film, when Alex is running loose amid the underbelly of society. However, as Alex is captured and moved outside his comfort zone, his voice-over loses its power and prominence over events in the story. This transfer coincides with the emergence of the look on Alex's face as he stares out over the Thames River, the earlier assumptions about his world having, at that point, been undermined and destabilized. Alex has lost his sense of the film's meaning. With Alex looking away in contemplation and depression, the look here also certainly contrasts with the opening shot of the film, where Alex's direct glare into the camera implicitly positions his attempts at storytelling as *A Clockwork Orange*'s earlier authoritative source of narrating. Like HAL and Jack in *The Shining* (the latter being Kubrick's one literally failed storyteller), Alex's embrace of physical violence offers the only means of restoring a sense of narrative order over others. Meanwhile, Joker and Pyle in *Full Metal Jacket* offer contrasting examples of the two Kubrickian narrators in the same film—the voice-over and the voiceless voice-over. Joker is the brash narrator who thinks initially he understands the world, while Pyle retreats quickly and quietly behind the look as he begins to sense the absence of cohesive, affirming meaning in the world. By the end of the film, though, one senses that Joker has moved a little closer to Pyle's understanding, revealed in part by the expression on his face after he kills the sniper and by the uncertainty evidenced in his final narration.

In contrast to earlier Kubrickian protagonists, Bill Harford in *Eyes Wide Shut* has no desire for physical violence and instead finally seems willing, albeit reluctantly and begrudgingly, to acknowledge his own narrative shortcomings over the course of the film. At first, Bill struggles unsuccessfully for narrative order. He makes assumptions about women and sex that prove inaccurate. Rather than act out violently, however, Bill attempts to use his own presumed powers of seduction to assert strength over others and their actions, but he fails embarrassingly. Throughout *Eyes Wide Shut*, Bill implicitly attempts to narrate his own story about the meaning of a prostitute's death, his wife's fantasies, and his own flashbacks, while also believing in his own impending danger at the hands of powerful strangers and murderous thugs. However, he must ultimately confront the limits of his own perceptions and efforts at understanding.

When he promises to "tell [her] everything," finally emerging from behind the look, Bill ends up narrating to his wife the only story he and Kubrick's films know how to tell for sure—the story of an inability to tell a story. Such a revelation proves to be the ultimate achievement of narrators in Stanley Kubrick's films, the last exhaustion of quixotic quests through the country of the mind. Kubrick's body of work suggests that verbal narration cannot truly achieve narrative authority, that the eerie stillness of the fractured and expressionistic images in *The Shining*, of the silence of *2001*, and of the blank faces in *Eyes Wide Shut* come much closer to thematic clarity. Yet "reality" (whatever that could be) still remains outside cognition, in the realm of the affective, the unrepresentable—no longer within the grasp of those narrators who first attempted such endeavors at the beginnings of the early films.

In the present project, I simply wish to conclude by foregrounding, however elusive, how *something* does happen even before critics begin to deploy the auteur as a means of justifying a particular director, or a particular film, even if we cannot quite explain it. By reintroducing *Fear and Desire* (and other new insights) into the discourse on this particular auteur, I do not aspire to the final, definitive look at Stanley Kubrick, something that will never be achieved in my lifetime; rather, I just hope that this particular map will point in some new directions, those still waiting to be explored. And yet I do not wish to be marooned with my own expressions and assumptions about Stanley Kubrick, either. And so—as I finish my work—I want to argue for how others have sensed Kubrick and extended his presence even beyond his own body of work. Focusing on how the *experience of Kubrick continues* is what I hope to illuminate as I conclude this intervention. And to do so necessarily means moving beyond even *Eyes Wide Shut*. In other words, I have finished my narrow intervention into the experience of his films here. But I cannot tie this project up so cleanly. I cannot quite end the conclusion here because a sense still remains. In order to stress how the possibilities of Kubrick continue, my conclusion itself must be still another introduction. "Kubrick" still remains. For me, yes, but for others, too. "Kubrick" pushes us further. . . .

SENSING STANLEY KUBRICK

The craft is impeccable. Every film he's ever made, the craft is impeccable. . . . Nobody could shoot a movie better than Stanley Kubrick in history. That was impeccable. But the way he told stories was sometimes antithetical to the way we are accustomed to receiving stories.

—Steven Spielberg[3]

Around the end of the twentieth century, many people offered their final thoughts on Stanley Kubrick, a tribute propelled in part by the release of his final film, *Eyes Wide Shut*, in July, but more important, by his unexpected death four months earlier. His friend, fellow filmmaker Steven Spielberg, was among the many who praised both his career and his life, highlighting such supposed attributes as Kubrick's "vision of hope" during a tribute speech at the 1999 Academy Awards. Spielberg even appeared on the 2000 DVD edition of *Eyes Wide Shut*, discussing his long friendship with the director, which went all the way back to the late 1970s. It was during this time that the Well of the Souls set in *Raiders of the Lost Ark* took over the soundstage in England that had just finished housing the large lobby of *The Shining*'s Overlook Hotel. Spielberg applauded Kubrick's consummate "craft," pointing out many of the technical skills Kubrick had mastered; however, embedded within Spielberg's praise was also the observation that the "way [Kubrick] told stories was sometimes antithetical to the way [audiences] are accustomed to receiving stories." Considering the source, this remark could be a slight criticism of the elder filmmaker, one who later de-emphasized the same rhetorical devices—such as voice-over narration and emotional musical scores—Spielberg has himself often relied on to make movies not "antithetical to the way" people are "accustomed" to receiving them. At the very least, Spielberg's comment brings into relief Kubrick's distinctive style of filmmaking and how it was usually received. By being antithetical, I believe Spielberg is articulating how one senses the absence of meaning in his films.

And yet one still senses it. It is not, by itself, absent. The films themselves create such a style of cinematic storytelling. By stripping away the use of voice-over narration and signifying music, Kubrick indeed did make films "antithetical to the way we are accustomed to receiving" them, a quality that Spielberg would be likely to note, given his own stylistic tendencies.[4] Interestingly, Spielberg—in the same interview—recalled how he, with family and friends, spent the night Kubrick died watching the heart-wrenching finale of *Paths of Glory*, where the German girl (played by Kubrick's real-life wife, Christiane [as Susanne Christian]) sings to a crowd of hostile French soldiers, only to move them to tears as they eventually sing along. Tim Kreider argues that "Spielberg loves tear-jerking scenes like that favorite in *Paths of Glory*,"[5] but he also adds that Spielberg takes the scene out of its context. He notes, "Those misty-eyed lugs are the same soldiers who, in a previous scene, stood dutifully in formation . . . as three of their comrades were ceremoniously tied to posts and shot."[6] Although we do have this irony Kreider highlights, I still think Spielberg's reading of the sequence remains a fair one; the moment, while genuinely moving, is also one of the most overt instances of emotional manipulation (right next to *Spartacus*'s concluding crucifixion scene, where the dying hero sees his son for the first time) ever put forth in a Kubrick film. And it is not entirely inappropriate that Spielberg would respond well to this sequence, for it is *not* "antithetical to the way" American audiences were accustomed to receiving mainstream films.

Kreider, moreover, goes on to assert that Spielberg "hasn't shown much of the subtlety, restraint, and layered irony that make Kubrick's work so rich and open to interpretation."[7] In fairness to Spielberg, though, Kubrick's early films—from way back to *Fear and Desire*, all the way up to *Spartacus*—often do not show "much . . . subtlety, restraint, and layered irony," either. The sequence in *Paths of Glory* serves, in an otherwise extremely cynical and downbeat antiwar film, as an unexpected moment of humanity and hope not typically offered at the end of Kubrick's films (even the moment of reconnection at the end of *Eyes Wide Shut*, while relatively hopeful, is still tinged by the awareness that nothing, including love, lasts "forever"—an assertion far removed from the typical assumptions of Hollywood romance). This stylistic tension between Kubrick and Spielberg over differing ways of telling stories and how audiences receive them, meanwhile, is best explored in the one project they "collaborated" on—*Artificial Intelligence: AI* (2001).[8] Specifically, Spielberg's way of framing the story events in *AI* recalls the formal narrative authority projected in Kubrick's pre-*Dr. Strangelove* films. In other words, there is *a sense of a certain Kubrick* in *AI*.

> In the past two years, I've seen only one big-budget Hollywood production in a cineplex (Spielberg/Kubrick's *AI: Artificial Intelligence* [2001]) that was interesting enough for me to want to write something about it.
>
> —James Naremore[9]

As a final commentary on Kubrick's cinematic relationship to the country of the mind and on the experience of his work, I offer an analysis of Spielberg's *AI*[10] through the critical lens of Kubrick's stylistic trends—reconsidering Kubrick's formal qualities under the assumption that Spielberg's narrative divergence from the elder's style helps further bring into relief both Kubrick's later unique antithetical style, and how it is received, as well as relocating Kubrick's assertion in 1966 that audiences "react primarily to direct experience and not to abstractions." Put another way, I hope to offer one way (among many possibilities) in which we can still feel a trace of Kubrick in *AI*. While I believe that *AI* is undisputedly Spielberg's (as much as one film could be labeled singularly as such), I work yet again under the assumption that Kubrick is an affect, a sense that floats somewhere alongside, before, after, or within the film, and thus propels us to reengage the issue of the country of the mind, even as it extends (necessarily) beyond the Cinema of Stanley Kubrick. As Naremore writes, "Kubrick is therefore figured as the ghost in the machine and Spielberg as his eulogist. Some commentary on the two seems inevitable as a way of accounting for *AI*'s particular way of achieving closure and its unusual commentary on gods, humans, and robots."[11] My discussion of Kubrick's own films is about the affective work, the effects, that his films accomplish as spectacle and as narrative. My brief concluding discussion of Spielberg's *AI* intends to do likewise—to intuit "the ghost in the machine" of the sci-fi epic.

Interestingly, biographical discourses on the last years of Stanley Kubrick's life seem to be filled more with the projects Kubrick was about to tackle[12] than with the projects—*Full Metal Jacket, Eyes Wide Shut*—he actually did. In this sense, the idea of Kubrick has always already been extended beyond his actual work, even before he passed away. But, if Kubrick's Napoleon or Holocaust projects never do come to fruition, such an ending would be just as well, for the last trace of Kubrick appropriately debuted in the calendar year 2001, even though the experience of Kubrick also exists beyond 2001 (and beyond *2001*). Such a coincidence is fitting, not only because the year recalls arguably Kubrick's most famous film but also because *AI* itself echoes the earlier sci-fi masterpiece on several levels. In other words, I do not read Kubrick into *AI* so much as I feel the latter film reveals traces of Kubrick and *2001* to me. And if one is tempted to consider my affective response to *AI* overly illusory, bear in mind that critical reactions at the time of *AI*'s initial release, not surprisingly, also focused in large part on Kubrick's possible presence in the film, even though the elder filmmaker's only work on the actual film was technically in the very early stages of preproduction. It wasn't even his script, but Spielberg's, that the production crew worked from. Nevertheless, the film creates in others a sense of Kubrick.

"What this [directorial] synthesis has wrought unquestionably will be debated at length"[13]—often not to Spielberg's advantage. Spielberg "tries for a new level of seriousness," writes Christopher Sharrett, "by melding the cynical nihilism of Kubrick's icy visual style with his own trademark mawkish sentimentality," adding that "this picture looks naïve, both cinematically and morally."[14] Joe Morgenstern considered the film a "grim disappointment for grown-ups, and far too violent for young kids. The product of an unprecedented collaboration between two great directors, . . . I found it to be clumsy, misanthropic and intractably lifeless."[15] Most harshly, however, Lucius Shepard hypothesizes:

In the hands of a great filmmaker, especially one of Kubrick's cold, meticulous sensibility, the movie might have avoided the excess of sentimentality inherent in the idea, but when Spielberg—who never met a button he failed to push— inherited the project and then rewrote the script, it was pre-ordained that the spirit of cutesy-poo would be invoked to the max.[16]

The overreduction here of the film as being a tension between the coldness of Kubrick and the sentimentalism of Spielberg was typical of reactions at the time. Though there is some truth there, neither filmmaker's style feels quite that simple. However, as with *Eyes Wide Shut*, some came to the film's aid, often by evoking, as its detractors also had, Kubrick himself. "Despite being freighted with clunky exposition, windbag moralizing and thumping self-importance," Peter Travers defends, "[*AI*] is a far darker and more disturbing piece of science-fiction than its market campaign lets on . . . preserving Kubrick's vision and adding much of [Spielberg's] own."[17] Richard Corliss adds that "Spielberg has the warmest of directorial styles; Kubrick's is among the coolest,"[18] but Rand Richards Cooper clarifies, "There's enough Kubrick in the genetic code of *AI*'s material to prevent the kind of sentimental ending that marred Spielberg's *Schindler's List* and *Saving Private Ryan*."[19] Moreover, Philip Kerr argues, the absence of Kubrick's direct touch "hardly detracts from the overall brilliance of Spielberg's movie and, although *AI* is not as good as *2001*—the benchmark against which all cinematic sci-fi must be measured—it's possibly the best, and certainly the most thoughtful, sci-fi film there has been since Kubrick's classic."[20] Kerr's praise seems excessive, but his defense of the film is a welcome respite from the formulation that *AI* is too much of a warm Spielberg and not enough of a colder Kubrick. In addition, the *New York Times*'s A. O. Scott regards the film as "not only the best movie of the year but also the most misunderstood."[21] In his article on the film (the most in-depth look yet at *AI*'s long preproduction and completed production history), Joe Fordham considers the film "alternately tender and chilling, playful and savage, visionary and apocalyptic . . . confound[ing] critics and divid[ing] audiences, just as many of Stanley Kubrick's films had done."[22] Or, as Kubrick's brother-in-law, business partner, and *AI* co-producer, Jan Harlan, simply puts it, "This will be a repeat of *2001*. . . . Some people will hate it. Never mind."[23] Ultimately, "Is it a Spielberg movie informed by the ghost of Kubrick?" asks David Ansen rhetorically (in metaphoric imagery that haunts me, Naremore, and others, and will continue to do so). "Is it a movie in which the sensibilities of the two most powerful cinematic personalities of our times—who couldn't be more different—conduct a 140-minute duel for dominance?"[24]

I hope, for my own part, to comment on this "duel" of styles, using my previous discussion of Kubrick's body of work as the theoretical framework under which to approach Spielberg's final product. Indeed, *AI* is largely, in terms of narrative theory, a Kubrickian story, filtered through Spielberg's discursive representation. Or, in postmodernist terms—it is Spielberg's remapping of Ian Watson's remapping of Kubrick's initial remapping of Brian Aldiss's original short story. That is to say, the original, the "true" *AI*, is unattainable, always already unrepresentable.[25] As the film's coproducer Kathleen Kennedy frames the tension, Spielberg "took Stanley's contribution and added that to his own. There's no question that this is a movie that has Steven Spielberg's sensibilities all over it. But the subtext is all Kubrick."[26] While I'm reluctant to agree with Kennedy's belief that the subtext is "all" Kubrick's, I would point out the ways in which even the film's producers (not only outside Kubrick supporters) seem to acknowledge that Kubrick was and is always there, somewhere, in and around the film. Narrative theory, the exploration of a film's tension between what is being represented and how it is represented, proves to be an effective method for pulling out how Spielberg's "sensibilities" impose narrative authority on the possibility of a Kubrickian "subtext" and for identifying the central instances, of effects, in *AI* of Kubrick's and Spielberg's respective minds. Adds visual effects technician Dennis Muren, "It's Steven's film, but it's still Stanley's story."[27]

Simply put, Kubrick affects the film. Or, better yet, the film effects Kubrick—compels us to feel Kubrick at the levels of sight and sound. *AI* actually suggests the possibility of a Kubrickian look, when the robot-child David (Haley Joel Osment), having been abandoned by both his family and his maker, sits on the edge of an old Manhattan skyscraper, contemplating his life. It is a moment strikingly close to one seen with, for example, Bill in *Eyes Wide Shut* or Jack in *The Shining*. Alienated by the diegetic world, his narrative understanding of how the world works having failed, the character completely withdraws into his own thoughts. Then, David throws himself into the ocean beneath, in a pseudo-suicidal move (as a machine, he cannot actually die). However, at this point in the narrative, Spielberg adds an interesting touch in terms of narrative authority—as David falls to the water, the film cuts to shots of Gigolo Joe (Jude Law), his companion on the journey, sitting in an amphibicopter, watching him as he descends. The frame first captures Joe's point of view as he observes David's drop, followed by a reverse shot of Joe's look of amazement as the image of a falling David reflects off the amphibicopter window. In this moment, *AI* captures both the viewer and the object of that gaze in the same shot (like Davy and the mirror in *Killer's Kiss*), taking the possibility of a Kubrickian look—the failure to find meaning in the story—and finding a way to frame it with an authoritative (if also implicit) narrator (Gigolo Joe), again reminding the audience of how to perceive this specific story event (namely, foregrounding the horror and tragedy of the moment).[28]

As another strong parallel to Kubrick's early professional instances of the country of the mind and authoritative narrators, *AI* opens with a voice-over narrator (Ben Kingsley) who seems to be in the third person initially but who in fact ends up being a character introduced very late in the film. Much like the mapping that occurs at the beginning of all early Kubrick films up to *Dr. Strangelove*, this narrator explains the background exposition to the story, pointing out how the ice caps had melted (because of global warming) and subsequently flooded most cities, thus causing massive starvation and limited resources across the world. Because of these changes, robots and androids— those who do not consume resources—were now more valuable to society than ever before. The information presented here is not particularly relevant to the narrative movement of the film; however, it does explicitly establish the (future) historical context for the story and, more important, allows Spielberg to construct an authoritative narrator in the discourse, one that will impose narrative order and make sure the audience can follow the events of the story. Certainly, this first mark of the country of the mind in *AI* recalls attempts by the earlier narrators in *Fear and Desire*, *Killer's Kiss*, *The Killing*, *Paths of Glory*, and *Spartacus* to construct films not "antithetical" to the way people were accustomed to receiving them. Moreover, this same narrator (actually, a Mecha from the future, presumably introducing the story as a flashback—not unlike Davy in *Killer's Kiss*) will return at several other points to explain the story to the audience, including the very end of the film, as though highlighting the voice-over narrator as a literal frame to *AI*'s story, contextualizing the beginning of the narrative and the end. At another crucial transition point, late in the film, David and his teddy bear companion are trapped in the amphibicopter—deep beneath the surface level of the sea— after a Ferris wheel collapses and suppresses them. With nowhere for David to go, and with his trying in vain to contact a Blue Fairy statue (which, in one of the film's many references to *Pinocchio*, he thinks will make him a real boy), the narrator returns and explains:

And David continued to pray to the Blue Fairy there before him—she who smiled softly forever, she who welcomed forever. Eventually, the floodlights [on the vehicle] dimmed and died, but David could still see her palely by day, and he still addressed her with hope. He prayed until all the sea anemones had shriveled and died. He prayed as the ocean froze and the ice encased the caged amphibicopter and the Blue Fairy, too, locking them together where he could still make her out—a blue ghost in ice, always there, always smiling, always awaiting him. Eventually, he never moved at all, but his eyes always stayed open, staring ahead forever in the darkness of each night and the next day, and the next day. Thus, 2,000 years passed by.

Again, the authoritative narrator returns, stating in no uncertain terms how David went from being trapped under the ocean to being in a position, two millenniums later, where Mechas—the only survivors since the humans died out—could uncover him as an artifact. Certainly, the voice-over narrator here does not pass along information that the audience could not glean from the events themselves. The fact that most people could figure out how the humans had all died out, without the narrator explicitly saying so, speaks to the superfluousness of the narration. However, this passage does allow Spielberg to reaffirm the role of a narrative authority through an overt mediator between audience and story. Moreover, the sudden jump ahead 2,000 years directly recalls a similar transition in *2001*, when the film—in a simple visual cut from flying bone to floating spaceship—moves from the time of apes to the title year, without any additional, extraneous expository tools.

In fact, comparing the different cinematic representations of the massive chronological jumps in both *AI* and *2001*—how they are or are not narratively framed—serves as a good centering point for contrasting Spielberg's narrative authority with Kubrick's move toward narrative minimalism. On a larger scale, the entire ending of *AI*, in fact, recalls the ending of *2001* and suggests perhaps the most focused point for comparing Kubrick's country of the mind with Spielberg's. The striking similarities in story events (if not as much in representation) between the endings of both films offer the strongest opportunity for analyzing conflicting notions on how audiences receive filmic narrations amid territories marked by the country of the mind. After following its individual protagonists through the second and third acts of the narrative, both *AI* and the earlier *2001* end with, respectively, David and Bowman (whose first name is also David) isolated and alienated from the human community that first fostered them. They conclude their respective films by living out eternity in an artificial set directly constructed, by outside observers, from their respective thoughts and memories. Far from the realm of the figurative, both Davids literally end their journey in something very close to a highly subjective country of their own minds. Whereas the aliens build the pseudo-classical apartment for Bowman to inhabit as he lives out his "human" existence in *2001*, David returns to a reconstruction of his foster parents' home.

Further connecting the two films, the transition to both final sets is also first marked by close-ups of each characters' eyes—Bowman's flickering in a bright, orange filter and David's blue eyes, meanwhile, opening slowly, slipping open an overexposed white background. Moreover, both sets are visually represented as slightly off from their original referents—while Bowman's apartment seems to suggest a pastiche of various Earth-bound architectural styles, thrown together in a disorienting manner, David's "home" is initially filtered by the camera through a blue lens, reminding both character and audience that this setting is not quite the place David used to live (much) earlier in the film. They both walk around their new diegetic settings cautiously, surveying the unexpected surroundings—vaguely familiar to them, yet not quite something they have ever seen before. In both cases, these off-putting differences highlight their artificial, abstract reconstruction, filtered from both Davids' respective minds through the distorting lens of a third party.

Yet there are also profound differences in the way both sequences are presented to audiences. For one, a soft nondiegetic piano score—as though signaling the procession of his homecoming after a long journey through the dark forests, Rogue City, and Manhattan—creeps into the discourse as David begins walking around the set. In *2001*, only the sounds of the disembodied alien voices, as they watch Bowman, can be heard. And this latter reading, while valid, is by no means absolute, thus further speaking to the earlier film's ambiguity. This is particularly important in contrast to *AI* because we *do* see the source of those watching him (the Mechas) in the later film. For another, David continues to talk about the environment to Teddy—by declaring, "Teddy, we're home," and then calling out for his mother—specifically positioning the setting for audiences. In *2001*, a silent Bowman is followed by the audience, presumably as confused and disoriented as he. Also, there are differences in how the outsiders present themselves to the protagonists—while the Mechas materialize first as the Blue Fairy (again, extracted from David's memory) and then as the Mecha who had been narrating the film all along, *2001* offers only the Monolith as a manifestation of the alien presence. As I noted earlier, the very fact that we see not only a Mecha itself but also the other Mechas watching David in his new home also departs greatly from the representation of the aliens in *2001*, who are never seen, only heard in a dialect unintelligible to human ears anyway. The Blue Fairy's and the Mecha's collective role, meanwhile, also foregrounds a significant stylistic shift from how Kubrick frames the final events of *2001*. Both characters largely serve the function of explaining the rather confusing sequence of events—how David got there, what "there" is, and how his Mother can suddenly appear for one, and only one, final day—not only to the protagonist himself but also, more important, to the film's audience.

2001, on the other hand, offers little explanation to its viewers (and thus takes much less screen time); the audience itself must impose narrative order on the story events—mapping what is, or may be, happening to Bowman from what little narrative assistance is offered. "If I do have a criticism [of *AI*]," Kerr astutely notes, "it is that the end is too literal, too explicatory. Kubrick, directing the same film, would have enigmatised his ending, as anyone who would have seen the oblique ending of *2001* would understand."[29] Of course, we do not know what would have happened had Kubrick directed the film, and this fact in some ways makes watching *AI* all the more exciting. It is our sense of Kubrick himself that has been further "enigmatised" by the film's production—Spielberg's direction thus makes Kubrick and his "vision" all the more elusive. But, certainly, there does appear to be significant evidence for examining how Spielberg's *AI* receives Kubrick in very different ways and how the film foregrounds a particular urgency when discussing the country of the mind as a larger cinematic practice, beyond the diegesis in *Fear and Desire*. It is the insistence on being "too literal" that lends *AI* its vision of a country of the mind—its vision of taking the meaning of life too seriously—a destination for David that will allow everything in the film to finally make sense for him.

Such a vision, this distinction between "too literal" and an "enigmatised ending," is perhaps best represented by the return, one final time, of the voice-over narrator in *AI*, who reasserts his authoritative presence—guiding audiences back out of the diegesis—by telling the audience that the love of David's adopted mother was "the everlasting moment he had been waiting for" (as though the film seeks the narrative and thematic closure *2001* avoids) and by reminding them (as though it demanded repeating at this point) that Monica would never return after she fell asleep at the end of the one day. The Mecha also assures audiences, however, that such a contingency was "okay" emotionally because David had now received personal satisfaction from her—or from her representation's (the distinction is never made clear)—admission of love for him. Like Jack at the end of *The Shining*, David could now go "to the place where dreams are born," inside this country of his own mind, which thus reinforces and rewards his surrender to the Mecha's narrative authority. In *2001*, though, the audience has only the Star Child and *Also Sprach Zarathustra*—a nondiegetic device possibly signaling destruction ahead in the narrative—to discern the meaning of the film's final events, where a similar surrender means the end of the human race. But, as I said before, *2001* is ultimately meaningless. *AI*, on the other hand, *thinks* it's filled with meaning. But if there is any meaning in this later film, it is ultimately in its ability—as with *2001*—to effect meaning in us.

Spielberg's *AI* certainly presents a good example of at least attempting to remap a filmic story not antithetical to how audiences receive it, although such a quality is brought into particular relief when analyzed through the lens of Kubrick's post-*Dr. Strangelove* films—especially, *2001*. In *AI*, David and the third-person narrator successfully impose narrative order and meaning on the story events, an area in which Kubrick's later protagonists routinely fail. Thus they must either embrace their own narrative authority violently (HAL, Bowman, Alex, Jack, and Pyle) or retreat from the diegetic world outside them, with inconclusive results (Redmond Barry and Bill Harford). Perhaps Kubrick's inability to find a way to have David "fail" in this respect—to see the poor boy come face to face with the misleading, even cruel narrative deception of the country of his own mind—is why he never could quite commit to making the film. Gregory Feeley labels the project "the masterpiece a master could never get right."[30] It may also be why Kubrick distracted himself instead with other projects. But that hypothesis may again be moving too far into the unrepresentable, the "there" we can imagine only from here, as audience and readers. Whatever the original intention (in fact because of its notable absence in so many of Kubrick's films), the audience thus struggles to understand the meaning and emotions in the experience of his films, a quality with which Spielberg's audiences, for better or worse, do not struggle nearly as much. *AI* may stand as an extraordinarily suggestive post-*2001* instance of the type of authoritative narrators Kubrick embraced early in his career, as a way to transmit unambiguously the meanings of his stories to audiences (as in the *Paths of Glory* finale Spielberg so warmly embraced), and how much the late Kubrick, as filmmaker, differed from many of his contemporaries.

When Kubrick declared in 1966—putting the verbal intensities of *Dr. Strangelove* behind him and looking forward to the ambiguity of *2001*—that audiences respond to cinematic "direct experience" and not to abstractions (as mentioned at the beginning of chapter 5), he outlined a formal approach to filmmaking that the director would seem to embrace all the way to *Eyes Wide Shut*. Kubrick's films reveal a distrust toward narrative authority whose attempts at subjective order and meaning reify in the form of cinematic abstractions—voice-overs, expressionist montages, signifying music, and so forth. He may have likewise assumed audiences felt the same way (the interview suggests he does, anyway). Yet, for better or for worse, I suspect Spielberg was right about Kubrick's films, and equally important, Kubrick was wrong about abstractions. It seems as if Spielberg's films are routinely more successful, at least on initial release, because they embrace the same abstractions Kubrick felt audiences could not relate to, abstractions necessary to make films not "antithetical to the way audiences are accustomed to receiving" them. When he resists overt meaning, such as in *Munich* (2005), the film bombs. *AI*'s commercial failure, meanwhile, spoke as much to the "train wreck"[31] of styles at work—to Spielberg's attempts to impose abstractions on top of Kubrick's initial idea for a story—as to Spielberg's style in and of itself. The marquee attraction of Kubrick and Spielberg may have spelled a big opening weekend, but the film fizzled quickly afterward. Indeed, what does *AI* mean?

Whatever their merits overall, Spielberg's films have often foregrounded the facade, the aspiration to clearly identify the emotional importance of events in the diegesis and to impose explicit meaning in those moments. To bring everything to the surface. The divergent levels of success point toward the possibility that forms of overt narrations and mapping are important to audiences in our current historical moment—that perhaps the cinematic events cannot, today, stand alone. *2001, A Clockwork Orange*, and *The Shining* highlight these cinematic abstractions as instances approximating the country of the mind, but only as a means to criticize the solitary, asocial nature of the protagonists, those who embraced a need for absolute narrative authority instead of narrative resignation and the need for interaction with other characters—that is to say, competing narrators. *Barry Lyndon* and *Eyes Wide Shut* attempt to resist these abstractions entirely, with the result that audiences could not easily receive each film's version of cinematic "direct experience"— that attempt to reach unobstructed and unfiltered the possibilities of the story world. As Martin Scorsese and Mario Falsetto note, mostly all of Kubrick's films were initially misunderstood. Audiences and critics, however, subsequently became more receptive to his films, including *Eyes Wide Shut*, because they moved beyond the need for, as Michel Chion states, the "narrative scaffolding" that overtly pieced events of the film together through various levels of narrative. Of course, my research here has been its own form of *scaffolding*, its own facade, hoping to suspend and sustain for others the cinematic instances I thought I experienced. As fans, critics, and scholars begin to travel back there, into the films of Stanley Kubrick, they might instead start to embrace the possible visions offered through the country of their own minds as a way to impose order and meaning on his films. Or, equally effective, they may wish to negate these maps entirely, instead opening themselves up to the affective possibilities of those cinematic moments—as a way to move beyond the facades and begin (re)experiencing the films of Stanley Kubrick.

In that way, then, Kubrick may have actually been right about direct experience. Audiences still reacted, but through the body and not so much through the mind. It could just be that audiences were consciously unaware of how the films were affecting them or of how they were reacting. And perhaps the respect for Kubrick's films will be amplified with time because some audiences (myself included) slowly but surely become increasingly aware of how they felt when they saw the film in question. I didn't think much when I first saw *Eyes Wide Shut*, but I sure did feel something. And if the abstractions didn't convey the meaning explicitly, some then assumed there was no meaning. In fact, the opposite may just as easily hold true. It may be that we first consider only what the mind was telling us (nothing) instead of surrendering to the possibilities of an experience we were only feeling. Perhaps Kubrick's films aren't antithetical to how audiences receive them, after all— only antithetical to how we think about them. That's my sense of it, anyway.

NOTES

1. Keith Uhlich, "Stanley Kubrick," *Senses of Cinema*, at www.sensesofcinema.com/contents/directors/02/kubrick.html (accessed 7 January 2006).

2. Brian Massumi, *Parables for the Virtual: Movement, Affect, Sensation* (Durham, N.C.: Duke University Press, 2002), 213.

3. Spielberg's quote comes from an interview with the director on the 2000 DVD edition of *Eyes Wide Shut*.

4. In this respect, however, Spielberg may be evolving, and it would be unfair of me not to make note of it. His most recent film at the time of this writing, *Munich*, might be his best film in ten years, in no small part because I get the feeling he is deliberately trying to resist his own tendencies to overload his films with explicit meaning. There are many speeches in the film, of course, about the Israeli/Palestinian conflict, but the film always seems to be keeping them at a distance rather than aligning overtly with them. It is a wonderfully ambiguous film in the best sense of the word—it seems to recognize the frequent hollowness of various types of mindless intensities.

5. Tim Kreider, "*AI: Artificial Intelligence*," *Film Quarterly* 56, no. 2 (Winter 2002/2003): 32.

6. Kreider, "*AI: Artificial Intelligence*," 32.

7. Kreider, "*AI: Artificial Intelligence*," 32.

8. The two filmmakers did not actually work together on the project, though they did both work on the film's preproduction history at one time or another and often exchanged ideas on the project. According to the original 2001 studio press release, Kubrick purchased the rights to Brian Aldiss's short story, "Supertoys Last All Summer Long," in the early 1980s, consulting with Spielberg regularly—via faxes and phone calls—for advice on the project. In the 1990s, John Baxter recounts how Kubrick spent a great deal of time with Aldiss, attempting to develop a screenplay to little success, and then "decided to try other writers," including *2001* author Arthur Clarke, who, "as for working with Kubrick again . . .," he told Aldiss later, "[Kubrick] hasn't got that much money." *Stanley Kubrick: A Biography* (New York: Carroll & Graf, 1997), 357. By 1991, Kubrick had reportedly "abandoned [*AI*] . . . after two years of research," but in 1993, Warner Bros. announced it to be Kubrick's next project, supposedly because *Jurassic Park*'s "recent breakthroughs in computer and digital imaging . . . rekindled Kubrick's interest in the venture." Vincent LoBrutto, *Stanley Kubrick: A Biography* (New York: Fine, 1997), 498. Then, in 1995, Warner Bros. announced without warning that *Eyes Wide Shut* would in fact be Kubrick's next film, followed by *AI*, without any explicit acknowledgment of why the change was made

other than to suggest that the sci-fi epic's ambition as "one of the most technically challenging and innovative special effects films yet attempted" may have unexpectedly pushed back production (as quoted in LoBrutto, *A Biography*, 500).

On the other hand, Kubrick may well have ultimately lost interest in the project. According to the press release, Kubrick told Spielberg that the younger filmmaker would be better suited to direct the film, which was "closer to [Spielberg's] sensibility than [Kubrick's]." As stated by biographer Baxter, Kubrick's desire to do *AI* was initially spurred on by the success of Spielberg's *E.T.* (a film that Aldiss did not like nearly as much as Kubrick did), which echoed the possibilities of *AI* as also being a "sentimental, dreamlike . . . fable." *A Biography*, 355. The Kubrick biographies did not spend much time highlighting Kubrick's friendship with Spielberg and were printed before *AI* actually went into production. Whatever the ultimate bridge between the two filmmakers, Spielberg did not take over the project until after Kubrick's death, spurred on, according to the press release, by Harlan and Christiane Kubrick's pitch to Warner Bros. chief Terry Semel that *AI* be revived "with Spielberg at the helm." Eventually, Spielberg began writing the script himself, his first since 1977's *Close Encounters of the Third Kind*.

Perhaps the most interesting rumor about Kubrick's participation in the making of *AI* involves the following anecdote:

> Early in 1996, the rumour page on one Kubrick site on the Internet recorded: 'Kubrick has been filming two months of *AI* every five years. He's using a young actor and filming his progress as he grows older. So far Kubrick has filmed four months/ten years.' (Baxter, *A Biography*, 359)

There appears to be no evidence, however, to support that anecdote, as bizarre and intriguing as it may be.

9. James Naremore and Adrian Martin, "The Future of Academic Film Study," in *Movie Mutations*, ed. Adrian Martin and Jonathan Rosenbaum (London: British Film Institute, 2003), 131.

10. I label *AI* as "Spielberg's *AI*" not as part of the usual obligatory acknowledgment of the director's possession that is common among critical references to films but instead to explicitly foreground the 2001 sci-fi epic as specifically being the creative final product of Steven Spielberg himself. While I believe that Kubrick played a large enough role in the preproduction history of *AI* to warrant this critical look, I do not wish to suggest that *AI* is somehow, even if symbolically, Kubrick's final film. I tackle *AI* briefly only as a way to offer a fresh perspective on Kubrick's body of work from a previously unexplored point of view, not as a misguided attempt to appropriate Spielberg's achievement (which I believe to be critically underestimated) as really being that of Kubrick's. At best, Kubrick informs *AI* affectively (or vice versa)—that is, we can sense his presence. There may be something about the film that compels us to consider Kubrick. But *AI* is ultimately Steven Spielberg's.

11. James Naremore, "Love and Death in *AI: Artificial Intelligence*," *Michigan Quarterly Review* 94, no. 2 (Spring 2005): 266–67.

12. In addition to the scattered attention paid by biographers and scholars, Gregory Feeley wrote an entire essay around the time of *Eyes Wide Shut*'s initial release, detailing the projects Kubrick never finished, including the since realized *AI*. "The Masterpiece a

Master Couldn't Get Right," *New York Times*, 18 July 1999, 2.9. Kubrick, of course, had other projects besides the sci-fi epic. *Aryan Papers*, based on Louis Begley's novel *Wartime Lies*, was the name of the Holocaust film Kubrick worked on during the early 1990s that "afforded Kubrick the opportunity to tell the story in narration, while showing the World War II terror through [a] boy's eyes." LoBrutto, *A Biography*, 497. According to LoBrutto, *Aryan Papers* was shelved because of Kubrick's newfound interest in *AI*, which would become his next project (before he finally decided on *Eyes Wide Shut*); however, both LoBrutto and Baxter specifically posit the competition from Spielberg's *Schindler's List* as a possible reason for the project's collapse. "As Spielberg's production gained pace, and it became clear that it would open by Christmas 1993, Kubrick's interest in *Aryan Papers* waned" (Baxter, *A Biography*, 361), although LoBrutto also argues that this theory seems "unlikely since Kubrick made *Full Metal Jacket* after several major Vietnam releases, and his directorial vision on a project has never mirrored any other" (499). When *Full Metal Jacket* was originally conceived, though, only *Apocalypse Now* and *The Deer Hunter* had been made, and the film took more time than anticipated to make, finally debuting several years after originally planned. So, by the time Kubrick was aware of the rash of competing Vietnam films in the mid-1980s—*Platoon, Hamburger Hill*, and so forth—he was already well into actual production.

Napoleon, meanwhile, is perhaps Kubrick's most famous lost project, something he reportedly wanted to do after the groundbreaking success of *2001*. Thomas Allen Nelson, Baxter, and LoBrutto spend considerable time mentioning this labor of love—"Napoleon was a man after Kubrick's own rational heart" (Baxter, *A Biography*, 236)—which supposedly fell apart only because the lavish, big-budget spectacle proved to be too financially risky for studios to back, even then at the height of Kubrick's commercial success, having just completed *Lolita, Dr. Strangelove*, and *2001*. Beyond those financial concerns inherent with any massive epic, added Baxter, "the cinema, having largely ignored Napoleon for three decades, suddenly began to take interest. . . . None of these [other four] films made money, however, and the chances of anyone funding Kubrick's epic became even more remote. He turned his mind to other more realistic projects," presumably, *A Clockwork Orange* (240). In November of 2003, however, Jan Harlan, Kubrick's brother-in-law and business partner, announced that Kubrick's plan for the Napoleon project would be published through Warner Bros. books, with the hope that it may one day be made into a feature-length production.

Perhaps, most bizarrely, according to Baxter, Kubrick was also at one time connected to a big-budget pornographic film in the 1960s, a project introduced to him by *Dr. Strangelove*'s screenwriter, Terry Southern. *Blue Movie*, based on Southern's novel of the same name, detailed "the attempt of top arthouse director Boris Adrian to make *The Faces of Love*, Hollywood's first big-budget porn film, with stars visibly indulging in full penetrative sex, without doubles" (195). Baxter claims that Kubrick decided against the project because "he had neither the temperament for porn nor the patience to subjugate his invention to the rigid demands of erotic ritual," something that, interestingly, did not appear to be a problem for the orgy sequence in *Eyes Wide Shut* (195). Fellow biographer LoBrutto also mentions *Blue Movie* but offers a more amusing reason for Kubrick's ultimate rejection—"while he was reading the book, Christiane [his wife] picked it up and, after perusing the pages, said to her husband, 'Stanley, if you ever do this I'll never speak to you again'" (329–30).

13. Todd McCarthy, "*AI*: Mecha Movie Is Mega Mind-Blower," *Variety*, 8 July 2001, 19.

14. Christopher Sharrett, "Spielberg the Serious," *USA Today*, September 2001, 67.

15. Joe Morgenstern, "Artifice over *Intelligence*," *Wall Street Journal*, 29 June 2001, W1.

16. Lucius Shepard, "Films," *Fantasy & Science Fiction* 101, no. 6 (December 2001): 112.

17. Peter Travers, "*AI/Artificial Intelligence*," *Rolling Stone*, 19 July 2001, 54.

18. Richard Corliss, "*AI*: Spielberg's Strange Love," *Time*, 25 June 2001, 61.

19. Rand Richards Cooper, "Pinocchio Redux," *Commonweal*, 17 August 2001, 20.

20. Philip Kerr, "Ghosts in the Machine," *New Statesman*, 10 September 2001, 45.

21. A. O. Scott, "Spielberg's Pathos," *New York Times*, 23 December 2001, 2.13.

22. Joe Fordham, "Mecha Odyssey," *Cinefex: The Journal of Cinematic Illusions* 87 (October 2001): 93.

23. As quoted in Corliss, "Spielberg's Strange Love," 61.

24. David Ansen, "Mr. Spielberg Strikes Again," *Newsweek*, 25 June 2001, 84.

25. Taking that logic to the extreme, one could then posit that Kubrick's copy of *AI* is just as valid as Spielberg's. But I won't do that here.

26. As quoted in the film's original press release.

27. As quoted in Fordham, "Mecha Odyssey," 93.

28. Also facilitating the audience's reception of the story events in *AI* is John Williams's prominent musical score. Recalling the emotional manipulation of Gerald Fried's scores in *Fear and Desire*, *Killer's Kiss*, *The Killing*, and *Paths of Glory* (as well as Alex North's score in *Spartacus*), Williams's score serves as a reinforcement of an overt narrative authority in *AI*. In an article from the *New York Times*, Franz Lidz and Steve Rushdin quote filmmaker Lloyd Kaufman, who supposedly regards *AI* as "emotional pornography," as referring to Williams's work as "soaring, boring scoring." "How to Tell a Bad Movie from a Truly Bad Movie," *New York Times*, 5 August 2001, 2.1.

In a more thoughtful review, Jack Sullivan praises the score as Williams's "most ambitious and varied score since *Close Encounters of the Third Kind*," with a "melancholy sparseness," though he also points out that "my only complaint is the schmaltzy vocal style of . . . 'For Always,' which momentarily upsets the delicate balance between starkness and childlike warmth." "Williams: *AI*," *American Recording Guide* 64, no. 6 (November/December 2001), 212. The mere fact that Williams's score complements the events of *AI*, pointing out both the "starkness" and the "childlike warmth" of the film, suggests the signifying music of Kubrick's earlier films more so than later ones, which avoided a continuous nondiegetic score. Perhaps this is best highlighted by Kubrick's decision to remove North's score from *2001*, the Kubrick film *AI* most echoes.

29. Kerr, "Ghosts in the Machine," 45.

30. Feeley, "The Masterpiece," 2.9.

31. Patrick Goldstein of the *Los Angeles Times*, as quoted in Braden Philips, "*AI* Submerged in Awards Season Hoopla," *Variety*, 17 December 2001, 16.

Filmography

Day of the Fight (1951) (16 minutes)

CAST

Douglas Edwards	Narrator
Walter Cartier	Himself
Vincent Cartier	Himself
Nate Fleischer	Himself

CREW

Director/Photography/Sound	Stanley Kubrick
Writer	Robert Rein
Editing	Julian Bergman
Original Music	Gerald Fried
Distributor	RKO Radio

The Flying Padre (1951) (9 minutes)

CAST

Bob Hite	Narrator
Fred Stadmueller	Himself

CREW

Director/Photography/Editor/Sound	Stanley Kubrick
Producer	Burton Benjamin
Editing	Isaac Kleinerman

Original Music . . . . Nathaniel Shilkret
Sound . . . . Harold R. Vivian
Distributor . . . . RKO Radio

The Seafarers (1953) (30 minutes)

CAST

Don Hollenbeck . . . . Narrator

CREW

Director/Photography/Editor . . . . Stanley Kubrick
Producer . . . . Lester Cooper
Writer . . . . Will Chasen

FEATURE-LENGTH FILMS

Fear and Desire (1953) (68 minutes)

Stanley Kubrick Productions

CAST

Frank Silvera . . . . Sgt. Mac
Kenneth Harp . . . . Lt. Corby/Enemy General
Virginia Leith . . . . The Girl
Paul Mazursky . . . . Pvt. Sidney
Steve Coit . . . . Pvt. Fletcher
David Allen . . . . Narrator

CREW

Director/Photography/Editor/Producer . . . . Stanley Kubrick
Associate Producer . . . . Martin Perveler
Production Director . . . . Bob Dierks
Writer . . . . Howard O. Sackler
Direction Assistant . . . . Steve Hahn
Dialogue Director . . . . Toba Kubrick
Art Direction . . . . Herbert Lebowitz
Makeup Artist . . . . Chet Fabian

Music . . . . Gerald Fried
Distributor . . . . Joseph Burstyn

Killer's Kiss (1955) (64 minutes)
Minotaur Productions

CAST

Jamie Smith . . . . Davy Gordon
Irene Kane . . . . Gloria Price
Frank Silvera . . . . Vincent Rapallo
Jerry Jarret . . . . Albert
Ruth Sobotka . . . . Iris

CREW

Producers . . . . Stanley Kubrick, Morris Bousel
Director/Photography/Editor . . . . Stanley Kubrick
Writers . . . . Stanley Kubrick, Howard O. Sackler
Assistant Director . . . . Ernest Nukanen
Music . . . . Gerald Fried
Production Manager . . . . Ira Marvin
Assistant Editors . . . . Anthony Bezich, Pat Jaffe
Choreographer . . . . David Vaughan
Distributor . . . . United Artists

The Killing (1956) (83 minutes)
Harris-Kubrick Productions

CAST

Sterling Hayden . . . . Johnny Clay
Elisha Cook Jr. . . . . George Peatty
Marie Windsor . . . . Sherry Peatty
Jay C. Flippen . . . . Marvin Unger
Coleen Gray . . . . Fay
Vince Edwards . . . . Val Cannon
Joseph Turkel . . . . Tiny
Ted de Corsia . . . . Randy Kennan

Joe Sawyer . . . . Mike O'Reilly
Tim Carey . . . . Nikki
Kola Kwariani . . . . Maurice
James Edwards . . . . Track Parking Attendant
Jay Adler . . . . Leo

CREW

Producer . . . . James B. Harris
Writer/Director . . . . Stanley Kubrick
(adapted from the novel *Clean Break* by Lionel White)
Additional Dialogue . . . . Jim Thompson
Cinematography . . . . Lucien Ballard
Editor . . . . Betty Steinberg
Art Direction . . . . Ruth Sobotka Kubrick
Set Design . . . . Harry Reif
Costume Design . . . . Beaumelle
Music . . . . Gerald Fried
Sound Effects Editor . . . . Rex Lipton
Sound . . . . Earl Snyder
Special Effects . . . . David Koehler
Distributor . . . . United Artists

Paths of Glory (1957) (86 minutes)

Harris-Kubrick Productions

CAST

Kirk Douglas . . . . Col. Dax
Ralph Meeker . . . . Cpl. Paris
Adolphe Menjou . . . . Gen. Broulard
George Macready . . . . Gen. Mireau
Wayne Morris . . . . Lt. Roget
Richard Anderson . . . . Maj. Saint-Auban
Joseph Turkel . . . . Pvt. Arnaud
Timothy Carey . . . . Pvt. Ferol
Peter Capel . . . . Narrator/Colonel Judge
Susanne Christian . . . . German Girl
Bert Freed . . . . Sgt. Boulanger
Emile Meyer . . . . Priest

John Stein . . . . Cpt. Rousseau
Ken Dibbs . . . . Pvt. Lejeune
Jerry Hausner . . . . Café Owner
Harold Benedict . . . . Captain Nichols

CREW

Producer . . . . James B. Harris
Director . . . . Stanley Kubrick
Writers . . . . Stanley Kubrick, Calder Willingham, Jim Thompson
(adapted from the novel by Humphrey Cobb)
Cinematography . . . . George Krause
Editing . . . . Eva Kroll
Assistant Editor . . . . Helene Fischer
Costume Design . . . . Ilse Dubois
Art Direction . . . . Ludwig Reiber
Music . . . . Gerald Fried
Special Effects . . . . Erwin Lange
Sound . . . . Martin Müller
Distributor . . . . United Artists, Byrna Productions

Spartacus (1960) (196 minutes)

Byrna Productions

CAST

Kirk Douglas . . . . Spartacus
Laurence Olivier . . . . Marcus Crassus
Jean Simmons . . . . Varinia
Charles Laughton . . . . Gracchus
Peter Ustinov . . . . Batiatus
John Gavin . . . . Julius Caesar
Tony Curtis . . . . Antoninus
Nina Foch . . . . Helena
Herbert Lom . . . . Tigranes Levantus
John Ireland . . . . Crixus
John Dall . . . . Marcus Glabrus
Charles McGraw . . . . Marcellus
Joanna Barnes . . . . Claudia
Harold J. Stone . . . . David

Woody Strode . . . . Draba
Peter Brocco . . . . Ramon
Paul Lambert . . . . Gannicus
Robert J. Wilke . . . . Captain of Guard
Nicholas Dennis . . . . Dionysius

CREW

Executive Producer . . . . Kirk Douglas
Producer . . . . Edward Lewis
Directors . . . . Anthony Mann, Stanley Kubrick
Writer . . . . . . Dalton Trumbo (adapted from the book by Howard Fast)
Cinematography . . . . Russell Metty
Additional Photography . . . . Clifford Stine
Assistant Directors . . Marshall Green, Joseph E. Kenney, Foster Phinney
Editor . . . . Robert Lawrence
Assistant Film Editors . . . . Robert Schultz, Fred Chulack
Music . . . . Alex North
Costume Design . . . . Valles
Wardrobe . . . . Ditta Peruzzi
Miss Simmons's Costumes . . . . Bill Thomas
Production Design . . . . Alexander Golitzen
Art Direction . . . . Eric Orbom
Set Decoration . . . . Russell A. Gausman, Julia Heron
Title Design Consultant . . . . Saul Bass
Historical and Technical Advisor . . . . Vittorio Nino Novarese
Music Director . . . . Joseph Gershenson
Music Editor . . . . Arnold Schwarzwald
Sound . . . . Joe Lapis, Waldo O. Watson, Ronald Pierce, Murray Spivack
Distributor . . . . Universal Pictures

Lolita (1962) (153 minutes)
Seven Arts/Anya/Transworld

CAST

James Mason . . . . Humbert Humbert/Narrator
Sue Lyon . . . . Lolita Haze
Peter Sellers . . . . Clare Quilty
Shelley Winters . . . . Charlotte Haze

Diana Decker .... Jean Farlow
Jerry Stovin .... John Farlow
Suzanne Gibbs .... Mona Farlow
Gary Cockrell .... Dick Schiller
Marianne Stone .... Vivian Darkbloom
Cec Linder .... Dr. Keegee
Lois Maxwell .... Nurse Mary Lore
William Greene .... Mr. Swine
Maxine Holden .... Ms. Fromkiss
James Dyrenforth .... Mr. Beale
Roberta Shore .... Lorna
Colin Maitland .... Charlie Holmes
Marion Mathie .... Miss Lebone
John Harrison .... Tom

CREW

Producer .... James B. Harris
Director .... Stanley Kubrick
Writer .... Vladimir Nabokov (adapted from his own novel)
Cinematography .... Oswald Morris
Assistant Directors .... Roy Millichip, John Danischewsky
Editor .... Anthony Harvey
Art Direction .... Bill Andrews
Costume Design .... Gene Coffin
Set Design .... Andrew Low, Peter James
Makeup Artist .... George Partleton
Original Music .... Nelson Riddle, Tom Adair, Bob Harris
Sound Recordists .... H. L. Bird, Len Shilton
Distributor .... Metro-Goldwyn-Mayer

Dr. Strangelove or: How I Learned to Stop Worrying and Love the Bomb (1964) (94 minutes)

Hawk Films

CAST

Peter Sellers .... Group Capt. Lionel Mandrake,
                        President Merkin Muffley, Dr. Strangelove
George C. Scott .... General "Buck" Turgidson

Sterling Hayden . . . . General Jack D. Ripper
Keenan Wynn . . . . Col. "Bat" Guano
Slim Pickens . . . . Maj. "King" Kong
Peter Bull . . . . Russian Ambassador Alexi de Sadesky
Tracy Reed . . . . Miss Scott
James Earl Jones . . . . Lt. Lothar Zogg
Glen Beck . . . . Lt. W. D. Kivel
Shane Rimmer . . . . Capt. G. A. "Ace" Owens
Jack Creley . . . . Mr. Staines
Frank Berry . . . . Lt. H. R. Dietrich

CREW

Producer/Director . . . . Stanley Kubrick
Associate Producer . . . . Victor Lyndon
Writers . . . . Stanley Kubrick, Terry Southern, Peter George
(adapted from the novel *Red Alert* by Peter George)
Cinematography . . . . Gilbert Taylor
Editor . . . . Anthony Harvey
Assistant Editor . . . . Ray Lovejoy
Production Design . . . . Ken Adam
Art Direction . . . . Peter Murton
Makeup Artist . . . . Stewart Freeborn
Special Effects . . . . Wally Veevers
Original Music . . . . Laurie Johnson
Technical Advisor . . . . Capt. John Crewdson
Sound . . . . John Cox
Distributor . . . . Columbia Pictures

2001: A Space Odyssey (1968) (141 minutes)
Metro-Goldwyn-Mayer

CAST

Keir Dullea . . . . David Bowman
Douglas Rain . . . . HAL
Gary Lockwood . . . . Frank Poole
William Sylvester . . . . Dr. Heywood Floyd
Daniel Richter . . . . Moon-Watcher
Leonard Rossiter . . . . Dr. Andrei Smyslov

Margaret Tyzack .... Elena
Robert Beatty .... Dr. Ralph Halvorsen
Sean Sullivan .... Dr. Bill Michaels
Frank Miller .... Mission Controller

CREW

Producer .... Stanley Kubrick
Director .... Stanley Kubrick
Writers .... Stanley Kubrick, Arthur C. Clarke
(adapted from Clarke's short story "The Sentinel")
Cinematography .... Geoffrey Unsworth
Additional Photography .... John Alcott
Editor .... Ray Lovejoy
Special Photographic Effects Supervisors .... Wally Veevers,
Douglas Trumbull, Con Pederson, Tom Howard
Special Photographic Effects .... Colin J. Cantwell, Bryan Loftus,
Bruce Logan, John Jack Malick, Frederick Martin, Donald Osborne
Production Design .... Tony Masters, Harry Lange, Ernie Archer
Art Direction .... John Hoesli
Set Decoration .... Robert Cartwright
Makeup Artist .... Stuart Freeborn
Nonoriginal Music .... Richard Strauss, Johann Strauss,
Aram Khachaturyan, György Ligeti
Wardrobes .... Hardy Amies
Sound Mixer .... H. L. Bird
Sound Editing .... Winston Ryder
Distributor .... Metro-Goldwyn-Mayer

A Clockwork Orange (1971) (137 minutes)
Warner Bros./Hawk Films

CAST

Malcolm McDowell .... Alex
Patrick Magee .... Mr. Alexander
Michael Bates .... Chief Guard
Warren Clark .... Dim
James Marcus .... Georgie
Michael Tarn .... Pete

John Clive . . . . Stage Actor
Adrienne Corri . . . . Mrs. Alexander
Carl Duering . . . . Dr. Brodsky
Paul Farrell . . . . Tramp
Clive Francis . . . . Joe
Michael Gover . . . . Prison Governor
Miriam Karlin . . . . Miss Weathers
Aubrey Morris . . . . Mr. P. R. Deltoid
Godfrey Quigley . . . . Prison Chaplain
Philip Stone . . . . Dad
Sheila Raynor . . . . Mum
Madge Ryan . . . . Dr. Branom
John Savident . . . . Conspirator
David Prowse . . . . Julian
Anthony Sharp . . . . Minister of the Interior
Pauline Taylor . . . . Dr. Taylor
Margaret Tyzack . . . . Conspirator
Steven Berkoff . . . . Constable
Lindsay Campbell . . . . Inspector
Carol Drinkwater . . . . Nurse Feeley

CREW

Producer/Director . . . . Stanley Kubrick
Executive Producers . . . . Max L. Raab, Si Litvinoff
Associate Producer . . . . Bernard Williams
Assistant to Producer . . . . Jan Harlan
Writer . . . Stanley Kubrick (adapted from the novel by Anthony Burgess)
Cinematography . . . . John Alcott
Editor . . . . Bill Butler
Assistant Editor . . . . David Beesley
Production Design . . . . John Barry
Art Direction . . . . Russell Hagg, Peter Sheilds
Nonoriginal Music . . . . Ludwig van Beethoven, Edward Elgar,
       Gioacchino Rossini, Henry Purcell, Nacio Herb Brown,
       Nikolai Rimsky-Korsakov
Original Electronic Music . . . . Walter Carlos
Costumes . . . . Milena Canonero
Makeup Artists . . . . . Barbara Daly, George Partleton, Fred Williamson
Paintings and Sculptures . . . . . . Herman Makkink, Cornelius Makkink,
       Liz Moore, Christiane Kubrick

Production Assistant . . . . Andros Epaminondas
Sound Editor . . . . Brian Blamey
Distributor . . . . Warner Bros.

Barry Lyndon (1975) (185 minutes)

Warner Bros./Hawk Films

CAST

Ryan O'Neal . . . . Barry Lyndon
Marisa Berenson . . . . Lady Lyndon
Patrick Magee . . . . The Chevalier de Balibari
Hardy Kruger . . . . Capt. Potzdorf
Michael Hordern . . . . The Narrator
Marie Kean . . . . Mrs. Barry
Steven Berkoff . . . . Lord Ludd
Gay Hamilton . . . . Nora Brady
Leon Vitali . . . . Lord Bullington
Diane Koerner . . . . Lischen
Murray Melvin . . . . Reverend Runt
Godfrey Quigley . . . . Capt. Grogan
Leonard Rossiter . . . . Capt. John Quinn
Frank Middlemass . . . . Sir Charles Lyndon
Andre Morell . . . . Lord Gustavos Adolphus Wendover
Arthur O'Sullivan . . . . Capt. Feeny
Philip Stone . . . . Graham

CREW

Producer/Director . . . . Stanley Kubrick
Executive Producer . . . . Jan Harlan
Associate Producer . . . . Bernard Williams
Writer . . . . Stanley Kubrick (adapted from the novel
by William Makepeace Thackeray)
Cinematography . . . . John Alcott
Film Editing . . . . Tony Lawson
Production Design . . . . Ken Adam
Art Direction . . . . Roy Walker
Casting . . . . James Liggat

Nonoriginal Music . . . . . . J. S. Bach, Frederick the Great, G. F. Handel,
    W. A. Mozart, Giovanni Paisiello, Franz Schubert, Antonio Vivaldi
Music Adaptation . . . . Leonard Rosenman
Original Music . . . . The Chieftains
Costumes . . . . Ulla-Britt Söderlund, Milena Canonero
Makeup Artists . . . . Alan Boyle, Ann Brodie, Jill Carpenter,
    Yvonne Coppard, Barbara Daly
Sound Editing . . . . Rodney Holland
Assistant Sound Editor . . . . George Akers
Assistant Director . . . . Brian Cook
Distributor . . . . Warner Bros.

The Shining (1980) (145 minutes)

Warner Bros./Hawk Films

CAST

Jack Nicholson . . . . Jack Torrance
Shelley Duvall . . . . Wendy Torrance
Danny Lloyd . . . . Danny Torrance
Scatman Crothers . . . . Dick Hallorann
Barry Nelson . . . . Stuart Ullman
Philip Stone . . . . Delbert Grady
Joe Turkel . . . . Lloyd, the Bartender
Anne Jackson . . . . Doctor
Tony Burton . . . . Larry Durkin
Lia Beldam . . . . Young Woman in Bath
Billie Gibson . . . . Old Woman in Bath
Barry Dennen . . . . Bill Watson
David Baxt . . . . Forest Ranger #1
Manning Redwood . . . . Forest Ranger #2
Lisa Burns . . . . Grady daughter
Louise Burns . . . . Grady daughter
Alison Coleridge . . . . Suzie, Ullman's Secretary
Jana Sheldon . . . . Stewardess
Kate Phelps . . . . Receptionist
Norman Gay . . . . Injured Guest

CREW

Associate Producers (The Producer Circle Company) . . . . . Robert Fryer,
    Martin Richards, Mary Lea Johnson

Producer/Director . . . . Stanley Kubrick
Executive Producer . . . . Jan Harlan
Writers . . . . Stanley Kubrick, Diane Johnson
(adapted from the novel by Stephen King)
Cinematography . . . . John Alcott
Steadicam Operators . . . . Garrett Brown, Ray Andrew
Editing . . . . Ray Lovejoy
Production Design . . . . Roy Walker
Nonoriginal Music . . . . Béla Bartók, György Ligeti, Krzystof Penderecki
Original Music . . . . Wendy Carlos, Rachel Elkin
Art Direction . . . . Les Tomkins
Costume Design . . . . Milena Canonero
Assistant Directors . . . . Brian Cook, Terry Needham, Michael Stevenson
Assistant to Producer . . . . Andros Epaminondas
Personal Assistant to Director . . . . Leon Vitali
Distributor . . . . Warner Bros.

Full Metal Jacket (1987) (117 minutes)

Warner Bros.

CAST

Matthew Modine . . . . Pvt. Joker/J. T. Davis
R. Lee Ermey . . . . Gun. Sgt. Hartman
Vincent D'Onofrio . . . . Pvt. Gomer Pyle/Leonard Lawrence
Adam Baldwin . . . . Animal Mother
Dorian Harewood . . . . Eightball
Kevyn Major Howard . . . . Rafterman
Arliss Howard . . . . Pvt. Cowboy
Ed O'Ross . . . . Lt. Touchdown/Walter J. Schinoski
John Terry . . . . Lt. Lockhart
Kieron Jecchinis . . . . Crazy Earl
Kirk Taylor . . . . Payback
Tim Colceri . . . . Doorgunner
John Stafford . . . . Doc Jay

CREW

Producer/Director . . . . Stanley Kubrick
Executive Producer . . . . Jan Harlan

Associate Producer . . . .   Michael Herr
Coproducer . . . .   Philip Hobbs
Line Producer . . . .   Bill Shephard
Writers . . . .   Stanley Kubrick, Michael Herr, Gustav Hasford
              (adapted from *The Short-Timers* by Gustav Hasford)
Cinematography . . . .   Douglas Milsome
Editing . . . .   Martin Hunter
Original Music . . . .   Abigail Mead
Nonoriginal Music . . . . Jeff Barry, Tom T. Hall, Lee Hazlewood,
              Mick Jagger, Keith Richards, Domingo Samudio
Production Design . . . .   Anton Furst
Casting . . . .   Leon Vitali
Art Direction . . . .   Keith Pain, Rod Stratford, Les Tomkins
Set Decoration . . . .   Barbara Drake
Costume Design . . . .   Keith Denny
Makeup Artists . . . .   Christine Allsopp, Jennifer Boost
Assistant to Director . . . .   Leon Vitali
Sound . . . .   Steve Bartlett
Sound Editors . . . .   Nigel Galt, Edward Tise
Special Effects Supervisor . . . .   John Evans
Assistant Sound Editors . . . .   Paul Conway, Peter Culverwell
Steadicam Operator . . . .   Jean-Marc Bringuier
Assistants to Producer . . . .   Emilio D'Alessandro, Anthony Frewin
Technical Advisor . . . .   R. Lee Ermey
Distributor . . . .   Warner Bros.

Eyes Wide Shut (1999) (159 minutes)

Warner Bros.

CAST

Tom Cruise . . . .   Dr. Bill Harford
Nicole Kidman . . . .   Alice Harford
Sydney Pollack . . . .   Victor Ziegler
Jackie Sawiris . . . .   Roz
Todd Field . . . .   Nick Nightingale
Peter Benson . . . .   Bandleader
Marie Richardson . . . .   Marion Nathanson
Rade Sherbedgia . . . .   Mr. Milich
Alan Cumming . . . .   Hotel Desk Clerk

Leelee Sobieski . . . . Milich's Daughter
Madison Eginton . . . . Helena Harford
Thomas Gibson . . . . Carl Thomas
Leslie Lowe . . . . Illona Ziegler
Brian W. Cook . . . . Tall Butler
Tres Hanley . . . . Coffee Shop Manager
Vinessa Shaw . . . . Domino
Fay Masterson . . . . Sally
Leon Vitale . . . . Red Cloak

CREW

Producer/Director . . . . Stanley Kubrick
Executive Producer . . . . Jan Harlan
Coproducer . . . . Brian W. Cook
Writers . . . . Stanley Kubrick, Frederic Raphael
        (adapted from the novel *Traumnovelle* by Arthur Schnitzler)
Editing . . . . Nigel Galt
Production Design . . . . Les Tomkins, Roy Walker
Set Decoration . . . . Lisa Leone, Terry Wells Sr.
Art Direction . . . . John Fenner
Casting . . . . Leon Vitali, Denise Chamian
Makeup Artists . . . . Robert McCann
Production Manager . . . . Margaret Adams
Costume Design . . . . Marit Allen
Assistant to the Director . . . . Leon Vitali
Supervising Sound Editor . . . . Paul Conway
Assistant Sound Editor . . . . Iain Eyre
Back Projection Supervisor . . . . Charles Staffell
Assistant Editor . . . . Claire Ferguson
Assistants to Stanley Kubrick . . . . Anthony Frewin, Emilio D'Alessandro
Distributor . . . . Warner Bros.

Artificial Intelligence: AI (2001) (146 minutes)
Dreamworks/Warner Bros.

CAST

Haley Joel Osment . . . . David
Frances O'Connor . . . . Monica Swinton

Jude Law . . . . Gigolo Joe
William Hurt . . . . Professor Hobby
Sam Robards . . . . Henry Swinton
Jake Thomas . . . . Martin Swinton
Ken Leung . . . . Syatyoo-Sama
Ashley Scott . . . . Gigolo Jane
Brendan Gleeson . . . . Lord Johnson-Johnson
Enrico Colantoni . . . . The Murderer
Robin Williams . . . . Dr. Know (voice)
Ben Kingsley . . . . Narrator/Mecha (voice)
Meryl Streep . . . . Blue Fairy (voice)

CREW

Director . . . . Steven Spielberg
Producers . . . . Bonnie Curtis, Kathleen Kennedy, Steven Spielberg
Executive Producers . . . . Jan Harlan, Walter F. Parkes
Writer . . . . Steven Spielberg (adapted from the short story
                "Supertoys Last All Summer Long" by Brian Aldiss)
Screen Story . . . . Ian Watson
Cinematography . . . . Janusz Kaminski
Film Editing . . . . Michael Kahn
Production Design . . . . Rick Carter
Art Direction . . . . . . Richard Johnson, Jim Teegarden, Thomas Valentine
Casting . . . . Avy Kaufman
Original Music . . . . John Williams
Nonoriginal Music . . . . . . Irving Berlin, Frank Loesser, Henri Salvador,
                Richard Strauss, Harry Warren
Costumes . . . . Bob Ringwood
Set Decoration . . . . Nancy Haigh
Makeup Artists . . . . Richard Alonzo, Bill Corso, Jene Fielder,
    Mark Garbarino, Kevin Haney, Joel Harlow, William Huff, Patty Miller,
Kenny Meyers, Greg Nelson, Douglas Noe, Joni Powell, Margaret Prentice,
                Sandra Rowden, Richard Snell, June Westmore
First Assistant Director . . . . Sergio Mimica-Gezzan
Assistant Art Directors . . . . Ramsey Avery, Liz Lapp, Andrew Menzies,
                Harry Otto, Patrick Sullivan, Susan Wexler
Set Designers . . . . Dawn Brown Manser, Pamela Klamer,
    Masako Masuda, Richard Mays, Thomas Minton, Steven Schwartz,
                Easton Smith, Patte Strong-Lord, Darrell L. Wight
Storyboard Artists . . . . Phil Keller, Peter Ramsey

Sound Effects Editors . Kyrsten Comoglio, Terry Eckton, Chris Scarabosio
Supervising Sound Editors . . . . Richard Hymns, Gary Rydstrom
Robot Characters Design . . . . Stan Winston Studio
Special Visual Effects and Animation . . . . Industrial Light & Magic
Special Effects Supervisor . . . . Michael Lantieri
Special Effects . . . . Robert DeVine
Special Effects Technicians . . . . Thomas Brown, Greg Bryant,
   Richard Cory, Kim Derry, Chris Eubank, John Fleming, Keith Haynes,
   Robert Johnston, Jay B. King, Jeffrey Knott, Jimmy Mena, Joel Mitchell,
   Ralph Peterson, James Rollins, Thomas Rush, Agustin Toral, Steven Scott
                                      Wheatley, Larry Zelenay
Visual Effects Supervisors . . . . Scott Farrer, Dennis Muren
Stunt Coordinator . . . . Doug Coleman
Distributor . . . . DreamWorks, Warner Bros.

Selected Bibliography

Agel, Jerome, ed. *The Making of Kubrick's* 2001. New York: Signet, 1970.

Alleva, Richard. "Final Curtain." *Commonweal*, 10 September 1999, 22–23.

Ansen, David. "Mr. Spielberg Strikes Again." *Newsweek*, 25 June 2001, 84.

Argent, Daniel. "Steven Spielberg as Writer: From *Close Encounters of the Third Kind* to *AI*" *Creative Screenwriting* 8, no. 3 (May/June 2001): 49–53.

Barlow, Arthur H. *The Films of Stanley Kubrick: A Study in Generative Aesthetics.* PhD dissertation, Penn State University, 1996.

Baxter, John. *Stanley Kubrick: A Biography.* New York: Carroll & Graf, 1997.

Bernstein, Jeremy. "How about a Little Game?" *The New Yorker*, 12 November 1966, 70–110.

Bier, Jesse. "Cobb and Kubrick: Author and *Auteur*." *Virginia Quarterly Review* 61 (1985): 453–71.

Bizony, Piers. *2001: Filming the Future.* London: Aurum, 1994.

Bogdanovich, Peter. "What They Say about Stanley Kubrick." *New York Times Magazine*, 4 July 1999, 1–22.

Boyd, David. "Mode and Meaning in *2001*." *Journal of Popular Film and Television* 6, no. 3 (1978): 202–15.

Branigan, Edward. *Narrative Comprehension and Film.* New York: Routledge, 1992.

Brown, John. "The Impossible Object: Reflections on *The Shining.*" In *Cinema and Fiction: New Modes of Adapting, 1950–1990*, edited by John Orr and Colin Nicholson, 104–21. Edinburgh: Edinburgh University Press, 1992.

Burgoyne, Robert. "Narrative Overture & Closure in *2001: A Space Odyssey.*" *Enclitic* 5 (Fall/Spring 1981/1982): 172–80.

Caldwell, Larry W., and Samuel J. Umland. "Come and Play with Us: The Play Metaphor in Kubrick's *Shining.*" *Literature/Film Quarterly* 14 (1986): 106–11.

Carducci, Mark. "In Search of Stanley Kubrick." *Millimeter* 3 (December 1975): 32–37, 49–53.

Castle, Alison, ed. *The Stanley Kubrick Archives.* Los Angeles: Taschen, 2005.

Chatman, Seymour. *Story and Discourse: Narrative Structure in Fiction and Film.* Ithaca, N.Y.: Cornell University Press, 1978.

Chion, Michel. *Kubrick's Cinema Odyssey.* Translated by Claudia Gorbman. London: British Film Institute, 2001.

————. *Eyes Wide Shut.* Translated by Trista Selous. London: British Film Institute, 2002.

Ciment, Michel. *Kubrick: The Definitive Edition.* Translated by Gilbert Adair. New York: Faber and Faber, 2001.

Clarke, Arthur C. *2001: A Space Odyssey.* New York: Signet, 1968.

————. *The Lost Worlds of 2001.* New York: New American Library, 1972.

Cocks, Geoffrey. *The Wolf at the Door: Stanley Kubrick, History, and the Holocaust.* New York: Peter Lang, 2004.

Cocks, Geoffrey, James Diedrick, and Glenn Perusek, eds. *Depth of Field: Stanley Kubrick, Film, and the Uses of History.* Madison: University of Wisconsin Press, 2006.

Collins, Floyd. "Implied Metaphor in the Films of Stanley Kubrick." *New Orleans Review* 16 (Fall 1989): 96–100.

Combs, Richard. "Kubrick Talks!" *Film Comment* 32 (September/October 1996): 81–84.

Cooper, Rand Richards. "Pinocchio Redux." *Commonweal,* 17 August 2001, 20–21.

Corliss, Richard. "*AI*: Spielberg's Strange Love." *Time,* 25 June 2001, 60–62.

Cosgrove, Peter. "The Cinema of Attractions and the Novel in *Barry Lyndon* and *Tom Jones.*" In *Eighteenth-Century on Screen,* edited by Robert Mayer, 16–34. New York: Cambridge University Press, 2002.

Coyle, Wallace. *Stanley Kubrick: A Guide to References and Sources.* Boston: Hall, 1980.

Crone, Rainer, ed. *Stanley Kubrick, Drama and Shadows: Photographs, 1945–1950.* New York: Phaidon, 2005.

Crowther, Bosley. "*Fear and Desire.*" *New York Times,* 1 April 1953, 35.2.

Cunneen, Joseph. "Bored *Wide Shut.*" *National Catholic Reporter,* 3 September 1999, 19.

Deer, Harriet, and Irving Deer. "Kubrick and the Structures of Popular Culture." *Journal of Popular Film* 3 (1974): 232–44.

Deleuze, Gilles. *Cinema 2: The Time-Image.* Translated by Hugh Tomlinson and Robert Galeta. Minneapolis: University of Minnesota Press, 1989.

Denby, David. "Last Waltz." *The New Yorker,* 26 July 1999, 84–87.

De Vries, Daniel. *Kubrick: The Films of Stanley Kubrick.* Grand Rapids, Mich.: Eerdmans, 1973.

Duncan, Paul. *Stanley Kubrick: The Complete Films.* Los Angeles: Taschen, 2003.

Falsetto, Mario. *Stanley Kubrick: A Narrative and Stylistic Analysis,* 2nd ed. Westport, Conn.: Praeger, 2001.

————, ed. *Perspectives on Stanley Kubrick.* New York: Hall, 1996.

Feder, Barnaby J. "A Revolution More Bland than Kubrick's *2001.*" *New York Times,* 30 June 2001, C1.

Feeley, Gregory. "The Masterpiece a Master Couldn't Get Right." *New York Times,* 18 July 1999, 2.9.

Feldmann, Hans. "Kubrick and His Discontents." *Film Quarterly* (Fall 1976): 12–19.

Fordham, Joe. "Mecha Odyssey." *Cinefex: The Journal of Cinematic Illusions* 87 (October 2001): 62–93.

Gans, Herbert J. "Kubrick's Marxist Finale." *Social Policy* 30, no. 1 (Fall 1999): 60–62.

Geduld, Carolyn. *Filmguide to 2001: A Space Odyssey.* Bloomington: Indiana University Press, 1973.

Gelmis, Joseph. *The Film Director as Superstar.* Garden City, N.Y.: Doubleday, 1970.

Genette, Gerard. *Figures of Literary Discourse.* Translated by Alan Sheridan. New York: Columbia University Press, 1982.

Gennusa, Chris. "Kaminski Fuses Kubrick, Spielberg." *Variety,* 15 January 2002, A6.

Gilbey, Ryan. *It Don't Worry Me: The Revolutionary American Films of the Seventies.* New York: Faber & Faber, 2003.

Giuliani, Pierre. *Stanley Kubrick.* Paris: Rivages, 1990.

Gorbman, Claudia. *Unheard Melodies: Narrative Film Music.* Bloomington: Indiana University Press, 1987.

Gorlin, Alexander. "Of Tragedy and the Movie Monolith." *New York Times,* 30 December 2001, 4.6.

Gross, Larry. "Too Late the Hero." *Sight and Sound* 9, no. 9 (September 1999): 20–23.

Herr, Michael. "Completely Missing Kubrick." *Vanity Fair,* April 2000, 260–72.

———. *Kubrick.* New York: Grove, 2000.

Hoberman, J. "I Wake Up Dreaming." *The Village Voice,* 27 July 1999, 59.

———. "The Dreamlife of Angels." *Sight and Sound* 11, no. 9 (September 2001): 16–18.

Houston, Penelope. "Kubrick Country." *Saturday Review,* 25 December 1971, 42–44.

Howard, James. *Stanley Kubrick Companion.* London: Batsford, 2000.

Hughes, David. *The Complete Kubrick.* London: Virgin, 2000.

Jameson, Fredric. *Signatures of the Visible.* New York: Routledge, 1992.

Jameson, Richard T. "Sonata." *Film Comment* 35, no. 5 (September/October 1999): 27–28, 54–56.

Jenkins, Greg. *Stanley Kubrick and the Art of Adaptation: Three Novels, Three Films.* Jefferson, N.C.: McFarland, 1997.

Kagan, Norman. *The Cinema of Stanley Kubrick.* New York: Holt, Rinehart and Winston, 1972.

Kawin, Bruce. *Mindscreen: Bergman, Godard and First-Person Film.* Princeton, N.J.: Princeton University Press, 1978.

Kemp, Philip. "Stanley Kubrick 1928–1999." *Sight and Sound* 9, no. 4 (April 1999): 3.

Kerr, Philip. "Ghosts in the Machine." *New Statesman,* 10 September 2001, 44–45.

Klawans, Stuart. "Long, Slow Buildup: Kubrick Was the Master." *New York Times,* 2 May 1999, A2.

Klein, Michael. "Narrative and Discourse in Kubrick's Modern Tragedy." In *The English Novel and the Movies,* edited by Michael Klein and Gillian Parker, 95–107. New York: Ungar, 1981.

Kloman, William. "In 2001, Will Love Be a Seven-Letter Word?" *New York Times,* 14 April 1968, D15.

Kohler, Charles. "Stanley Kubrick Raps." *Eye* (August 1968): 84–86.

Kolker, Robert Philip. *A Cinema of Loneliness: Penn, Kubrick, Scorsese, Spielberg, Altman,* 3rd ed. New York: Oxford University Press, 2000.

Kozloff, Sarah. *Invisible Storytellers: Voice-Over Narration in American Fiction Film.* Berkeley: University of California Press, 1988.

Kreider, Tim. "*Eyes Wide Shut.*" *Film Quarterly* 53, no. 3 (Spring 2000): 41–48.

———. "*AI: Artificial Intelligence.*" *Film Quarterly* 56, no. 2 (Winter 2002/2003): 32.

Kroll, Jack. "Kubrick's View." *Newsweek*, 22 March 1999, 66–68.

Kubrick, Christiane. *Stanley Kubrick: A Life in Pictures*. Boston: Little, Brown, 2002.

Kubrick, Stanley. "Kubrick Dissects the Movies." *Newsweek*, 2 December 1957, 96–97.

———. "Director's Notes: Stanley Kubrick Movie-Maker." *The Observer* (London), 4 December 1960.

———. "Words and Movies." *Sight and Sound* 30 (Winter 1960/1961): 14.

Leff, Leonard, and Jerold L. Simmons. *The Dame in the Kimono*, 2nd ed. Lexington: University of Kentucky Press, 2001.

Lidz, Franz, and Steve Rushin. "How to Tell a Bad Movie from a Truly Bad Movie." *New York Times*, 5 August 2001, 2.1.

LoBrutto, Vincent. *Stanley Kubrick: A Biography*. New York: Fine, 1997.

Lyman, Rick. "A Director's Journey into a Darkness of Heart." *New York Times*, 24 June 2001, 2.

Magistrale, Anthony, ed. *The Shining Reader*. Mercer Island, Wash.: Starmont, 1991.

Mainar, Luis M. Garcia. *Narrative and Stylistic Patterns in the Films of Stanley Kubrick*. Rochester, N.Y.: Camden House, 1999.

Manvell, Roger, and John Huntley, eds. *The Technique of Film Music*, 2nd ed. Revised by Richard Arnell and Peter Day. New York: Hastings House, 1975.

Martin, Adrian, and Jonathan Rosenbaum, eds. *Movie Mutations: The Changing Face of World Cinephilia*. London: British Film Institute, 2003.

Maslin, Janet. "A Visionary, a Mindblower, Kubrick Never Failed to Stun." *New York Times*, 14 March 1999, AR30.

———. "Bedroom Odyssey." *New York Times*, 16 July 1999, E1.

Massumi, Brian. *Parables for the Virtual: Movement, Affect, Sensation*. Durham, N.C.: Duke University Press, 2002.

McCarthy, Todd. "*AI*: Mecha Movie Is Mega Mind-Blower." *Variety*, 8 July 2001, 19, 26.

McCormick, Patrick. "If They Only Had a Heart." *U.S. Catholic Reporter* 66, no. 10 (October 2001): 44–46.

McDougal, Stuart Y., ed. *Stanley Kubrick's A Clockwork Orange*. New York: Cambridge University Press, 2003.

Menand, Louis. "Kubrick's Strange Love." *New York Review of Books* 46, no. 13 (12 August 1999): 7–8.

Morgenstern, Joe. "There's Plenty of Sex, but *Eyes Wide Shut* Never Hits a Climax." *Wall Street Journal*, 16 July 1999, A1.

———. "Artifice over *Intelligence*." *Wall Street Journal*, 29 June 2001, W1.

Munday, Rod. *The Kubrick Site*, 2006, at www.kubrick.com (accessed 2 February 2006).

Nabokov, Vladimir. *Lolita*. New York: Everyman's Library, 1992.

Naremore, James, and Adrian Martin. "The Future of Academic Film Study." In *Movie Mutations: The Changing Face of World Cinephilia*, edited by Adrian Martin and Jonathan Rosenbaum. London: British Film Institute, 2003.

———. "Love and Death in *AI: Artificial Intelligence*." *Michigan Quarterly Review* 94, no. 2 (Spring 2005): 257–84.

Nelson, Thomas Allen. *Kubrick: Inside a Film Artist's Maze*, 2nd ed. Bloomington: Indiana University Press, 2000.

Nordern, Eric. "*Playboy* Interview: Stanley Kubrick (1968)." In *Stanley Kubrick Interviews*, edited by Gene D. Phillips, 47–74. Jackson: University Press of Mississippi, 2001.

Ordway, Frederick I. "Perhaps, I'm Just Projecting My Own Concern about It." In *The Making of Kubrick's* 2001, edited by Jerome Agel, 193–98. New York: Signet, 1970.

Phillips, Braden. "*AI* Submerged in Awards Season Hoopla." *Variety*, 17 December 2001, 16–17.

Phillips, Gene. *Stanley Kubrick: A Film Odyssey*. New York: Popular Library, 1975.

Phillips, Gene D., and Rodney Hill, eds. *The Encyclopedia of Stanley Kubrick*. New York: Facts on File, 2002.

Polan, Dana. *The Political Language of Film and the Avant-Garde*. Ann Arbor, Mich.: UMI Research Press, 1985.

———. "Materiality and Sociality in *Killer's Kiss*." In *Perspectives on Stanley Kubrick*, edited by Mario Falsetto. New York: Hall, 1996.

Preussner, Arnold W. "Kubrick's *Eyes Wide Shut* as Shakespearean Tragicomedy." *Literature/Film Quarterly* 29, no. 4 (2001): 290–96.

Rapf, Maurice. "A Talk with Stanley Kubrick." *Action* (January/February 1969), 15–18.

Raphael, Frederic. *Eyes Wide Open: A Memoir of Stanley Kubrick*. New York: Ballantine, 1999.

———. "A Kubrick Odyssey." *The New Yorker*, 14 June 1999, 40–47.

Rasmussen, Randy. *Stanley Kubrick: Seven Films Analyzed*. Jefferson, N.C.: McFarland, 2001.

Rodowick, D. N. "The Difficulty of Difference." *Wide Angle* 5, no. 1 (1982): 4–15.

Romney, Jonathan. "Exclusion Zone." *New Statesman*, 13 September 1999, 43–44.

Rozen, Leah. "*Eyes Wide Shut*." *People*, 26 July 1999, 35.

Sarris, Andrew. "*Eyes* Don't Have It: Kubrick's Turgid Finale." *New York Observer*, 26 July 1999, 29.

Schickel, Richard. "Art Was His Fragile Fortress: Stanley Kubrick: 1928–1999." *Time*, 22 March 1999, 100.

———. "All *Eyes* on Them." *Newsweek*, 5 July 1999, 66–70.

Schwarzbaum, Lisa. "Sci-Fi Channel." *Entertainment Weekly*, 29 June 2001, 109–10.

Scott, A. O. "Opening *Eyes* to a Kubrick Masterpiece." *New York Times*, 16 April 2000, 2.9.

———. "Spielberg's Pathos." *New York Times*, 23 December 2001, 2.13.

Seesslen, Georg, and Fernand Young. *Stanley Kubrick und seine Filme*. Marburg: Shüren, 1999.

Shargel, Raphael. "Kubrick's Final Odyssey." *The New Leader*, 9 August 1999, 18–19.

Sharrett, Christopher. "Spielberg the Serious." *USA Today*, September 2001, 67.

Shaviro, Steven. "Regimes of Vision: Kathryn Bigelow, *Strange Days*." *Polygraph* 13 (2001): 59–68.

Shepard, Lucius. "Films." *Fantasy & Science Fiction* 101, no. 6 (December 2001): 112–17.

Shklovsky, Victor. *Russian Formalist Criticism: Four Essays*. Translated by Lee T. Lemon and Marion J. Reis. Lincoln: University of Nebraska Press, 1965.

Siegel, Lee. "*Eyes Wide Shut*: What the Critics Failed to See in Kubrick's Last Film." *Harper's*, October 1999, 76–82.

Silber, Irwin. "Film: *Barry Lyndon* Finds History Meaningless." *Guardian*, 17 March 1976, 19.

Sperb, Jason. "The Country of the Mind in Kubrick's *Fear and Desire* (1953)." *Film Criticism* 29, no. 1 (Fall 2004): 23–37.

Staiger, Janet. *Perverse Spectators: The Practices of Film Reception*. New York: New York University Press, 2000.

Stang, Jonathan. "Film Fan to Film-Maker." *New York Times Magazine*, 12 October 1958, SM34, 36, 38.

Strick, Philip. "*AI: Artificial Intelligence*." *Sight and Sound* 11, no. 10 (October 2001): 38.

Sullivan, Jack. "Williams: *AI*." *American Record Guide* 64, no. 6 (November/December 2001): 212.

Svetkey, Benjamin. "Stanley Kubrick, 1928–1999." *Entertainment Weekly*, 19 March 1999, 14–17.

Taylor, John Russell. *Directors and Directions: Cinema for the Seventies*. New York: Hill and Wang, 1975.

Thissen, Rolf. *Stanley Kubrick: Der Regisseur als Architekt*. Munich: Heyne, 1999.

Travers, Peter. "*AI/Artificial Intelligence*." *Rolling Stone*, 19 July 2001, 54–55.

Usai, Paolo Cherchi. "Checkmating the General: Stanley Kubrick's *Fear and Desire*." *Image* 38, no. 1/2 (Spring/Summer 1995): 3–31.

Vitali, Leon. "Kubrick Questions Finally Answered." *DVD Talk*, 2002, at www .dvdtalk.com/leonvitaliinterview.html (accessed 5 February 2006).

Walker, Alexander. *Stanley Kubrick Directs*. New York: Harcourt Brace Jovanovich, 1972.

———. *"It's Only a Movie, Ingrid": Encounters On and Off Screen*. London: Headline, 1988.

Walker, Alexander, Sybil Taylor, and Ulrich Ruchti. *Stanley Kubrick, Director: A Visual Analysis*. New York: Norton, 1999.

Weinberger, Gabriele. "Spielberg's *Artificial Intelligence*: Millennial Mother and Son." *West Virginia University Philological Papers* 49 (2002–2003): 104–9.

Wheat, Leonard F. *Kubrick's 2001: A Triple Allegory*. Lanham, Md.: Scarecrow, 2000.

White, Susan. "Male Bonding, Hollywood Orientalism, and the Repression of the Feminine in Kubrick's *Full Metal Jacket*." *Arizona Quarterly* 44 (Autumn 1988): 120–44.

Whitinger, Raleigh, and Susan Ingram. "Schnitzler, Kubrick, and 'Fidelio.'" *Mosaic: A Journal for the Interdisciplinary Study of Literature* 36, no. 3 (September 2003): 55–71.

Williams, Tony. "Narrative Patterns and Mythic Trajectories in Mid-1980s Vietnam Movies." In *Inventing Vietnam: The War in Film and Television*, edited by Michael Anderegg, 114–39. Philadelphia: Temple University Press, 1991.

Young, Toby. "I Wish I Hadn't Seen It." *The Spectator*, 11 September 1999, 48.

Žižek, Slavoj. *The Fright of Real Tears: Krzysztof Kieslowski between Theory and Post Theory*. London: British Film Institute, 2001.

Index

Allen), 20, 24–25; plot summary of, 23; praise for, 31; rivers as metaphor for alienation in, 25, 115; voice-over narration in, 2, 10, 19–26, 39, 41, 43, 50, 65, 68, 102–103, 105, 123n13, 137, 145
Feeley, Gregory, 149, 152n12, 154n30
feeling. *See* affect
film noir, 37, 43
"Fletcher" (Steve Coit), 26–27
Ford, John, 14n9
Fordham, Joe, 143, 154n22, 154n27
formalism, 5, 33n9, 93
"Frank Poole" (Gary Lockwood), 87–88, 90–91, 94
Fried, Gerald, 23, 44, 46, 154n28
Full Metal Jacket (Kubrick), 9, 11, 23, 24, 26, 30, 48–49, 63–65, 75–76, 102–104, 106–111, 119, 121–122, 138, 142, 153n12; as a remake of *Fear and Desire* (Ciment), 30; interviews in, 24; Kubrickian look in, 9, 11, 63, 108–110, 138; relation to other Vietnam films, 106, 153n12; voice-over narration in, 64, 75–76, 102–104, 106–109, 119, 121–122, 138

"General Broulard" (Adolphe Menjou), 48–49
"General Mireau" (George Macready), 48–49
"General Ripper" (Sterling Hayden), 3, 10–11, 56, 65, 68–69, 71–75, 76n6, 94, 105–106, 109, 111, 116, 129, 138
"General Turgidson" (George C. Scott), 3–4, 10, 56, 66–68, 70–71, 73, 75, 94, 116
"George Peatty" (Elisha Cook), 44
"Georgie" (James Marcus), 113–114
"Gigolo Joe" (Jude Law), 144–145
"Glabrus" (John Dall), 51–53
"Gloria" (Irene Kane), 38, 40–41
Goldstein, Patrick, 154n31
Gorbman, Claudia, 32n4, 33n4
"Gracchus" (Charles Laughton), 51, 52

"Group Captain Mandrake" (Peter Sellers), 66, 72, 74
"Gunnery Sergeant Hartman" (R. Lee Ermey), 103–107, 110, 121

"HAL," 87–88, 90–92, 94–96, 100, 129, 137–138, 149
Hamburger Hill (Irvin), 153n12
Harlan, Jan, 143, 152n8, 153n12
Harris, James B., 34n18
"Hello, Vietnam" (Wright), 106
"Heywood Floyd" (William Sylvester), 87, 89
Hitchcock, Alfred, 14n9
Hoberman, J., 133n5, 133n13
"Humbert" (James Mason), 54–58, 60n10, 60n11, 60n12, 61n13, 61n15, 106, 137

intention. *See* auteur theory
Inventing Vietnam: The War in Film and Television (Anderegg), 122n4
Invisible Storytellers: Voice-Over Narration in American Fiction Film (Kozloff), 13n2
"Iris" (Ruth Sobotka), 26, 40

"Jack Torrance" (Jack Nicholson), 1–4, 8–13, 19, 26–27, 63, 99–103, 105, 108, 112, 120–121, 122n2, 128–129, 138, 144, 148–149
Jameson, Fredric, 8, 15n18, 111, 122n2
Jenkins, Greg, 60n10
"Joe" (Clive Francis), 115
"Joker" (Matthew Modine), 11, 102–107, 109–111, 119, 121–122, 135, 138
"Johnny Clay" (Sterling Hayden), 38, 44–46, 65
Jurassic Park (Spielberg), 151n8

Kagan, Norman, 21, 28, 33n9, 34n12, 34n13, 35n29, 35n30
Kaufman, Lloyd, 154n28
Kennedy, Kathleen, 144
Kerr, Philip, 143, 148, 154n20, 154n29

About the Author

Jason Sperb teaches in the Department of Communication and Culture at Indiana University, Bloomington. In addition to his work on Kubrick for *Film Criticism*, *Storytelling*, *Interactions*, and www.kubrick.com, he has contributed to such journals as *Quarterly Review of Film and Video*, *Biography*, *Studies in the Literary Imagination*, and *Bright Lights Film Journal*. He also serves as an advisory editor and contributor for *Kritikos*, a journal of postmodern culture based out of Florida State University. He is finishing a manuscript on a certain cinema of late postmodernity and will soon began coediting a scholarly collection of essays on cinephilia and computer-generated imagery with Scott Balcerzak.